Yaqui Homeland and Homeplace

Yaqui Homeland and Homeplace

The Everyday Production of Ethnic Identity

Kirstin C. Erickson

The University of Arizona Press   Tucson

The University of Arizona Press

Library of Congress Cataloging-in-Publication Data

Erickson, Kirstin C., 1966–
  Yaqui homeland and homeplace : the everyday
production of ethnic identity / Kirstin C. Erickson.
      p. cm.
  Includes bibliographical references and index.
  ISBN 978-0-8165-2734-2 (hardcover : alk. paper)—
  ISBN 978-0-8165-2735-9 (pbk. : alk. paper)
    1. Yaqui women—Mexico—Sonora (State)—
Social conditions.   2. Yaqui Indians—Mexico—Sonora
(State)—Ethnic identity.   3. Sonora (Mexico : State)—
Social conditions.   4. Yaqui River Valley (Mexico)—
Social conditions.   I. Title.
F1221.Y3E75   2008
305.897'4542—dc22   2008018867

Publication of this book is made possible in part by the proceeds
of a permanent endowment created with the assistance of a
Challenge Grant from the National Endowment for the
Humanities, a federal agency.

Contents

Illustrations

Acknowledgments

This book is the culmination of more than ten years of research and writing, none of which would have been possible without the intellectual give-and-take, support, and encouragement of my family and many colleagues, mentors, friends, and collaborators. To all of those who have seen this project through, I offer my deepest thanks.

I am most grateful to the Yaqui tribal authorities in Potam, who supported my research endeavors, approved my residence in Potam Pueblo, and aided my efforts in innumerable ways. My work in Sonora was greatly facilitated by UNISON (Universidad de Sonora) and by INAH (the Instituto Nacional de Antropología e Historia). Both institutions provided academic support and library access, and INAH provided me with institutional affiliation. Through INAH I had the privilege of meeting historian Raquel Padilla Ramos and sociolinguist José Moctezuma Zamarrón. I thank them for their enthusiasm for all things Yaqui and for their interest in my work. Preliminary research in the summer of 1995 was made possible by a Tinker/Nave Fund Summer Research Grant. A generous financial gift from my father, Peter Christenson, helped fund my research during the 1996–97 field season.

The writing of this book was facilitated by a fellowship at the Anderson Center for Interdisciplinary Studies in Red Wing, Minnesota. The Anderson Center provided a creative and stimulating environment in which I had time to write, think, and test ideas among a supportive group of artists and writers—Heid Erdrich, Rachel Weinstein, Betsy Markowski, and Tia Blassingame. Thanks to the center's director, Robert Hedin, for this opportunity. My time at the Anderson Center centered around a collaborative project with textile artist Dawn Zero Erickson. The project, *Material Devotions*, was her brainchild. I thank Dawn for her creativity, her attention to ethnographic detail, and her companionship. Dawn's intellectual curiosity and artistic sensibility are unsurpassed.

I owe a debt of gratitude to my mentors and professors at the University of Wisconsin–Madison, especially Katherine Bowie, Richard Flores,

Jack Kugelmass, Maria Lepowsky, Florencia Mallon, Peter Nabokov, Francisco Scarano, and Steve Stern. These individuals made anthropology and Native American and Latin American studies come alive; they challenged me to become a critical thinker and a better writer.

My graduate advisors, Richard Flores and Peter Nabokov, continue to be true mentors. Both have fostered my intellectual growth and have demonstrated an interest in me and my family. Richard Flores's passion for critical theory, his capacity to imagine anthropology's social possibilities, and his commitment to ethical research have been inspirational—they are standards to which I aspire. Following my fieldwork in Sonora, my husband, Brad Erickson, and I lived in Austin, Texas. Richard and Christine Flores and their daughters graciously shared their home and their extended family with us and helped us learn to maintain the delicate balance between family and intellectual pursuit that is so often overlooked in academic life. We are deeply thankful for their continued friendship and example. Peter Nabokov's expansive knowledge of Native American ethnography and history, his ability to cultivate concise, evocative writing, and his insatiable scholarly curiosity have been instrumental in shaping the scholar I have become. I thank Peter for visiting me in Potam in 1997. My Yaqui friends and I still fondly remember his visit.

I offer a special word of thanks to Lorrie Lincoln-Babb, who took me to Sonora for the first time and paved my way with introductions and personal connections. I also owe a debt of gratitude to those scholars of the Yaqui whom I have had the privilege of meeting. Thanks to Larry Evers, Evelyn Hu-DeHart, and David Delgado Shorter for their words of advice, camaraderie, and rich, nuanced scholarship.

At the University of Wisconsin and during my time spent at the University of Texas fellow students, now colleagues, provided moral support, a stimulating intellectual cohort, and precious feedback on my ideas, my research, and my writing. My deepest appreciation to Cheryl Allendoerfer, Marc Anderson, Kevin Bohrer, Ben Chappell, Hank Delcore, Rebecca Furth, Patty Gray, Calla Jacobson, Sarah Jessup, Rachel Meyer, Maria Moreno, Kathleen Mulligan-Hansel, Ken Price, and Julie Walsh; thanks for your abiding friendship and critical insights.

Many friends have remained enthusiastic supporters of my research. All of them have patiently listened to my stories about the Yaquis, and many have commented on my work, holding me accountable for clarity and honesty in what I write. Thank you, Beth Ashbrook, Sreekala and Dilpreet Bajwa, Amy Farmer, Christine Flores, Kate Graney and Sean Loftus, Molly Jensen and Alan Ostner, Sarah Jensen, Thom Johnson, Hannah Levine, Matt Quinn, Gina and Jeff Smith, Jennifer Tabola and Ted Adams, and Lise Wall. Colleagues at the University of Arkansas have also expressed interest in and support of my research, including Lynda Coon, Michael Pierce, Luis Fernando Restrepo, Reina Ruiz, Kathryn Sloan, Tricia Starks, and Ted Swedenburg. My thanks to JoAnn D'Alisera and David Chaudoir; both read and responded thoughtfully to portions of this book. I am most grateful to JoAnn for her continued camaraderie, and I thank her for her willingness to challenge and reinvigorate my work. Steve Striffler read my manuscript and provided careful, detailed commentary and insightful recommendations at a critical juncture in the writing process; his feedback was invaluable and is greatly appreciated.

As I have conducted research, traveled to Sonora, and written this book over the past ten years, my family has offered unwavering support. I thank my parents, Peter and Jacqueline Christenson, for their interest in the Yaquis and for their support of my decision to study anthropology. My mother has opened her Tucson home to Mexican friends, driven me to the border more times than I care to count, and helped me with the monumental task of gathering supplies and gifts before each of my trips to Potam. Her house was my home base and occasional retreat when I was living in Sonora. My father visited my field site in 1997 and has, ever since, been connected to Potam and my Yaqui "family." His enthusiasm for this project and my work is greatly appreciated. I am grateful to Donald and Joanna Erickson for their steadfast encouragement and for posing perceptive and timely questions. My mother-in-law, Elaine Erickson, passed away before this book could be completed. I will always be grateful for her interest in my work and her loving support. My thanks to Tim and Simone Christenson, Kris and Kurt Anderson, Steve Erickson and Christine Boyer, and Tomm Vittoria for their indulgence and willingness to listen and learn along with me.

Earlier versions of chapters 2, 3, and 4 appeared in the *Journal of American Folklore* 116(462):465–482 (University of Illinois Press, 2003); *Anthropology and Humanism* 28(2):139–154 (copyright American Anthropological Association, 2003, reprinted with the permission of the American Anthropological Association, Arlington, VA); and *Cuadernos de Literatura* 11(22):32–45 (Bogotá, Colombia: Fundación Fumio Ito, 2007). They are reprinted here with permission.

I would like to thank the director of the University of Arizona Press, Christine Szuter, and my editors, Allyson Carter and Nancy Arora, for their expert guidance, enthusiasm, and utter professionalism in bringing this book to publication. I am indebted to the anonymous reviewers of my manuscript for their careful reading, pointed comments, and helpful critique. My thanks to M. Jane Kellett at the University of Arkansas Archeological Survey for her map work and admirable sense of design. I am also greatly indebted to my copy editor, Mary M. Hill, for her engagement with the Yaqui material, her painstaking work on the manuscript in its final stages, and her patience in guiding me through the copyediting process.

Brad has done more than anyone to bring this project to fruition. He has supported me, demonstrated unwavering confidence in my abilities, and often altered or postponed his plans in order to help me realize my own. My deepest thanks to him for his love, his abiding companionship, and his interest in the things about which I am passionate. My thanks to my daughters, Ruby and Linnea Erickson, who put up with my absence more often than makes me comfortable, knowing that "Mommy has to work on her book . . . again!" Their acceptance, love, and energy make it all worthwhile.

I would like to express my heartfelt gratitude to the immediate and extended family of Virginia Jacobo de Cruz and Saúl Cruz in Ciudad Obregón and in Aguascalientes. Virginia, Saúl, Lupita, Renán, Alma, Marisela, Vicki, Saúl, Norma—you were my anchors, my biggest cheerleaders, and my second family in Obregón. Finally, I would like to thank the Yaqui women and men in Potam, Rahum, Vicam, and Loma de Bacum with whom I lived and worked and from whom I continue to learn. Unfortunately, those from whom I gained the most in respect to this project are the ones who must remain nameless in order to assure anonymity. Thank you for accepting me into your lives, opening your homes, treating me like a member of your families, and enduring thousands of questions and intrusions. Your care and your devotion to this project have made it a reality. *Dios emchiokoe utte'esia*. This book is dedicated to Brad, to Ruby and Linnea, and to my esteemed Yaqui companions.

Yaqui Homeland and Homeplace

1

"How Fine It Was"
Memory and the Production of Ethnicity

> Like that, at times, I begin to remember. I tell myself how I had
> believed that everything would be the same. But it turns out
> that no, no. Things have changed. As I tell the girls, when
> I was little, I never knew hunger. I never went hungry.
> —Josefina Vila Echeverría

Hurrying home from an interview on a blazing summer afternoon, my
gaze fixed on the ground as I negotiated Potam's deeply rutted roadways,
I imagined the cool water I would splash on my face when I arrived at
the house. The streets were silent; other people were indoors, eating their
midday meal or resting, waiting until the sun sank in the sky before ven-
turing out to do laundry, visit friends, gather firewood, or sweep their
patios. I walked through yards and alleyways along footpaths littered
with candy wrappers, horse manure, and shards of brown glass from
broken beer bottles. As I rounded one corner, cutting close to the high
carrizo (river cane) fence surrounding someone's yard, an inquisitive
voice broke through the quiet: "¿Adónde va?" (Where are you going?).
She startled me, made me jump. An elderly woman, her head covered
with a checkered cotton *rebozo* (shawl), leaned against the inside of a
gatepost that towered over her compact body. The white-hot sun was
blinding, and I put up my hand to shade my eyes. In a few seconds the
face beneath the shawl materialized, dark and deeply etched with expressive wrinkles. "Where are you going," she repeated, "and why are you
out in the sun?" She raised knowing eyebrows: "You are going to get
overheated."

I tried to remember where I had met her while I explained that I
had spent the morning interviewing someone in the neighborhood of
Mérida. "Yes," she smiled, "Carlota told me that you were going to visit
today." Embarrassed, I suddenly realized that this was Josefina, Carlota's

mother, and that she and I had met several months previously. I inquired about her health, and we chatted briefly. Before I left I asked if she would be willing to talk to me about her childhood, her family, and her work. She agreed, and we arranged to meet the following afternoon.

Josefina Vila Echeverría is a mother of eight who lives with one of her daughters, several granddaughters, and her unmarried son on the east side of Potam, a Yaqui Indian pueblo in southern Sonora, Mexico. A thick gray braid rests heavily on the curved length of her spine, and a smile almost always tugs at the corners of her mouth. She was 69 years old at the time of our first interview in June 1997. During this initial interview we sat side by side on Josefina's double bed inside her carrizo-and-mud-walled bedroom. A broken television, dwarfed by an over-stuffed wood-veneer wardrobe, occupied one corner. Josefina pointed to the photographs of her grandchildren on the walls and complained about the rats, indicating her solution: underneath the bureau was a large wooden trap with menacing steel teeth and a piece of tortilla as bait. Wiping the sweat from her brow, she asked me to adjust the fan, and then I turned on the tape recorder.

I urged Josefina to describe what Potam was like when she was young. She explained:

> It was different back then. There were not so many Yoris [non-Yaqui Mexicans]. Then, back when I was a girl, as I tell my daughters, my granddaughters, when I was a kid, one never heard that "So-and-so is a thief," that "So-and-so is a pothead . . . a drug addict." None of that. Pure work and farming. There weren't so many *malditos* [trouble-makers]. Back then, no. There were dances; there were celebrations . . . they celebrated birthdays with little dances, but with the Victrola! [She grinned broadly, tracing an imaginary turntable with her finger.] With a little mariachi music, like that, with accordion. They did it very well. . . . They didn't fight. . . . And now, no! Now when they have dances, they go about on horseback, assaulting the people, fighting, doing harm. And before, no.
>
> Back then, everything was very inexpensive. And everyone farmed. Everyone farmed. Look, we did not have to buy *frijoles* [beans]. We did not have to purchase *maíz* [maize]. My uncle had a little room in which he put the frijol harvest. He had his sacks of frijol, his maíz. . . . My grandmother raised pigs, and so when people arrived with the urge to eat *chicharrones* [pork rinds] or meat, she would have a pig

killed so that they might eat. . . . We didn't have to purchase pork lard. She had jars of lard, the meat *adobada* [preserved], like this, with chile. She had beef, because a butcher came and would say, "María Dolores, aren't you going to want meat?" "Yes, of course!" She had a big tray, my grandmother—*full* of meat they would give it to her. For three pesos! And now how much does a kilo of meat cost? You see what a good life we had! For that reason I say now that I didn't grow up in wretchedness. . . . I never went hungry like we do now. Now that I am old, I occasionally go hungry. When I was a girl, I didn't know need. . . . In those times we didn't have to purchase anything. We only had to buy flour. We ate huge tortillas and chicharrones. A pot full to the brim, to the brim with chicharrones, and with *carnitas* [chopped barbecued pork], and you can see how fine it was. I never would have believed that my life would be like it is now.

When I asked her why she thought things had changed, Josefina shrugged. "Well, who knows? But the Yoris began to come. They took my uncle's land."

Josefina continued her story. She told about her marriage at the age of 25 to a Yaqui rancher. They eventually separated when she would no longer tolerate his infidelities. She talked about her children: "All born at home. . . . All *indios de aquí* [Indians from here (Potam)]," she chuckled. Josefina always made a living by taking in laundry, by making and selling food and other goods. I asked her to describe how she earned money to support her family.

Me? Well, from *falluquera* [street vending], and I would take things to Guaymas [the nearest port city] to sell, chickens or *panelas* [rounds of fresh cheese], things like that. I took things to sell, as my daughter—this one here—now does. She sells panelas, *pinole* [cornmeal drink], and she makes some big *empanadas* [fruit-, vegetable-, or meat-stuffed pastries].

Josefina still makes and sells *menudo* (tripe soup), tacos, enchiladas, and *gorditas* during the shrimp harvest in the fishing village of Lobos. As a younger woman Josefina was selected to be a *fiestera*, one of eight hosts of the four-day celebration in honor of the Santísima Trinidad (Holy Trinity), Potam's patron. As is customary among the Yaquis, once one has faithfully performed her role as fiestera (a yearlong series of duties that culminate in the celebration of the fiesta), the role becomes a title with which that person is always associated. Josefina is respected in the community, and, now in poor health, she is well cared for by her children and grandchildren in Potam.

During our talk Josefina's narrative continually circled back to the past, to her childhood. She described weekend visits from relatives:

> On Sundays the older people visited each other. My grandmother had relatives on ranches who had cattle. And they would arrive on Sundays. My grandmother used to get up early. And she would say to me, "*Ándale* [get going], grab the broom. I want you to sweep the entire yard." And to my uncle, "And you, get busy watering; clean up, because my relatives are going to come." And she would put the food on [to cook]. She made *carne con chile* [beef in chile sauce] and at times *mole* [sauce made from a mixture of chiles that may include chocolate and peanuts]. She made flour tortillas. . . . And then they arrived . . . and they were here the whole day. My grandmother had a *ramada* [shelter] where she received her visitors. There they would be, lying down; there she would place her cots. And then in the afternoon they would leave. . . . And since they also cultivated sugarcane, garbanzos, green beans . . . they would bring things. Well, my uncle also farmed, at times bringing watermelon, melons. . . . See how good we had it?

During our interview that day and again nearly every time we had a chance to talk Josefina articulated fond memories of her childhood, painting a nostalgic vision of the past. Her memory of abundance is a narrative of plenitude, but it is also a commentary—about her family's struggles and about her own identity—in the present.[1] She insists that when she was a girl, things were different. "There were not so many Yoris." People were not assaulted on their way home from the dances that have now become like discos. There was less crime. There were fewer drug addicts. She associates the coming of non-Yaqui Mexicans with changes in the pueblo's culture and agricultural practice; her narrative references the accelerating integration of Yaquis into the Mexican cash economy and the unsettling displacement of subsistence farmers. She compares a time when there was plenty to eat (homemade chicharrones and carnitas, watermelon and mole), a time when guests arrived laden with produce from their own fields ("sugarcane, garbanzos, green beans") to a present in which food has to be purchased and an elderly woman still has to sell tacos and menudo in order to make ends meet. "Back then, everything was very inexpensive. . . . Everyone farmed. Look, we did not have to buy frijoles. We did not have to purchase maíz. . . . She had a big tray, my grandmother—*full* of meat they would give it to her. For three pesos! And now how much does a kilo of meat cost? You see what a good life we had!"

Josefina's memories are shaped by her specific experience of the present, and part of that contemporary reality is the persistent marginal status of the Yaqui people within the dominant Mexican society. Josefina's is a moral discourse that reconstitutes and reinforces categories of identity, representing Yaquis as fundamentally different from non-Yaquis. "My grandmother said that in the past it was not so much like this, like it is now. The people were very innocent, the Yaquis. The good people were still here."

"The Richest Tribe in Mexico"

This book is a study of the ways in which Yaqui individuals, living in a series of pueblos located within the boundaries of their reclaimed aboriginal territory in northern Mexico, construct, negotiate, and continually reimagine their own ethnic identity today. It is about how Yaquis create a sense of identity and belonging, ensuring the survival of their community and carving a space for themselves as an indigenous people of modern Mexico. Material necessity, economic distress, ethnic opposition, and racial inequalities are the realities that shape people's lives and underpin narratives like the one shared by Josefina Vila. Such conditions are rooted in a very specific historical experience. The Yaquis, an indigenous people renowned for their elaborate religious ceremonialism, ethnic pride, and cultural persistence, have also faced tremendous hardship since the Spanish conquest. From the moment of the first Yaqui–European encounter in 1533 the Yaqui experience has been characterized by conflict over their identity and their ancestral land.[2] Upon the designation of their territory as a Jesuit mission in the early 1600s the Yaquis endured massive relocation, a fundamental transformation of their mode of production, and Catholic indoctrination. The Jesuit period, which ended in the mid-1700s, was followed (over the next one and a half centuries) by a Mexican rush for Yaqui land, decades of war, and Yaqui outmigration. The Yaqui River had, for centuries, carried and deposited loamy soils from high in the sierra, enriching an already lush desert. The fertile Yaqui River valley became one of the most contested pieces of land in all of northern Mexico, and the nineteenth century witnessed the displacement of nearly the entire Yaqui population as Yaqui fields were forcibly colonized by government-backed settlers and developers of export-oriented agriculture. Some Yaquis joined the resistance, spawning the "Yaqui Wars" of the late 1800s, while others fled the violence in their pueblos, scattering throughout Sonora. At the turn of the twentieth century, perceived as a military and social threat to President Porfirio Díaz's vision of a thoroughly modernized Mexico, Yaquis were subjected to removal from their land, constant surveillance, deportation, even random execution. It was a systematic persecution approaching genocidal proportions that subsided only after the outbreak of the Mexican Revolution in 1910 and the removal of Díaz from power.

After the Mexican Revolution, displaced Yaquis began to return to their ancestral land, resettling the pueblos along the Yaqui River. But territorial repossession did not guarantee the Yaquis freedom from state interference. Chief among the forces transforming productive life in the Yaqui pueblos during the postrevolution period was the state's decision to construct a modern dam in the mountains to the east of Yaqui territory. Before 1950 subsistence farming was the norm, and Yaqui families cultivated their plots manually. The river overflowed its banks biannually, and when irrigation was needed, shallow impermanent channels were dug to direct the flow of water into the fields. With the completion of the Álvaro Obregón Dam in 1952, the waters of the Yaqui River were henceforth contained in an extensive reservoir behind thick cement walls.[3] Substantial amounts of water were diverted to the Yaqui Valley (to the south, outside the boundaries of Yaqui territory). Yaqui fields, once watered and fertilized in abundance by the river, now received irrigation solely through a series of narrow canals. As Cynthia Hewitt de Alcantara notes, the channeling of water to non-Yaqui commercial fields to the south of nearby Ciudad Obregón "wreaked havoc with subsistence plots on the north bank of the river" (1976:267).

In a place where productive activity is centered on agriculture, raising cattle, and fishing, the river and its impact on agrarian life have been inscribed in cultural discourses; concerns about the river and water loss surface frequently as important topics in people's recollections of the past. Older Yaquis remember occasional floods that required evacuation, but, more often, they express anger at the taking of their river. Seventy-eight-year-old Manuel Valencia Valenzuela's declaration, "The Río Yaqui is dead," echoes a wealth of bitterness and loss. Yaqui elders articulate memories of idyllic country scenes in which children played alongside the river, of fields where watermelons, beans, sweet potatoes, bananas, and sugarcane grew in abundance.

Figure 1. The Yaqui River near Potam, Sonora

The "opening" of the Mexican economy in the 1980s and the implementation of NAFTA (North American Free Trade Agreement) in the 1990s have only exacerbated the economic disparity between indebted Yaqui farmers and the successful commercial farms for which Sonora is famous. The place known as the Yaqui Valley, once tribal territory but now lying outside of the Zona Indígena (Indigenous Zone) directly to the south of Ciudad Obregón, is an example of the shape taken by most Sonoran agriculture. Those who farm on a large scale have prospered from the neoliberal policies of the 1980s. Immense privately owned and corporate farms stretch across the absolutely flat plain of the valley floor. Maize, cotton, tomatoes, wheat, and cucumbers are grown there year-round.

Most Yaqui farms are small by comparison, and although they are located within the Zona Yaqui, they have become dependent on Mexican banks and beholden to the dictates of the market. The 1950s brought the end of subsistence farming for Yaquis. Facing the need to purchase water, the majority of Yaqui farmers joined credit societies that depended upon bank loans; mechanization, integration into the "green revolution," and tight regulation of Yaqui planting schedules soon followed (Hewitt de Alcantara 1976:266–278). Since that time modernization has continued apace, further undermining Yaqui self-sufficiency. What Thomas McGuire noted in the 1980s still rings true today: "Yaquis retain political control over the lands of the zone, yet they lack economic control; they are at the mercy of the outside financiers" (1986:121). Indeed, the appearance of abundance in the verdant fields covering the valley floor of the Zona Indígena belies a more complicated reality. During my year in Potam, numerous Yaqui farmers described to me the one bad harvest that prevented repayment of a bank loan and their subsequent loss of credit.

"The Yaquis are the richest tribe in Mexico" was an assertion made to me by nonindigenous Mexicans in casual conversations and during interviews, on buses and at parties. It was something I heard repeatedly. Southern Sonorans, their awareness sharpened by proximity, would describe to me the size of the landmass belonging to the tribe, reminding me of the Yaquis' exclusive rights to the ocean resources along the shores of the reserve. They would speculate aloud, imagining a wealth of mineral resources lying dormant, unexploited in the foothills of the reserve's Bacatete Mountains. Beneath such declarations ran a persistent subtext, an unspoken critique of Yaqui lifestyle and poverty.

Yaquis are aware of and are keenly affected by such discourses—talk that focuses on seemingly self-evident "realities," talk that ignores the historically generated structures that perpetuate inequalities and poverty. Mestizo claims about Yaqui nonproductivity are countered by Yaquis who go to great lengths to contextualize the predicament of their existence. A young Yaqui seminarian explained, "The reality is that the Yaquis are not rich. They have the land but not the means to work it."

Today there are an estimated 32,000 Yaquis living in Mexico's state of Sonora (Solidaridad 1995:15–16), the majority of whom reside within the boundaries of their federally granted reserve, a portion of their original homeland. This territory—known variously as the Yaqui Zona Indígena (Indigenous Zone), the Reserva Yaqui (Yaqui Reserve), or the Comunidades Yaquis (Yaqui Communities)—encompasses 485,000 hectares of land and is located 400 kilometers directly south of the international border separating Sonora from Arizona. Clustered in the desert landscape around the Yaqui River are eight historic pueblos (Vicam, Potam, Torim, Bacum, Belem, Rahum, Huirivis, and Cocorit), collectively referred to as the Ocho Pueblos (Eight Towns) or the Ocho Pueblos Sagrados (Eight

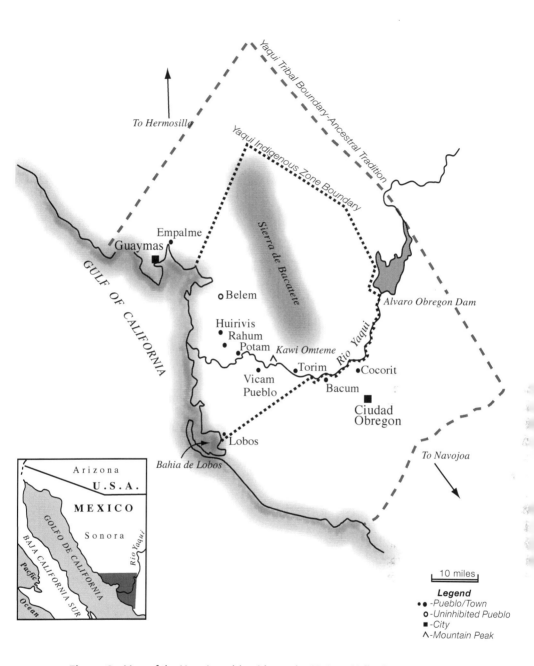

Figure 2. Map of the Yaqui pueblos (drawn by M. Jane Kellett)

Sacred Towns). Several of these Yaqui towns, established in the early seventeenth century under the Jesuit program of *reducción* (reduction, or gathering Indian inhabitants of small communities into larger pueblos) and consecrated by Yaqui oral tradition, continue to form the economic backbone of the Yaqui community. They are central to Yaqui social and ceremonial life and, as "sacred" pueblos, remain an important symbol of Yaqui cultural continuity.

The Yaqui Zona Indígena is an economically marginal pocket within a state known for its prosperity, a place where underemployment and unemployment are pervasive, where non-Indian Mexican farmers with the means to purchase tractors, expensive seed, and fertilizer till the vast tracts of Indian land lost to debt. Anyone who has traveled International Highway 15, which passes directly through the Yaqui Zona, has witnessed the crumbling walls of wattle-and-daub houses, their tarpaper roofs held down with rocks and bottles and soil, the dirt roads that wind away from the main thoroughfare, the conglomeration of cramped, dusty stores, rusted bicycles, and limping cars. An awareness of the history of displacement and persecution of the Yaqui people (Hu-DeHart 1981, 1984; Padilla Ramos 1995; Spicer 1980) and their economic and political marginalization within the nation (Lutes 1987; McGuire 1986) is important to identity scholarship. This context continues to shape Yaqui senses of self, social difference, and the connections to place that permeate ethnic narratives today.

Parameters of Difference

This book is based on 16 months of ethnographic research conducted in Potam and several of the other Yaqui pueblos and outlying communities. I traveled to the Yaqui Zona Indígena in the summer of 1995 to do a short-term field project on Yaqui women, work, and identity. When I returned for fieldwork in the autumn of 1996, I was prepared to continue my investigation of Yaqui women's gender through a study of women's economic practices and narratives. It was only a matter of weeks before I came to the realization that while gender was indeed a significant organizing feature of Yaqui society, Yaqui women's gendered identity was frequently overdetermined by ethnicity. Yaqui consultants were adamant that I understand the distinctions, as they perceived them, between themselves and Yoris, the history of conflict between these two groups, and the persistence of economic and social inequalities. They endeavored to illustrate what "Yaquiness" meant to them by talking about the importance of their places—and their homeland—and by calling attention to certain ways of behaving and believing. Interviews seemed to include an inevitable mention of ethnicity, and casual conversations were awash with references to identity. Following the lead of Yaquis with whom I worked, I redirected my focus. I turned to an examination of narratives and behaviors that might provide some insight into the ways in which Yaquis give meaning to, construct, and present their own ethnic identity. Within that framework I also hoped to come to a better understanding of women's gender and its articulation with ethnicity.

Ethnicity is a historically constructed, highly situational aspect of identity foregrounded in certain contexts and downplayed in others. While ethnic identity often becomes associated with a set of cultural values, symbolic practices, and geographic location, it is not a static entity. It is, rather, a relation of selves to others, embedded in power and continually in process (Vincent 1974; Wilmsen and McAllister 1996a). The cultural "stuff" with which members of an ethnic group are identified (or identify themselves) may, over time, undergo a dramatic transformation, while the boundaries of the ethnic group remain largely intact (Barth 1969). And although we understand the constructed, historically emergent nature of ethnicity (Comaroff and Comaroff 1992:60; Hall 1996:446), we may at the same time accept as legitimate (and potent) the political and moral meanings attached to ethnicity (Sharp 1996), its emotional component, as well as its tangible effects (Wilmsen 1996:2).[4] As Wilmsen and McAllister write, "The potency of ethnicity is palpable, but not easily explained. Part of its enticement lies in its diffuse and unspecified simplifications of the social world—its capacity to represent the complexities of class inequality, for example, in the emotive language of identity, being, and belonging" (1996b:viii).

The Yaquis I know distinguish themselves from non-Yaquis in many ways, but the parameters of difference are drawn most clearly through the terminological categories Yoeme and Yori, two words in the Yaqui language that epitomize a relation born in counterpositionality, two deceptively clear terms at the nexus of which accumulate strands of thickly intertwined meanings. An examination of the practical use of these terms reveals a variety of narrative strategies of belonging and exclusion through which distinctions are drawn between Yaqui selves and cultural others. The indigenous word for a Yaqui individual is Yoeme (sometimes pronounced Yoreme), meaning "person" or "human being." The plural

form, Yoemem, means "people." "Yoeme" is contrasted most strongly
with "Yori," the Yaqui word used to identify a non-Yaqui Mexican. Yori
simultaneously signifies "foreigner," "stranger," and "white person" and
can even imply "nonperson" (see Evers and Molina 1993:42; Figueroa
Valenzuela 1992:140).[5] Yorim (commonly Hispanicized to Yoris) is the
plural form of Yori. Anthropologist Edward Spicer notes:

> Yoemem was the word which embodied the Yaqui sense of being the
> real and essentially human beings of their region. . . . When yorim first
> came into use we do not know. What we know is that during the late
> nineteenth century it had the meaning of everything evil and inhuman
> that could be attributed to men and women. Its meaning was shaped by
> the violence that Yaquis experienced at the hands of Mexicans, and its
> usage intensified Yaqui feelings about the great worthiness and essential
> human qualities of themselves. [1980:349]

The foremost non-Yaqui academic expert on Yaqui language and culture
in the twentieth century, Spicer has hypothesized that, while the Yoeme–
Yori distinction entered into common parlance during the nineteenth-
century wars fought between these two groups, the word Yoeme itself is
far older. Grounding his claim in linguistic evidence, Spicer writes, "In
view of the extensive employment of the root in words for the language
and other related concepts, it seems likely that Yaquis used the word
Yoeme long before the 1600s" (1980:306). The root of the word Yoeme,
yoem, is used to form many other words in the Yaqui language; *yoemra*
(humanity), *yoemtu* (to be born, to become an adult), and *yoem-noki*
(Yaqui language) are just a few examples.[6] Although Yaquis acknowledge and take pride in the fact that they too are citizens of Mexico, non-
Yaqui Mexican nationals are still referred to as Yoris, often defined by
Yaquis with whom I spoke as "strangers" or "whites." Frequently, the
distinction is spatialized; a Yori is described as "one from the outside."

Yaqui (Yoeme) and Yori are the identity labels that are most commonly employed in Yaqui discourse, and they are the terms that contrast most starkly with one another. However, there are other degrees of
ethnic difference denoted in Yaqui talk. When I asked Ana Ochoa, the
Yaqui woman with whom I lived, if Mayos, Tarahumaras, Guarijios, and
Pimas (other indigenous groups in northern Mexico) were also "Yoris,"
she shook her head. "They are *otros Yoremes* [other Yoremes]," people
culturally similar enough to be designated Yoreme, like the Yaquis. I
then asked if she would classify me as a Yori; after all, I was definitely

an outsider, and the topic of my "whiteness" surfaced frequently in casual conversation. Again Ana shook her head. "You are *norteameri-cana* [North American]," she smiled, "a gringa, one from *el otro lado* ['the other side' of the border]. You are not a Yori." And, aside from "la Kristi," that in fact was how I most often overheard myself referred to: as the one from "el otro lado." My experiences confirm what Spicer noticed half a century ago: Yori is a term that designates a specific kind of otherness, carrying with it an unstated reference to the fraught history between Yaquis and Mexicans.

The question of ethnicity has figured prominently in the work of numerous scholars of Yaqui culture. Spicer, who conducted fieldwork among the Sonoran Yaquis during the 1940s, was the first and best-known anthropologist from the United States to study Yaqui culture. Spicer's prolific writings on Yaqui communities in Sonora and Arizona demonstrate a concern for history and a fine-tuned understanding of the political and religious organization of Yaqui society (see Spicer 1954, 1980, 1984). Spicer claims that, like the Basques and other "enduring" peoples (1980:337), the Yaquis' "persistent identity" is forged in opposi-tion to an encompassing, more powerful state (1971:797). He argues that it is within symbolic systems (including language and expressive culture) that those historically generated ethnic distinctions are maintained. Spicer produced works oriented around ceremonialism and social orga-nization; his studies of the deer dance, Semana Santa (Holy Week), and the fiesta system emphasize the performative aspects of Yaqui identity. Historian Evelyn Hu-DeHart (1981, 1984) has also written about identity in her examination of the centuries-long armed struggle of the Yaquis to retain their land and the impact of this experience on the Yaquis as a group. Alejandro Figueroa Valenzuela (1994) dedicated his life's work to a comparative investigation of Yaqui and Mayo ethnicity, focusing on history, social organization, and religious expression. David Shorter (2002) expands and complexifies Western notions of "writing" and "his-tory" through his study of Yaqui identity inscription in religious per-formance. And Thomas McGuire (1986) has written about the political economy of the Yaqui Zone, ethnic politics, and land claims.

McGuire's work emphasizes the ascriptive component of Yaqui eth-nicity. When he insists that an "individual's group membership—his identity as Yaqui—is founded upon genealogy" (1986:40), he is quite correct: one is a Yaqui because he or she is born a Yaqui. Yet while I agree with McGuire's premise that most Yaquis are secure in identifying themselves as such by virtue of their family heritage, I believe that he goes too far in his assertion, "Questions of ethnic identity . . . are *uninteresting* to contemporary Yaquis because that identity is largely unproblematic" (1986: ix–x, emphasis added). My own fieldwork, observations, and continued conversations with Yaquis have led to a very different set of conclusions: Yaquis may not see ethnic belonging itself as "problematic," but degrees of "Yaquiness" and indeed what it means to be Yaqui *are* significant social concerns. The recognition that one belongs to the ethnic group is merely a starting point. The cultural contents of Yaqui ethnic identity are negotiable, and most of the Yaqui individuals I know invest themselves deeply in the daily work of the production of ethnic identity.[7] Their narratives continually reiterate the connections between place and identity, and they exhibit a compelling concern with the contours of "acceptable" Yaqui behavior.[8]

Yaquis discuss identity all the time. They talk to one another and to outsiders about identity when narrating their lives and their history. Themes of identity emerge in stories concerning the special relationship Yaquis have to their homeland. And Yaqui individuals highlight important differences between themselves and Yoris in conversations about everything from religious concerns to practical matters. Yaquis call attention to those aspects of their behavior that make them *muy Yaqui* (very Yaqui) and to those practices or attitudes that are emblematic of a certain "authenticity." Indeed, an examination of Yaqui ethnic identity reveals it to be, most fundamentally, a "cultural identity" (Linnekin and Poyer 1990), constituted even as it is performed (Butler 1990, 1999), narrated, and embodied (Taussig 1993).

Overview

This book is best conceived as a story about the interplay between ethnicity, place making, and women's identity-constituting practices. It is an examination of how Yaquis make their way in the world and remind themselves—through narrative and through culturally prescribed behaviors and practices—of who they are. My primary interest is not the representation of identity through political oratory, official histories, or the intricacies of the Yaqui civil–ceremonial system (Spicer 1954, 1980). Rather, I am concerned with the details of everyday life and the cumulative impact of seemingly mundane conversations, stories, household rituals, and spatial practices upon identity concepts—in short, *how* identities are continuously created and contested by Yaqui individuals. Specifically, this study examines two interconnected areas of Yaqui identity production: the simultaneous processes of place making and ethnic identification, and the inseparability of ethnicity from female-identified spaces, roles, and practices.

Over the past 20 years an awareness of the social production of space (Lefebvre 1991) has come into its own in academia, fostering an anthropology of place and space (Low and Lawrence-Zuñiga 2003), with topics as diverse as the study of spatial relations and power (Gupta and Ferguson 1992; Harvey 1990; Soja 1989, 1996), narrative and place making (Basso 1996; Stewart 1996), and the connections between place and memory (Gordillo 2004; Nora 1989; Shaw 2002). Drawing on this scholarship, I analyze the complex interplay of place making and Yaqui identity constitution with the intention of extending anthropological understandings of the ways in which identity is spatially imagined.

Part I of the book explores how the experience of place and space impinges upon the expression of Yaqui social histories, shaping the narrative construction of a modern Yaqui subject. Peter Wade writes that "ethnicity is, of course, about cultural differentiation, but it tends to use a language of *place* (rather than wealth, sex, or inherited phenotype)" (1997:18). Location and geography figure prominently in the identity narratives of the Yaquis, a people whose aboriginal territory has been a source of contention since colonial times. Their removal from their aboriginal territory, enslavement in southern Mexico, life in exile, and struggle to return to their homeland have become central themes in the narratives that are the fabric of Yaqui social history. As portrayed in myths focused on territory and borders, stories of ancestors who dwell underneath the hills, historical accounts of exile and return, and legends of enchanted caves and blessed springs, Yaqui ethnic–cultural identity has a decidedly spatial component.

Within the context of this place-centered sense of identity, part II then turns to an examination of how Yaqui ethnicity articulates with and powerfully affects notions of femaleness in Yaqui culture. At the same time, my focus shifts from the narrative construction of ethnicity (deemed important to local communities and anthropological observers alike) to more subtle (and frequently overlooked) forms of identity production: women's everyday "tactical" interactions (Certeau 1984), modes of relationality, and the creation of domestic spaces that are recognized as both gendered and utterly ethnic (Massey 1994; Moore 1986).

An examination of women's gender is crucial because Yaqui ethnicity is reproduced, in part, through the enactment of gender relations.

In previous scholarship on the Sonoran Yaquis, only one work focuses explicitly on Yaqui women's lives: Jane Holden Kelley's (1978) collection of four life histories. There has not yet been a study that addresses Yaqui women's particular actions and discourses—their agency, symbolic practices, place making, and social relations. In reaffirming their gendered identities and by creating and occupying female-gendered spaces (kitchens, household altars, and the spaces of ritual and refuge), women constitute Yaqui ethnicity in a way that is *as significant* as the actions taken by the (male) governors of the pueblos and through public ceremonialism. Women's "behind-the-scenes" ritual labor and networks of reciprocity become prime occasions for the reproduction and affirmation of Yaquiness.

Fieldwork

When I moved to Potam in October 1996, I rented a room in the home of a non-Yaqui woman. That first month my research progressed on schedule: I met new people every day, recorded interviews, visited schools, and attended church services. Still, something was missing. The Yaquis whom I met were polite and expressed interest in my project, but there was a distance and formality in these growing relationships that made me uncomfortable. I primarily attended daytime events and saw people during visits in which I was treated as a guest.

Three days after my arrival in Potam I met Ana Ochoa Bakasewa, a 34-year-old Yaqui woman who viewed the translation of Yaqui culture to an outsider as a serious responsibility and in whose house I would live for over a year. Ana and her husband, Marco Usacamea López, are both elementary school teachers, born and raised in Potam. They have three children. (When I began my research, Juan was 14 and Margarita was 11; baby Lila was born the following summer.) We began spending more time together, and at the end of October they invited me to move into their house. I did so and quickly experienced a new level of involvement and intimacy. Through Ana, Marco, their extended families, and their circle of friends and ritual kin I made new contacts and acquaintances. I was included in all family events. These relationships gave me access to a world I might not have experienced as fully had I continued to live "outside" the Yaqui community: dropping in to visit a new mother still sequestered at her natal home under the *cuarentena* (40-day postpartum quarantine); attending a midnight wake for a deceased grandmother; helping from start to finish with the preparations for a family wedding; conversing late into the night with Ana and her sisters about everything from husbands to ritual sequences, locally available medicinal plants, and pueblo politics.

Throughout my field study I interacted with and interviewed many people, male and female. The first portion of this book concerns the significance of place, concepts of locality, and discourses about the homeland in the construction of ethnic–cultural identity, and it relies heavily on the narratives of individuals of both genders. But the reader will notice a decided shift in the second half of the book, where my emphasis is primarily on women's voices and experiences. From the inception of this project my desire has been to present both women and men as creative cultural actors but also to draw attention to a topic that has previously received little attention—Yaqui women as significant agents in the production of Yaqui identity, true participants in the complex workings of pueblo cultural and ritual life.

On a very practical level, Yaqui social life and social spaces are intensely gendered. As a female ethnographer I found that everyone (Yaqui men, Yaqui women, and I myself) appeared to be more comfortable when I associated with groups of women. While I lived and conversed with male consultants, interviewed them, went places with them, and observed their behavior and interactions, I spent a greater amount of time with Yaqui women. I was more involved in women's daily lives and therefore privy to their conversations, points of view, and opinions.

The Yaqui individuals with whom I worked were not a random sampling of the pueblo's population. Quite simply, I was introduced to two women in 1995 and the fall of 1996 who were incredibly gracious, intellectually curious, and tolerant enough of me and my questions to invite me into their lives. They introduced me to their families, coworkers, and friends, who then introduced me to other ritual kin, acquaintances, and so on. This relationally oriented method of encountering and engaging informants is sometimes identified as "ego-centered" networking (Ellen 1984:268) or "snowball sampling" (Chavez 1998:7). In reality, however, the way I went about my fieldwork had much more to do with establishing relationships of trust and working within Yaqui communicative norms. In Yaqui practice every new introduction (especially those that precede formal inquiry or the exchange of cultural information) requires an intermediary. The Yaqui women who befriended me also interceded for me at nearly every turn, speaking first, smoothing the way—"speaking for" me, as they say—when I needed to talk with an elder or ritual specialist, when I appeared in front of the tribal council and governors of Potam to gain permission to conduct research, or when I simply wanted to meet someone new.

The descriptions in this book are as situated as my field experience. It is a work based upon formal and informal interviews, collected speech acts, historical narratives and life stories, and the various observations I made while visiting the Yaqui Zona Indígena during July 1995, while living in Potam from October 1996 through December 1997, and on several subsequent visits since that time. My fieldwork and interviews were conducted in Spanish, and the narratives and conversations that fill the pages of this book were spoken in Spanish. While many of my consultants and most of the elders I know are fluent in the Yaqui language and code-switch easily between Spanish and Yaqui, the Spanish language often predominates as the medium of discourse among those who live in Potam and other large towns in the Zona Indígena.

When I lived in Potam, I spent my waking hours immersed in Yaqui consultants' lives and concerns, attending baptisms and weddings, confirmations and funerary rituals. I participated in Lenten promenades, observed Holy Week performances, and helped out during lengthy pueblo fiestas. I participated in daily household and economic activities. My work is full of people's stories—their tales of family trouble and personal crisis, their memories of the past, their claims about identity and the meanings of their places.[9] As a partial and mediated account (Clifford 1986; Kondo 1990), this book paints one of a multitude of possible pictures of Yaqui life. Yet at the same time I believe it yields important insights into contemporary Yaqui realities and experience, revealing broader truths about Yaqui cultural discourses and the deeply historical, emplaced, and gendered processes through which Yaquis produce and reproduce identity.

Claiming Identity

Cultural belonging, behavior, and narrative are powerful modes through which self-identities are constituted. It is significant that the narrative with which I began—Josefina's story—is a nostalgic presentation of Yaqui life in the past and a moral discourse on being Yaqui in the present. Yet, tracing her genealogy, one would discover that Josefina actually has very little Yaqui "blood." Josefina was born in the state of Oaxaca in southern Mexico, her mother a Mayo Indian from Huatabampo, her father a mestizo and a soldier in the Mexican army. Her father died when she was very young, and her mother died shortly after bringing Josefina to Potam to live with her maternal grandmother. Her maternal grandfather had been at least part Yaqui; having spent most of his life in the Sonoran cities of Empalme and Guaymas, he had moved his family to Potam toward the end of his own life to claim a piece of land granted by tribal authorities to those of Yaqui heritage. With pride, Josefina recalled how as a girl she had learned the Yaqui language:

> Yes, they [her grandmother and mother] were Mayas [women of Mayo descent].[10] My mother hardly spoke Mayo but rather [used] Castilla [Spanish].[11] And in that way I became used to speaking in pure Castilla; I didn't speak in *la lengua* [literally, 'the tongue'; i.e., the Yaqui language].[12] . . . No, I didn't speak la lengua. I learned here. Some neighbor girls taught me, little girls. I had brought many little toys from Mexico City. My mother had bought them for me. She gave them all [to those girls] so that they might teach me.

Josefina may not have a substantial quantity of Yaqui "blood," but she boasts a lifetime invested in the pueblo in both senses of the Spanish word: pueblo as place (literally, "town") and pueblo as a "people." Josefina has anchored herself in Potam, one of the Eight Sacred Pueblos, a place of great significance to Yaqui identity. She spent the majority of her years living and working in Potam; she speaks the Yaqui language; and she gave birth to and raised eight children there. In her own words, they are "all *indios de aquí* [Indians from here (Potam)]." She has also firmly ensconced herself within the Yaqui community. A godmother many times over, Josefina is linked socially and economically to dozens of families. She has served her community by shouldering the arduous duties of the fiesta host.

She was born somewhere else, her father a mestizo soldier and her mother a Mayo Indian, but the sheer weight of evidence affirming Josefina's "Yaquiness" accumulates as her narrative progresses. It is when she shares her memories of better times that Josefina stakes her strongest yet most subtle claim to ethnic belonging. As Natalie Zemon Davis and Randolph Starn note, "Identity depends on memory, whether we mean by that a core self that remembers its earlier states or, poststructurally, the narratives that construct (and deconstruct) identities by comparing 'once upon a time' and 'here and now'" (1989:4). A narrative strategy of belonging, Josefina's life story recalls an idealized past, a time when things were different, a time of safety and abundance. By reflecting upon a time before there were so many Yoris in Potam, Josefina identifies and sets the Mexicans, the Yoris, as a group apart, as other—those who brought with them the changes that led to the deterioration of what was a comfortable and secure existence. In so doing she implicitly reinscribes her own identity as a Yaqui self. Just as Josefina's memories of the past are shaped by her experience and positionality as a Yaqui self (as opposed to a Yori other) in the present, so too her present-day identity is affected by her memories of the past.[13] The process is perpetual; it turns back on itself. Josefina's story subverts discourses of blood and belonging through memory and the narration of difference.

I
Narrating Place, Articulating Identity

2

"They Will Come from the Other Side of the Sea"
Prophecy, Ethnogenesis, and Agency in Yaqui Narrative

> Histories told and remembered by those who inherit them
> are discourses of identity; just as identity is inevitably
> a discourse of history.
> —Geoffrey White, *Identity through History*

I was waiting for a bus in the shade of a mesquite tree on a Sunday morning in June 1997 when an opportunity presented itself. I had been conducting research in the Yaqui pueblo of Potam for ten months. Despite my efforts at maintaining a rigorous interview schedule, regular rounds of visiting, and attendance at important pueblo ceremonies, it seemed that the most interesting ethnographic prospects simply materialized unbidden; fortunately, this one wasn't difficult to recognize. A man in his late sixties approached me, and although I had never been formally introduced to Ramón Hernández Leyva, he always made polite conversation when we happened to bump into one another. On that warm spring morning Ramón greeted me in the Yaqui language and asked where I was going. I told him I was on my way to Sonora's branch of INAH (Instituto Nacional de Antropología e Historia, the National Institute of Anthropology and History) in Hermosillo to use the library. After that I would be going to Tucson, Arizona. Ramón smiled and said that he himself had been to "Tucsón" several times to give talks about the Yaqui tribe. "I know much about history," he declared, adding that he had been "recorded" at the University of Arizona and had participated in a symposium in the town of Ajo, near the Tohono O'odham Reservation. "I know many things," he added. "Come to my house when you return from el otro lado."

It was not until September 1997 that Ramón and I were able to have the first of our three lengthy interviews. Sitting in his adobe house in Potam, Ramón switched on a clattering fan and attached the microphone to his lapel while I set up the tape recorder. Recalling his enticing claim that he knew "much about history," I began with a query about Yaqui resistance to the colonization of their land by Mexican settler farmers and the ensuing "Yaqui Wars" of the nineteenth century. Ramón's response was both unexpected and illuminating:

> The Mexicans? The Mexicans, well, they are just Mexicans. And throughout time, well, that is, they have brought many consequences upon us, the Mexicans. Throughout time, in times past, the Yaqui tribe was one single tribe. Nothing more. One single tribe. Yes. Before the Spaniards came. But yes, they had been told, no? By their gods, the Yaqui tribe. And by means of their dreams, they were told. They understood that certain disasters were to follow. The sun was the father of all. He was like a father, a *papá*, the sun. And the moon, well, that too, they treated her as if she were their *mamá*. They respected her greatly. The moon, yes. And over time then, before the Spaniards arrived, they had a vision by means of their own wisdom. They already had their own customs, but very ancient, hmm? And later, a Yaqui poetess said that with the passage of time there would come another generation in another form. And with all this knowledge, no? They understood it well by means of their thoughts and by talking—with the stars and with all classes of animals.

I had inquired about the Yaqui Wars, expecting a conventional history or perhaps a family story—a Yaqui's perspective of a familiar tale. Instead, Ramón alluded to a narrative that I immediately recognized from my readings (Evers and Molina 1993; Giddings 1993; Painter 1986; Sands 1983; Spicer 1980; Valenzuela Kaczkurkin 1977) as a version of what Edward Spicer first called the "myth of the Talking Tree" (1980:172). The Talking Tree story prophesies the arrival of Europeans, foretells a radical conversion of the Yaquis to Christianity, and ultimately describes the transformation of this people's cultural identity when confronted with a dominating other.

This chapter explores Ramón Hernández's Talking Tree story as a constitutive narrative event—a contextualized and self-creative "telling" that articulates some important (one might even say "core") ideas about the past and Yaqui ethnic origins. On that searing September afternoon I asked Ramón about Yaqui resistance during the nineteenth century. He chose to begin with a story about a time before Yaqui–European contact, a revealing narrative about prophecy, impending invasion, and the consequences of difference. This story remains significant to tribal historians—people like Ramón—because it concerns the ethnogenesis (the coming-into-being) of the Yaqui people—the very inception of Yaqui identity. But also, and perhaps more critically, I argue that the Talking Tree story is an alternative history, one that presents Yaquis as agents rather than victims, one that *refigures* the relation of Yaqui selves to Yori others in the process of ethnogenesis.

Ramón's Talking Tree History

In the first decades of the sixteenth century Spaniards exploring the northwestern edge of New Spain encountered roughly 30,000 people practicing agriculture on the floodplain of the Yaqui River (Pérez de Ribas 1944:64; Spicer 1980:5). Hot summers and insufficient rainfall made this desert lowland along the Gulf of California inhospitable to human habitation with the exception of river valleys like the Yaqui, a green oasis in an arid region otherwise home to groves of thorny mesquite and acacia, aloes and spiny cacti. At the time of European contact aboriginal Yaquis lived in 80 semipermanent hamlets scattered along the lower 100 kilometers of the Yaqui River. There they cultivated maize, beans, pumpkins, squash, and cotton in soft alluvial soils and supplemented their farming with hunting, fishing, and gathering (Hu-DeHart 1981:9–11; Pérez de Ribas 1944:64; Spicer 1969:787, 1980:5–9).

In 1533 Capt. Diego de Guzmán and his soldiers attempted to enter Yaqui territory and claim it for the Spanish Empire, but they were violently repelled by Yaqui warriors. During the first decade of the 1600s Capt. Diego Martínez de Hurdaide and his forces were repeatedly defeated by Yaquis defending their land. Despite the fact that the Yaquis had successfully fended off European invaders, the Spaniards made it clear that assaults would continue. The Yaquis acquiesced, agreeing to allow Jesuit missionaries to live in their midst (Hu-DeHart 1981:14–16, 25–27; Spicer 1980:5, 13–17).[1]

And so it was in 1617 that Fathers Andrés Pérez de Ribas and Tomás Basilio set out for the Yaqui River valley to convert Yaquis to Christianity and transform Yaqui aboriginal territory into a Jesuit mission. From the beginning the missionaries implemented the standard Jesuit practice of reducción. Historian Evelyn Hu-DeHart describes the Jesuit strategy for a massive relocation and reorganization of the "loose federation"

(1981:23) of Yaqui-speaking communities: "First of all, they had Indian assistants from established missions transport prodigious quantities of food to the new mission site. They needed these provisions to entice Yaquis from distant, dispersed *rancherías* [hamlets] to leave their homes and fields to take up new residence ... along the river" (1981:32). The missionaries directed the construction of eight churches, the building of which "was designed to set in motion a process of change in physical location of the whole Yaqui population" (Spicer 1980:27), and by 1623 the Jesuits claimed to have baptized all of the Yaquis in the surrounding region (Hu-DeHart 1981:33). The missionaries introduced domesticated cattle and goats, novel crop varieties, and new irrigation techniques to Yaqui farmers (Hu-DeHart 1981:36–38; Spicer 1980:30). Spicer estimates that by the mid-1700s but possibly as early as the mid-1600s the majority of the 30,000 people who formerly inhabited 80 scattered hamlets had relocated to the eight large pueblos of Potam, Vicam, Cocorit, Bacum, Torim, Huirivis, Rahum, and Belem (1980:27).

The events described in the Talking Tree story occur on the eve of European–Yaqui contact, before the Spanish colonial presence in northwestern New Spain and the establishment of Jesuit missions. As such, this narrative marks what Spicer calls the "beginning of the Conquest" (1980:172) in the Yaqui historical imagination. The Talking Tree story continues to have a unique status in Yaqui oral literature. Kathleen Sands notes, "Unlike many other tribes, the Yaquis do not have a cohesive and comprehensive body of lore concerning their origins and identity. Though a great deal of Yaqui lore has been collected, no lengthy cycles or extended narrative texts have come to light" (1983:359). This story is the exception in that portions of it are well known by many older Yaqui people in the Sonoran Yaqui communities.[2]

During our interview Ramón Hernández talked about the presence of Jesuit missionaries, the introduction of Catholicism, the resistance to Mexican colonization of Yaqui territory led by his great-great-uncle Juan Maldonado Tetabiate in the 1890s, and a terrible flood that is also recounted in the Bible. At one point, in an attempt to draw him back to the narrative with which he began our interview, I asked Ramón to tell me what he knew about the ancestral Surem, the people who inhabited Yaqui territory when the mysterious Talking Tree first began to sound out its prophetic message.[3] In the following pages I present Ramón's version of the Talking Tree story, followed by an elaboration of some specific portions of the story and an analysis of its implications for understanding the negotiation of Yaqui identity through historical narrative.[4]

> RH: In those times, they passed the story along (but just by word of mouth, with words only) of the Surem. Well, about 5,000 years ago, those people lived here. . . .
>
> And at one time, down to there, down to Belem [one of the historic Yaqui pueblos], that place was ruled by, dominated by, the Pimas. The Pimas, no? Because they had not yet moved themselves farther north. They moved about out here, no? Farming. . . . And after some time, well, now the Spaniards arrived here. The Mexicans, the Yaquis. Already you have been spoken to many times, no? About los Ocho Pueblos.
>
> At that time the Pimas disappeared from here. But much earlier the Surem lived here. It is a theory. I have gone many places, no? Giving talks. Investigating, no? About the Surem. . . . And a long time ago, while walking about on the lands, I found a little *metate* [grinding stone] like this. [Ramón spread his hands about 30 centimeters apart, indicating the size of the metate.] A little metate like this. It is still out there. They were very short people, like this, the Surem. [Ramón held his hand less than a meter from the floor to demonstrate the stature of the Surem.] Hmm. And supposedly, they even say, hmm, the ancestors, that these people surely did exist. And that they were very, very wise as well. They knew that the Spaniards were going to come here. Some went up into the sierra, and others fled underneath, underneath the earth, here. Hmm? . . .
>
> There was a Yaqui poetess, no? They went for her. Here at Omteme Mountain, there in that place, there appeared a wooden pole. A wooden pole like that, tall. . . . It was like a telegraph, no? Like that. But no one understood it. And they went for a wise man who lived out there. And there were other wise ones, and they went for them too. . . . I believe that it became angry. It became angry because many people gathered. . . . They call it that, "angry," the Angry Mountain, Omteme. Kawi Omteme. They had to ask the question of all the animals, of all the birds who were there. They asked the question. . . .
>
> Here, something appeared, a pole, very tall. And in the afternoon, it sounded off in this way. And no one understood what it said. . . . And the ancestors knew that a warning was going to come. "Well, I believe that that is what this is. Get the wisest person in the land; look

for him here among the Yaquis."⁵ And they went out there. And so some little birds came. Little birds like this. They came and said they knew where the wise one lived. It was a woman. "This one," they said, "lives out there. Near the sea. Near the sea, that is where she lives, Maapol. Hmm. . . . One who is called Maapol. And this one will know."

"She lives there," said the smallest bird.

And so they went for the young woman, a Yaqui poetess. . . . And they arrived out there. And she accepted. She told them, "Tomorrow, very early in the morning, I will head over there. I've got to notify my papá and everyone." *In achai* [my father]. In achai. That is how they said the words "my father" at that time, "in achai." Hmm. . . . And they left and arrived.

And then in the morning, at about one o'clock in the morning there, the young woman got up, no? She grabbed her bow and her arrows, made a lunch, . . . *agua* [water], . . . and she wrapped it all up in a bundle. She told them that she was going out there. Coming over here. . . . "I have to go to help them because they don't know what is happening. Soon I will tell them. Now I am going over there."

It is when the Surem were there, no? They left. The Surem said to themselves, "Times are not going to be good from now on; other people are going to come." Many went away.

Now the Yaqui poetess took to the road. And she didn't arrive that same day. Until the next day, at 12 o'clock. At midday she arrived. But with her came her entire troop. Along with her came *mochomos* [ants], scorpions, ants. Hmm? And then they arrived there. And the animals arrived along with her. They were her soldiers. Many people were frightened. Many people disappeared when they saw these animals coming.

"*Bueno* [Well], here I am. Now I am here." And this was their salutation, no? "Haisa wewu, haisa wewu. Haisa wewu [*haisa*, 'how'; *wewu*, not translatable]." That was the greeting because they still didn't know Dios [God].

KE: Meaning they couldn't say, "Dios em chaniabu" [May God help you]?

RH: No. They still didn't know. And so they said "Haisa wewu. Haisa wewu." And now they gave her an explanation of what was happening there. "We don't understand anything. Let's see if you do." And now in the afternoon she began. She lit a *cigarro* [cigarette] of the *macuchus* [Yaqui tobacco, or *hiak vivam*]. And she began to smoke it. . . . "Well, gentlemen," she said, "now everything has come to me. It is nothing, this. Other people are going to come. They will come from the other side of the sea. People . . . like us. The same. It's just that they are from over there, and we are from here. But they are the same people. They have the same spirit, the same thoughts that we have. The same heart, the same eyes, the same nose. All of it. They are going to come here. And from here on, when these people arrive, there is going to be a change. A change, another way of life. They are going to bring a thing called religion. They shall bring an upright pole, crossed with another. [Ramón made the sign of the cross with his hand.] There is a person hanging there. And this is the way it will be. Now there will be no deaths. Everyone shall continue living. Hmm. And there is a person who died for all the people.

"We are not the only people. On the other side of the sea there are more people. And they are people like us. And now their customs shall come here. . . . And there is another Lord called God. He sent that one here to save the world. They will bring this knowledge to us, so that we might learn it. Hmm. . . . They are going to teach you with this [right] hand, to make a cross, to cross yourselves. They will teach you that he died for us. They are going to bring many things. And they will bring a green ball like this, with some seeds in the center, that you are going to learn to plant. And they are also going to bring with them a little bundle that looks like a little nose, a seed, and this you will also plant. You are going to plant garbanzo. And other things. And some other tiny seeds, to plant here. These people are going to come here. . . . You just need to prepare yourselves. You are going to need many things, bows. So that they don't grab you by surprise. Guard your territory here. Guard your territory. Mark your borders. Mark them. They are going to come." . . .

After awhile, she was with them for a while, "Now I am going back," she said. "I am going back." And she went out there, no? The poetess. Toward the south. And the poetess told the Yaquis to get their arrows, to raise their bows. [Ramón explained that they stood in a line and shot their arrows into the distance.] "Now it is marked. Now it is marked." And in fact, where the arrows landed, they surrounded it with some marks. "And now they are going to arrive here." [Ramón asserted that the boundaries abutted Mayo territory to the south and extended northward to the Río Colorado; they were marked everywhere an arrow landed.] "There shall come some bearded men, white; many of them have white hair." Hmmm. This is what the poetess said. . . . And they shot off some arrows over there. And from there, they came here. . . .

And that is what the Yaqui poetess said. Hmm? Hmm. And so the Surem who were there, they left. They wrapped up a piece of the Yaqui River, like this. [Ramón made a wrapping motion, as if bundling something with his hands.] Each one grabbed a piece of the river. This was the river that used to flow over there. Over there it flowed, 5,000 years ago. Hmm.

And so . . . New Spain was established. . . . And that is the way it happened. The Yaqui tribe has never left the Yaqui River. The government of Porfirio Díaz, and General Lorenzo Torres—they all wanted this land, the land of the Yaquis. They sent them to Yucatán, Oaxaca, the Valley [Valle Nacional]. But they couldn't finish them off. Many fled to Tucson, over there. And to this day they are there. They have their own reservation and are now recognized as a North American tribe. . . . And that is how it was.

According to Ramón, the Talking Tree's prophecy occurred "5,000 years ago," before the Pimas occupied this country, before the Spaniards arrived, before the "Mexicans [or] the Yaquis" were here. It is a story set in the mythic past, a time characterized by Karl Luckert (1975) as that of "pre-human flux" (Nabokov 2002:42). At the very beginning of our interview Ramón described an era when animals and humans were not sharply differentiated, when communication was not limited within single species: "And over time then, before the Spaniards arrived, they had a vision by means of their own wisdom. . . . They understood it well by means of their thoughts and by means of talking—with the stars and with all classes of animals." Through her research with the Yaqui communities in Tucson, Muriel Thayer Painter came to understand that the Surem "lived a nomadic life in a unitary world in which man and animals, insects, flowers, indeed, the whole world of nature and man, had a common psychic life" (1986:4). While the essence of this time is marked by the ability of people and animals to interact, the Talking Tree story is situated on and centrally concerns the boundaries of today's Yaqui territory. In his narrative Ramón connects the ancient past with the present-day homeland by mentioning places still familiar. He refers to Belem, one of the original Ocho Pueblos of the Yaquis, and he describes the place where the vibrating stick appeared—Kawi Omteme (Angry Mountain), a rocky peak located just east of Vicam Pueblo.

As Ramón explains, the Surem are the ancestral inhabitants of this land; they are short in stature and very wise. Stories of discovery—the small metates and tiny pots stumbled upon by Yaquis walking through the bush on their way to the fields or to a relative's home for a visit—are occasionally cited by older informants as physical proof, evidence of the continuing existence of these ancient people. The unexpected appearance of a tall wooden pole on Kawi Omteme, a pole that emitted a sound "like a telegraph," is the event that changes everything for the Surem, rupturing the contours of their existence.[6] In their perplexity and their determination to understand the message emanating from the pole, the Surem seek out the wisest person in the land to translate; they are informed by little birds that the wise one lives near the sea and that her name is Maapol.

The character Ramón calls Maapol is the only identifiable individual in this narrative. In some versions of the Talking Tree myth her name is Yomumuli (Giddings 1993).[7] Occasionally, she is described as twin girls, and at times she is called Sea Hamut (Flower Woman).[8] Regardless, in every recorded version the wise one is young and female. According to Ramón, Maapol lives with her father in the wilderness, significantly, near the sea, a place that Yaquis often associate with danger and power (Sands 1983:364).[9] The wise one breaks traditional Yaqui gender conventions: she prepares for her trip by gathering a bow and arrows (male hunting equipment), and she makes the long trek inland without accompaniment.[10] Maapol's association with the wilderness is reinforced by another detail in Ramón's story: she journeys to the country of the Surem with an army of dangerous and frightening insects.

When Maapol arrives at Kawi Omteme, she greets the Surem people and proceeds to smoke macuchis in order to gain an understanding of the wooden pole's strange humming. While some Yaqui storytellers have identified the young woman as a "prophetess" (Sands 1983:363), Ramón calls her a "poetess." Even if unintentional, the implication of Ramón's word choice is meaningful. Playing with sound, rhythm, syntax, and vocabulary, the poet fashions language into something out of the ordinary. He or she intensifies language to call the listener's attention to style so that style itself conveys meaning (Bauman and Briggs

1990:79; Herzfeld 1985; Jameson 1972). As Larry Evers and Felipe Molina point out, other forms of Yaqui narrative invoke this heightened relationship between sound and meaning:

> In a significant way, all beginnings in Yaqui oral history involve such recognitions. The sounds that need to be understood may come from fishes, caves, or invading Spaniards. They may be a part of what we call myth, history, vision, or dream, but time and again in Yaqui stories the people must understand sound from beyond the limits of the everyday language of their communities in order to continue. In this sense there are no creators in Yaqui tradition, only translators. All beginnings are translations. [1993:36]

The young woman foretells unimaginable changes: the arrival of people "from the other side of the sea," men with beards and white hair who will bring a religion symbolized by a cross and who will introduce new seed varieties. Maapol warns the Surem to delineate the boundaries of their land by standing in a line and shooting off arrows in all directions; the final landing place of those arrows would mark the full extent of the Surem's territory.[11] At several points during his narrative Ramón refers to the response of the Surem after they heard the prophecy. "The Surem said to themselves, 'Times are not going to be good from now on; other people are going to come.' Many went away." The ancestors of the Yaquis "knew that the Spaniards were going to come here. [And] some went up into the sierra, and others fled underneath, underneath the earth." Eventually, Ramón insists, the Surem simply left, taking with them pieces of the Yaqui River. Ramón's description of the disappearance of the Surem is not inconsistent with the explanations provided by other consultants. Many residents of Potam spoke to me about the descent of the Surem into the earth, their journey to "the North" or simply into the hills. Although there is no widespread consensus as to where the Surem went when they fled the invaders, it is generally agreed that they continue to exist in a world parallel to the visible world.[12]

Narrating Ethnogenesis

While it does not explain the creation of the world, the Talking Tree story typically outlines the ethnogenesis (the coming-into-being) of the group of people who today identify as Yaqui. In one version of the myth, recounted by Luciano Velasquez to Yaqui scholar Felipe Molina in 1982, the depiction of Yaqui ethnogenesis is quite explicit.[13] Upon hearing the translation of the tree's message, the Surem

> didn't really like some of the things they heard, so they planned a big meeting. . . . At this meeting some of the Surem decided to leave the Yaqui region, while others decided to stay and to see these new things. . . . [T]he Surem who were leaving cut up a portion of the Yo Vatwe [Enchanted River], wrapped it up in a bamboo mat, and took it north to a land of many islands. Other Surem stayed around and went into the ocean and underground into the mountains. There in those places the Surem now exist as an enchanted people. Those who stayed behind are now the modern Yaquis . . . the Baptized Ones. [Evers and Molina 1993:38]

The Talking Tree's prophecy marks a decisive moment: the differentiation of those who remain in their original form as immortal Surem (those who fled when the European invaders came) from those "modern" Yaquis who chose to await the newcomers and accept Christianity (Evers and Molina 1993:38; Spicer 1980:67, 172). Ramón's narrative does not categorically label those Yaquis who decided to stay the "Baptized Ones," yet his description of ethnogenesis is implicit within the text. He tells of the many Surem who "went away" upon receiving the prophecy, and he enumerates the great changes in store for those who remained behind.

At one point Ramón illustrates a shift in the Yaqui belief system by pointing to language itself: "And this was their salutation, no? 'Haisa wewu, haisa wewu. Haisa wewu.' That was the greeting because they still didn't know Dios." The reference is to the customary Yaqui greeting "Dios em chaniabu," a phrase that begins with Dios (also pronounced "Lios" by Yaqui speakers), a word directly adopted from the Spanish, meaning God. "Dios em chaniabu" may be loosely translated "May God help you." Ramón's declaration differentiates "before" (the Christian) God was known from "after," a distinction also embedded in his assertion: "They already had their own customs, but very ancient, hmm? And later, a Yaqui poetess said that with the passage of time there would come another generation, another generation in another form."

The Talking Tree story is about radical transformation, but change is not presented as unilaterally good or evil. As Jerome Bruner argues, the work of narrative is not to bring a problem to its seamless resolution but rather to facilitate "the comprehension of plight that, by being made interpretable, becomes bearable" (1991:16). The story of the Talking Tree demonstrates a capacity to register the deep ambivalence with which impending change is received. On the one hand, the prediction of the arrival of the whites is a prophecy of invasion: Maapol instructs the Surem to mark a border around their territory. The arrival of the foreigners precipitates division: some of the Surem leave with portions of the Yaqui River tucked under their arms, and a new type of Yaqui person emerges. On the other hand, the strangers from across the sea are to bring with them certain opportunities, including new seeds to plant and a chance to know a savior sent to "save the world."

This is a crucial point to remember when discussing the meaning of the Talking Tree story: Yaqui people today exhibit tremendous pride in being Catholic. Yet the Catholicism they practice is thoroughly syncretic, framed by their own unique indigenous cosmology. Yaqui Christianity has become an integral part of their identity as a people. That certainty is evident in the following version of the Talking Tree, narrated by Javier Choqui of Rahum Pueblo, recorded by María Trinidad Ruíz Ruíz and Gerardo David Aguilar during a cultural encounter in Potam in 1987. Javier Choqui explains the attitude of the Surem to the prophecy:

> The Surem refused the blessing, they did not accept it, they said that they did not want it, . . . so then they were told that some [Jesuit] fathers would come in order to bless those who had accepted, when the fathers arrived, the Surem scattered, but they did not go just anywhere, they remained here in the earth where they lived and continue living. . . . This is what remains for us of our ancestors, the blessing was made [accepted] by our ancestors . . . those who refused went down into the earth . . . all of us have seen but nobody likes this animal that wanders about below us, . . . he [who] comes from our ancestors, and they became like that because they did not accept the blessing, and we come from those who indeed did accept the blessing, it is for that reason that we believe in God and for that reason that we believe and listen to Him with attention. [Ruíz Ruíz and Aguilar 1994:31][14]

Like Javier Choqui, Ramón also portrays Yaqui Christianity as a positive outcome of the encounter between Yaquis and the Jesuits. While most accounts of the Talking Tree prophecy distinguish the immortal Surem from the mortal Yaquis, Ramón inverts the myth's story line, emphasizing that immortality became a possibility through Christ: "They shall bring an upright pole, crossed with another. There is a person hanging there. And this is the way it will be. Now there will be no deaths. Everyone shall continue living." For both Javier Choqui and Ramón Hernández the final division of the modern Yaquis from the

Surem is predicated on either the acceptance or the rejection of a new religion.

The Talking Tree story overlaps with other accounts of Yaqui ethnogenesis; however, the theories of non-Yaqui anthropologists and historians offer a slightly different perspective on this process of identity formation. Consider John and Jean Comaroff's assertion that "ethnicity has its origins in the asymmetric incorporation of structurally dissimilar groupings into a single political economy" (1992:54). Similarly, Spicer hypothesizes that Yaqui ethnicity was forged in a process of "opposition" (1971:796–797) during a historic encounter with a dominant other. Historians (Hu-DeHart 1981; Spicer 1980) tell us that the people living in hamlets along the Yaqui River, confronted in the sixteenth and seventeenth centuries with the persistent threat of military-aided invasion of their land and the prospect of becoming colonial subjects of New Spain, extended an invitation to missionaries, thus launching a chain of related events, including Jesuit reduction of their scattered communities into larger towns, religious conversion, and substantial changes in their practice of agriculture. This was a process that not only impacted the everyday life of the individuals living in the Yaqui River valley but, as Spicer (1971, 1980) and Hu-DeHart (1981, 1984) argue, also transformed the Yaquis' concept of the world around them, their relations to it, and their perception of their own collective identity. Hu-DeHart postulates that changes to identity occurred because of the abrupt concentration of the inhabitants of the rancherías and the simultaneous presence of Europeans: "When they reduced eighty widely scattered and loosely federated hamlets into eight mission communities, Jesuits heightened the Yaquis' incipient consciousness of being a nation—that is, a distinct cultural group with its own language, pueblos, and political boundaries. Their mission communities were coherent, well-defined, well-structured, economically self-sufficient, and segregated from the Spanish society outside" (1984:4).[15]

When placed side by side, the Talking Tree prophecy and academic analyses expose multiple understandings of a historical process. Nevertheless, it is clear that not all modes of historical representation are equally valued. About an hour into our first interview, when I asked him to tell me about the Surem, Ramón paused and prefaced his narrative of the Talking Tree prophecy with what I interpreted to be a disclaimer: "This is a *dicho* [saying], nothing more. It is a dicho that the Yaqui tribe, well, concerning the issue of history, they are very backward. In the questions of archaeology, the tribe is lacking, no? In the question of history. Very poor." Why would he start this way? Reluctant to interrupt him, I silently considered the possibilities as he began his story. Was Ramón reticent to share this narrative because I was a university student, someone who presumably had her own ideas about "legitimate" accounts of history?[16] Was he weighing the differences between the oral and the written, or were his remarks a performance of self-deprecation, a reflection of the modesty so culturally valued among the Yaqui people? It is impossible to know what he was feeling at that moment.

At the same time it was obvious to me that this narrative was extremely important to Ramón. He assured me that as a younger man, "while walking about in the lands … [he had] found a little metate," physical evidence of the existence of the Surem. Next, he said that the ancestors maintain that "these people surely did exist." Most significant, I believe, is the fact that at the very beginning of our interview, when I asked Ramón to tell me about the nineteenth-century wars between the Yaquis and the Mexicans, *this* was the story—a narrative about a poetess, some dreams, and a prophecy of radical change—that he offered.

Ethnicity and the Narrative Production of Agency

Discourses of history are not merely representations of past identities; they also construct identity in the present (White 1991:3). The Talking Tree prophecy is important because it is fundamentally about ethnic origins, rooted in the conflict and coexistence that characterize the history shared by Yaquis and mestizos. Although often perceived and presented as a reified or objectifiable "thing," ethnic identity is a relation, a negotiation of self and other. While theirs is a history of intermarriage, of economic and cultural exchange with their non-Yaqui neighbors, the Yaquis nevertheless strive to hold themselves apart geographically, linguistically, culturally, and religiously from non-Yaqui Mexicans, the Yoris. The distinction between Yaqui and non-Yaqui might appear to be straightforward, but the boundaries of culture and behavior that help shore up or exemplify such distinctions are fluid and are defined according to the speaker, the audience, and the context. Some claim that "authentic Yaquis" speak the Yaqui language with fluency. Others refer to the Yaqui history of resistance (first to Spanish conquistadors and then to Mexican farmer–settlers and the Mexican army) and the struggle to retain their ancestral land as the most significant factors. Many

Yaquis draw ethnic boundaries by emphasizing variations in practice, dress, and behavior. Still others identify Yaqui ethnicity with the elaborate folk–Catholic ceremonialism that characterizes pueblo fiestas, the Lenten season, and Semana Santa. In a multitude of creative ways and through the flourishing expressive culture of daily life, Yaqui individuals strive to reidentify *as Yaquis*—and both everyday discourse and formal narrative play a significant role in this process.

The present-day Yaqui social reality is one of constant mediation between inside and outside, between Yaqui self and Mexican (or Yori) other, a relationship that is immanent or implied in innumerable economic, communicative, and social interactions. The Mexican nation and the non-Yaqui other are ever-present realities for those living on an impoverished and beleaguered Indian reserve: educational discourse, the media, and trips to nearby urban centers produce compelling examples of "modernization" and success—incentives to assimilate. From the perspective of mainstream Mexican society, poverty is often equated with Indian identity, portrayed as a choice, and pressure is placed upon Yaquis to forsake their ethnic identity and to "fit in" with the national culture.

In the Talking Tree story the genesis of the Yaqui people is portrayed as part of a process of coming-into-relation with the outsider; the other is a persistent force, unavoidably connected to Yaqui selfhood. Through the description of a prophecy of impending change, the marking of territorial boundaries, and the ensuing flight of the ancestral Surem, Ramón's narrative gathers notions of differentiation and identity, linking ethnogenesis to the delineation of a cultural space and to a definitive choice.

As opposed to other narratives that might gloss over Yaqui agency in colonial times, the Talking Tree story depicts the acceptance of and preparation for change as a conscious decision. Although Ramón's narrative clearly resonates with other accounts that portray the emergence of Yaqui identity at the time of the coming of the Yoris, the story differs in one significant respect from histories produced within the academy. The Talking Tree prophecy locates the moment of ethnogenesis at a time *before* the whites came, portraying ethnogenesis not as a response but rather as a preparation, an informed anticipation. Yaquis are not presented as passive victims of transformation; rather, they insist upon their *own* historical agency in the establishment of their homeland, in the implementation of new modes of production, and in the integration and interpretation of Christian symbols, stories, and practices in terms of their own cultural logic (Morrison 1992; Shorter 2003). Stories about the prophecy of the Talking Tree and the exodus of the Surem describe the emergence of a new consciousness of group belonging formulated by the impending presence of a qualitatively different other. The narrative is doubly relevant in the present, as the prophecy of the arrival of the whites and the ensuing decision to *become* Yaquis mirrors and validates the continuing decision (in the face of tremendous pressures to change) to *be* Yaquis today.

Although it may indeed be one of several complementary modes of historical interpretation, the greater significance of Ramón's narrative lies in the way it figures the process of identity formation—in the power for self-fashioning it accords to Yaquis themselves. Perhaps this is why the Talking Tree survives in the shape of fully elaborated and well-practiced narratives such as Ramón's and in the form of scattered, oblique references made by other Yaqui informants: references to the use of arrows in the establishing of territorial boundaries and the ancestral "little people" who live under the hills, to the magic that affects those who venture to climb Kawi Omteme and the wise woman's prediction that eventually came to pass. A compelling example of "oral literature" (Evers and Molina 1993:11), the Talking Tree story illuminates narrative's flexibility as a powerful "technology" of identity (Lauretis 1987:19) and its immense potential as a discursive tool in the production of creative, agentive ethnic selves.

3
Moving Stories
Displacement, Return, and Yaqui Identity

The morning after the cyclone blew in from the sea, knocking down trees, washing mud under closed doors to coat the carefully polished cement floors of shops and homes, and transforming deeply rutted streets into a soft, treacherous terrain, I went to the town of Vicam to visit Luz García. By 9:00 the stagnant August air was already steamy. We sat in the shade beneath a fluttery mesquite tree, leaning into the breeze from a rotating fan and sipping syrupy coffee while Felipe, the youngest of her 11 children, played with his matchbox cars at our feet. Luz spoke into my tape recorder, describing the economic conditions on the Yaqui Reserve. Leaning forward in her chair, jabbing her finger into the air as if to punctuate her sentences, she railed against the scarcity of employment opportunities that drove her sons north to find work:

> Because the young people . . . the Yaqui youth, are once again nomads. They are leaving their pueblos because they need work. . . . Many, many modern young people, like I say, those who have studied, they are leaving the country, to the tribe which we have over there, in Tucsón.[1] Many Yaquis are going there. . . . They are no longer working in [professions related to] what they have studied, mind you. . . . Many of them studied to be agricultural engineers, architectural engineers, ecological engineers. . . . [Now] they have come to know this work of waiters, restaurant workers, or they simply work picking lemons or oranges or vegetables there in the United States. Yes.

The structure of Yaqui agriculture changed dramatically after 1952, when the Obregón Dam diverted the water of the Yaqui River into a series of irrigation canals. The majority of these cement-lined canals carried water southward to non-Yaqui farms outside of the Zona Indígena (Hewitt de Alcantara 1976; Hu-DeHart 1984:213). Yaqui subsistence farmers, once certain of a plentiful and free water supply for their fields of beans and corn, had no option but to purchase their water and involve themselves in a modernization project that ultimately organized them into credit societies. Mexico's Banco Nacional de Credito Ejidal (BNCE—National Cooperative Credit Bank) provided the necessary credit for highly mechanized farms that now required tractors and combines, new seeds and increased irrigation, but it also mandated that wheat and cotton be planted for sale on the commercial market (Hewitt de Alcantara 1976:267–271). This transformation, imposed largely from the outside and with little grassroots support among Yaqui farmers, was perceived as yet another imposition by a meddling government. Yaquis now found themselves fully integrated into the cash economy. Beholden to the bank and overextended in their credit, they became extremely vulnerable to disruptions in the harvest. Loans were defaulted on at an alarming rate (Hewitt de Alcantara 1976:271–279). Many Yaqui farmers, no longer able to obtain credit from the bank, found themselves forced to work as wage laborers on their own land, now rented out to non-Yaqui farmers who could afford the substantial capital input required for modernized agriculture.

When I conducted my fieldwork in 1996–97, well-informed consultants estimated that over 90 percent of Yaqui land was being rented out.[2] Other than farming, occupational options in the Zona Indígena are limited. Some families own a small number of milk cows or goats; 700 Yaqui men are members of the tribe's modest fishing cooperative; and men and women alike work off the reserve as day laborers on commercial vegetable farms or in canneries. But much of this work is seasonal, low paying, and uncertain. Women supplement family incomes by selling handicrafts, prepared food, or homemade cheese; they travel to the city to purchase dry goods and other groceries, selling them at a slight markup to neighbors and friends. Faced with continuing discrimination and a faltering job market in nearby urban areas, an increasing number of Yaqui young people are moving to distant border cities to work in factories. Rampant unemployment, poor infrastructure, and uncomfortable living conditions are prevalent on the Zona Indígena. The predicament of having to rent out the farmland inherited from one's parents and being forced to work as a poorly paid laborer for non-Yaquis on tribal land at times boils over in an expression of utter frustration.

Tears welled up in Luz's eyes, spilling down her cheeks. Her voice shook, and she began to speak faster and faster: "These [Yaqui] Mexicans are going [to the United States]—do you know why? Because this government is *taking* the land and is draining our territory of all its wealth. *Why?* So that we might be forced to wander about as *nomads*, once again. . . . We are again returning to a nomadic epoch. Of *nomads*." Luz's anger at the present situation is understandable: she has seen her sons, both college educated, move away from home in search of work. She blames the Mexican government for denying the tribe the financial aid they need, and she accuses those Yoris, the "whites" who have moved into the Zona Indígena, of throwing traditional Yaqui lifeways off balance.[3]

Throughout our interview Luz continually emphasized the word *nómada* (nomad), a polysemous term that, throughout Mexico, carries multiple situation-specific (but typically negative) connotations. Luz's assertion that the Yaqui people are "again returning to a nomadic epoch" indicates that the Yori system not only compels Yaquis to move away from their cherished homeland but also impedes the advancement of modern Yaquis into a future they deserve. While in another context, among non-Yaqui Mexicans, the word nómada might be a condensed reference to a broader discourse involving the savage–civilized dichotomy, this instance was different.[4] Luz is a Yaqui woman, and she prides herself on being a competent exponent of her people's history. Earlier, she and I had been talking about the Yaqui past. Luz's repeated use of the word nómada, in combination with her assertion that the Yaquis are being "forced to wander about . . . *once again*," was a specific reference to the Yaqui history of displacement—their forced exile from their aboriginal territory a century ago. As employed by Luz on that muggy morning, the word nómada encapsulated a whole range of emotion, articulating a sense of bitterness and injustice, highlighting a particular past.

Understandings of space and place play a critical role in the ethnic self-identification of the Yaqui people of southern Sonora. As they are created, occupied, traversed, and made meaningful by human activity, spaces and places are implicated in the constitution of the identities of the very actors that produce them (Certeau 1984; Feld and Basso 1996; Gupta and Ferguson 1992; Massey 1994; Soja 1989). During my time in Sonora I found that, when asked to talk about their own history or their perceptions of ethnic identity, Yaqui actors "accented" such discussions with a decided spatiality. Ethnic identification is accomplished not solely by association with a group of people but with the place that is the Yaqui homeland (see Evers and Molina 1992b, 1993).[5] And for most Yaquis the idea of homeland itself is intimately connected with (and cannot be understood in isolation from) a distinct set of cultural memories of displacement. The homeland with which Yaquis so strongly identify is conceptualized and continually constructed through social histories that focus on the Yaquis' exile from their land.

From the mid-nineteenth through the early twentieth centuries the Yaqui experience was characterized by long-distance movement. Removal from their land, life in exile, and the struggle to return have become central themes of Yaqui historical narrative. How have the Yaqui homeland and Yaqui ethnic identities become defined as meaningful, in part, by a history of movement away from and return to their land? What are the connections between narratives of movement and the Yaquis' emphasis upon rootedness and return in the present? Such stories shape the ways in which Yaquis conceptualize their ethnicity and its connection to the place they call their own.

Displacement

In the 1850s Mexico, still a fledgling nation-state, was undergoing immense change as liberal politicians implemented a comprehensive modernizing vision that included the assimilation of Indians, then perceived as backward and savage, into the citizenry and the privatization of collective landholdings (Alonso 1995:119–131; Lomnitz-Adler 1992:274–275; Radding 1989:332–333).

The rich soils deposited by the Yaqui River made the ancestral home of the Yaqui people one of the most coveted locations in all of northwestern Mexico. The valley, a veritable swath of green cutting across the desert landscape, promised to be an agricultural "Eden" to nonnative farmers and *hacendados*, owners of large landholdings (Harris 1908:5). Yaqui people were increasingly displaced as their towns and fields were colonized by non-Indian settlers backed by the Mexican military and three successive governors of the state of Sonora. Yaqui armed resistance gathered both momentum and organization in the 1880s. Due to the violence brought about by the occupation of their land, thousands of Yaquis fled. By 1890 less than one-quarter of the entire Yaqui population still lived in their home communities. Scattered throughout Sonora, these marginalized and landless Yaquis became a force in the expanding state economy as their labor came to be seen as invaluable to the mines, orchards, haciendas, ranches, and railroads of Sonora (Hu-DeHart 1974:77, 1984; Spicer 1980:149). The Yaqui resistance to Mexican colonization of their homeland in the 1890s was conducted primarily from the Sierra de Bacatete, a mountain range to the east of the Yaqui pueblos and the Mexican city of Guaymas. From where they lived in small groups in this sierra stronghold Yaqui warriors conducted raids on nearby villages and ranches (Hu-DeHart 1984).

Porfirio Díaz, elected to the Mexican presidency in 1876, was determined to extinguish the Yaqui resistance. As the century came to a close Díaz, in collaboration with the governors of Sonora, instigated a program of surveillance and removal and deported thousands of Yaqui men, women, and children to the state of Yucatán and the Valle Nacional in Oaxaca, where they were forced to labor on plantations. The beginning of the twentieth century, then, was a time of vast dispersal for the Yaqui people. Many of those who had been lucky enough to avoid execution or deportation to the south hid in the mountains or on farms and ranches; some disguised their identities in an attempt to "blend in" with the urban citizenry of Guaymas and Hermosillo, and others journeyed northward to Arizona seeking political refuge (Hu-DeHart 1974, 1984; Moisés, Kelley, and Holden 1971; Spicer 1980).

In order to understand the Yaqui production of a concept of homeland, we must frame it, as an overwhelming number of Yaquis do, within discourses that locate the intersection of a particular history with movement across socially and politically defined spaces.[6] Through ordinary social practices, particularly biographical narratives, Yaqui individuals produce the meaningfulness of *their place* by tracing a history of exile and return. Recounted as family histories or examples of fortitude, these stories of movement demonstrate how culturally informed senses of belonging to a specific place and to a particular people emerge in discursive constructions of the past.

When I met her, Inez Leyva Choqui was 77 years old and had retired to a comfortable existence in Potam, one of the eight principal Yaqui pueblos. A commanding presence, her wit and passion for detail made my work enjoyable as she told me about her childhood, her marriage, and the history of the Yaqui Wars. From birth Inez had enjoyed both economic security and a notable heritage. Her father had been a career soldier in the Mexican army, having fought in the Mexican Revolution under Gen. Francisco Indalecio Madero, and his ample military salary augmented the money the family earned from the sale of crops grown on his fields just outside of Potam. Inez's mother had been the granddaughter of the renowned and beloved nineteenth-century Yaqui resistance leader Juan Maldonado Tetabiate. From the beginning of our acquaintance it was evident that Inez was proud of her Yaqui heritage and especially of her relation to General Tetabiate.

When I asked her full name and the year in which she was born, she squared her shoulders, declaring into the microphone:

> I, . . . I, Inez Leyva Choqui, was born on the 11th of November 1920, in Potam, Río Yaqui, Sonora.[7] My . . . mother was a descendant of General Tetabiate and my father was a descendant of some cattle-ranching Yaquis. . . . [T]he general was the most honorable general that there was in the Yaqui tribe. Very honest, honorable. . . . And so there was talk in Mexico, with Porfirio Díaz, that the wealthy people wanted these lands of the Yaquis because they were very fertile. . . . Out there in Tetabiate he had his ranch. Out there they all were born: my family, my mother, all of them were born out there in the sierra, in Tetabiate.

Inez's grandmother had been Tetabiate's daughter, born on the mountainous eastern edge of the Yaqui territory in a scruffy makeshift wartime community. This was the late 1800s, at the height of the resistance, when the Yaquis' battle for their land was being transformed into a struggle for their very existence as a people. Inez's family history, then, was shaped by the Yaqui resistance against the Mexican government, and she focused her description of the past on those wars. She explained, "They depopulated Huirivis; they depopulated Rahum; they depopulated Belem.[8] All those people who could escape, they fled into the sierra. To fight, yes. Against the government. . . . [Tetabiate] was their leader."

By the early 1900s the Díaz regime's program of detention, surveillance, and deportation was accelerating despite the protests of prominent Mexican citizens who decried it as a violation of human dignity and a disruption of the production and commerce that depended so heavily on Yaqui labor. Yaquis designated for deportation were routinely taken by boat from Guaymas, a port city on the western coast of Sonora. Boats proceeded southward along the coast, occasionally stopping for supplies during the five-day journey. Yaqui prisoners disembarked in San Blas in the state of Nayarit and were marched to San Marcos, a 15- to 20-day walk through mountainous terrain. In San Marcos they boarded a train that took them through Mexico City to the east coast city of Veracruz, where they would be put on another boat to Yucatán, their final destination (Padilla Ramos 1995:126–135; J. Turner 1969).

As she recounted her history Inez continually defined her people in terms of the hardships they had endured. But what I found most compelling about her narrative was her attention to the details of Yaqui removal and her portrayal of their unwavering determination to return while in exile, an insistent reminder that Yaquis identify themselves not only in terms of the struggle for their homeland but also by virtue of their movements through the space of a modernizing nation. She continued:

> Before the revolution, now when the Yaquis had been sent off, when the government had deported the Yaquis to Mérida, to Veracruz, to Valle Nacional, to all of those ports, all those people were traded. The governor of the state asked for each Yaqui head two-fifty. In that way they were sold like slaves. . . . Out in the Valle Nacional, when the first Yaquis were taken—it is a valley, a desert. They took them tied here, look, from the hand like this. Men and women tied together by their hands. They took them in a line. And when they could no longer walk, the people, those who could no longer walk, they fell and they died out there. And they left them; like animals, they tossed them. The government, the soldiers. And purely with beatings, they got them up, so that they might walk. Until they reached where they had to arrive. To be slaves.

This narrative does not simply trace the route of travel to Yucatán; it evokes the human experience of a journey into exile in all of its violence, discomfort, and utter exhaustion. As Inez recalled the deportations she emphasized how the people were separated from their land and their families to be sold "like slaves," "traded" like commodities.[9]

Her concern with history and movement resonates with stories shared by other Yaqui consultants. While I elicited several narratives about Yaqui displacement and exile in the context of formal interviews, the details of this experience also emerged as spontaneous offerings in the context of casual discussions I had with consultants about Yaqui self-identity. It is clear that these stories exist and are employed independently of anthropological inquiry about the past. I occasionally heard adults refer to the Yaqui displacement when talking to young people about the importance of "tradition" or when correcting behavior they felt was unbefitting a proper Yaqui youth. In such cases narratives of movement were not fully elaborated. Rather, they were referenced through the use of a few lines or even a place-name, seemingly intended to make a point about Yaqui fortitude or to emphasize ethnic difference. If "selves" are, indeed, created as they are performed (Butler 1999; Goffman 1959), and if a broader "language" of identity is composed of discrete utterances (Bakhtin 1986), then it makes a great deal of sense to follow Richard Bauman's suggestion and examine "the spontaneous, unscheduled, optional performance contexts of everyday life" (1977:28).

The fact that narratives of displacement and return told by Yaquis today do not arise from personal experience, that they are retellings of the memories of others—grandparents, great-grandparents, great-aunts, and neighbors—is not insignificant, for it highlights the existence of an informal narrative tradition. Those memories, personal histories of movement, are shared with children and grandchildren, neighbors and ritual kin. As such, these stories circulate broadly in this southern Sonoran river valley; deeply embedded in the Yaqui historical consciousness, they readily surface when Yaquis are called upon to talk about their ethnic identity or their land.[10]

A good example of the significance of movement in Yaqui narrative self-identification is the story that Enrique Sanchez told about his grandfather. Enrique was 54 years old at the time of our conversation. He had grown up near Phoenix, but his family was originally from Bacum, a Yaqui pueblo southeast of Potam. Like a dwindling number of Arizona Yaquis, Enrique is trilingual; Yaqui, Spanish, and English had been spoken in his childhood home. One evening, as we talked and warmed ourselves next to the fire, he shared two narratives epitomizing the horrors of displacement.

Enrique explained that his grandfather José's earliest memories were of flight from Bacum, his home pueblo. One day when he was a young boy, José had been tending to the family's watermelon patch when an old man came by and urged, "Run, little boy, they are killing your family back there!" Enrique said that José chose to remain, thinking to himself, "This old man just wants to steal these watermelons." And so he stayed behind. Later, another person came to the watermelon patch. This time it was a woman who pleaded, "Come with me, little boy, they are killing people back there." José decided to trust the woman and went with her. She took him to a place near Phoenix, where they settled among other Yaqui refugees and where José was eventually reunited with some members of his family.

The story Enrique shared about Manuela, a relative's grandmother, also concerned the war years and was similarly brief yet stirring. During the early 1900s, when Manuela was a little girl, her family fled from the fighting in the Yaqui pueblos. As they walked north through the desert toward the town of Magdalena Manuela's sister suddenly became very ill. Enrique shrugged and shook his head, declaring that "they were not thinking clearly" when they decided to turn around and head back to the Yaqui territory. He explained how the family put the sick child on the back of a donkey and walked home. When they arrived, they were detained by Mexican soldiers. The girl died, and Manuela was taken into custody. She was separated from her family and was sent to the state of Yucatán, where she was forced to live and work on a plantation.

Both of these stories, sparse in detail and offered spontaneously, show movement to be an important facet of Enrique's identity. By demonstrating that his family had not only originated in the Sonoran homeland but had also endured displacement, these narratives establish a historical connection through shared experience. Perhaps the reduced and sudden nature of Enrique's narratives index the disorientation of war, the colonization of Yaqui land, and indiscriminate massacres in the Yaqui pueblos. Perhaps the very style of those narratives, stark and abrupt, reflects the feeling of those times: when families in panic "were not thinking clearly," inadvertently delivering themselves into the hands of the soldiers; when people had to flee their pueblos, leaving maize and beans, melons and squash, to rot in the fields.

Stories about forced movement across the landscape of the nation locate Yaqui ethnic identity firmly within a domain of unequal power relations. As the Yaqui resistance to the Porfirian government's attempts to colonize their lands grew in the late 1800s, Díaz, with the help of a "triumvirate" of wealthy Sonoran governors (Hu-DeHart 1984:157–158), succeeded in driving the majority of the Yaquis from their communities. What began as the exiling of Yaqui guerrillas after the Battle of Mazocoba in 1900 (Padilla Ramos 1995:66) escalated into the deportation of entire families of Yaqui noncombatants to a place far from their beloved homeland (Hu-DeHart 1984:163–190).[11]

The ultimate destination of the Yaquis was influenced in large part by the political economy of henequen (sisal hemp), an agave-type cactus with stiff spiny leaves.[12] From the mid-1800s forward the haciendas of Yucatán were transformed into commercial plantations as demand for the henequen they grew increased dramatically. The fiber of this desert plant was exported primarily to the United States for use in the manufacture of twine and for the cables and riggings of ships (Joseph 1988:13–23). By the 1870s henequen monoculture dominated the peninsula, and Yucatecan entrepreneurs found themselves indebted to the North American cord manufacturers who provided the finances to keep the farms operating. As a full-blown "business," the cultivation of henequen required not only large amounts of capital but also labor—a need filled by Mayan residents, Korean indentured workers, Mexican political dissidents, and Yaqui deportees (Joseph 1988:29–30). In cooperation with Sonoran governors who desired an end to their "Yaqui problem," Yucatecan businessmen arranged for the transport of thousands of Yaquis to their plantations (Padilla Ramos 1995:90). Families were often split apart, either being assigned to different plantations or becoming separated on the long journey south.

As prisoners of an internal war, the Yaqui deportees were "sold" by the government to plantation owners upon arrival on the peninsula.[13] The Sonoran Indians were treated like slaves, working under brutal conditions. Apart from having to cut henequen from sunup to sundown in the tropical heat, workers received little or no remuneration for their labors. Records show that many Yaquis died from smallpox and yellow fever contracted during transit through Mexico City and in Yucatán (Padilla Ramos 1995:81–83, 142–143). *Patrones* (bosses, plantation owners) typically prohibited workers from marrying outside of the plantation. Even if they were already married to someone from whom they had been accidentally separated, Yaqui women were often "forced to cohabit" with Asian or Mayan laborers "in order to produce more children for the fields" (Hu-DeHart 1984:182). The data collected by John Kenneth Turner (1969) suggests that the division of labor between men and women created by plantation owners was a division between the productive and the reproductive; men labored in the fields to harvest henequen and keep the farms financially viable, while women were supposed to produce offspring as future slaves for the plantations. Workers were housed in cramped dwellings and forbidden to leave the premises, and there were no schools provided for their children. Disobedience or failure to meet production quotas often resulted in floggings, and laborers consistently suffered from hunger (Joseph 1988:71–77; Padilla Ramos 1995:132–152). The conditions on henequen plantations for Yaqui deportees were so deplorable that "two-thirds could be expected to die within their first year in Yucatán" (Joseph 1988:78).

The stories of flight and forced exile told by the Yaqui descendants of those slaves depict a historical moment of land hunger, rapid modernization, racist discourse, and state coercion in which the Porfirian government's attempt to solve the "Yaqui problem" manifested the attributes of genocide. Such narratives illuminate for us the human aspects of a historical conjuncture in which Yaqui deportation was the convenient solution to two problems: it eradicated the presence of rebellious and tenacious Indians, and it alleviated a serious labor shortage for the world's largest supplier of henequen. However, oral histories of exile are balanced by more hopeful stories. Narratives about the Yaquis' struggle to return to their homeland abound, describing the endurance of individuals and families and thereby celebrating the resilience of the Yaqui people.

The Journey Home

The end to Yaqui slavery in Yucatán came in 1915 with the arrival of the revolution in that state, when Gen. Salvador Alvarado abolished all forced labor (Joseph 1988:103). While former henequen peons would now be free to seek work wherever they wanted, most Yaquis decided to return to their homeland. With little or no savings, some men, at times accompanied by their Yaqui wives and children, joined various revolutionary battalions in Mexico City, returning home only after the war (Padilla Ramos 1995:156).

A young woman at the end of the revolution, Manuela—whose sister's sudden illness led to her own detention and deportation to Yucatán—was one among the many Yaquis who worked their way north, stopping at various points along the way in order to earn sufficient money to continue their journey. Manuela eventually made it home to Potam, where she married, raised a family, and lived out her remaining years.

Luz García presented a compelling version of a narrative of movement when she shared a neighbor's story of wartime in the early twentieth century. Now deceased, Luz's neighbor had been forcibly removed from her home in the Yaqui community of Vicam as a young girl and deported along with other Indian "undesirables" to the state of Chihuahua. Luz spoke about how the Yaqui land had been invaded by Mexican soldiers, about deportation and racial difference: "They [the soldiers] took with them a little of the Yaqui race. Many from the Yaqui race. And they took them out there, to the south, to Mexico City." When I interjected to ask why they were taken away, Luz repeated a familiar story about enslavement, mistreatment, and the difficulties of returning home. She began forcefully, "Well, to make other *criollos* [creoles]![14] With the same Mexican race but other criollos. And they treated them badly. . . . They worked a lot. They beat them as well. They treated them like slaves. Like slaves." Luz then recounted the "very beautiful history" that her neighbor had shared with her:

> [That] woman told me that they returned on foot, from Chihuahua. Yes, walking. And at times they stayed in the caves, like that, in the caves, until

they reunited with the Yaqui tribe. Until they arrived here. They came walking. How they suffered! Hunger. Very hard. And some of their family died as well, on the way, and there they remained. But they finally arrived. She, this señora, was 98 years old, . . . and she remembered it all. . . . They had taken her. She had been taken there, out there to Chihuahua. They had taken others as well, and they had just dumped them there. That is what they say! . . . They established themselves there for a while, but they had the desire to return again to the Yaqui tribe. And they came! On foot. Walking. *Pobrecitos* [Poor things]. . . . Yes, she told me everything. She told me how they came, what they ate out there, just leaves, roots—*quelites* [wild edible greens], as we say here. . . . In the wilderness! In the wilderness, because there were no roads, just wilderness . . . with all the Yaquis who were there, all grouped together. And they came walking, walking, walking, from out there, from Chihuahua to here. To Sonora. . . . And then they arrived in their own land, here.

In retelling her neighbor's story Luz emphasized the demands of a journey through the wilderness—the hunger they experienced, living in caves, the necessity of picking their way through the desert, the people who died along the way. It may seem ironic that she introduced this narrative as "a very beautiful history." Yet for Luz the beauty of this story may well inhere in its outcome: a young Yaqui resisted displacement, braved the wilds of Chihuahua's rugged sierra, and ultimately returned to her natal village, where she married, raised a family, and lived to the age of 98. Indeed, Luz equated the return to the homeland with a decision to remain Yaqui, with a refusal to "make other criollos" (to have children with non-Yaquis, thereby diluting Yaqui blood).[15] For me the "beautiful history" was made even more poignant by the poetics of Luz's rendering. The cadence of her repetition of certain words and phrases— "walking, walking, walking" and "On foot. Walking. Pobrecitos"—gives us a feel not only for the relentlessness of their suffering but also for the sheer determination with which the young woman and her Yaqui companions were able to return home.

Whether they attest to Yaquis' strategies of work or enlistment or describe the utter resolve to walk home over mountains and across a desert, stories of return maintain an important place in the Yaqui ethnic imagination, demonstrating that identity is determined not solely by structural factors or by victimhood to the powers that be. Rather, narratives illustrating the will to return from exile confront a nation's "topography of power" (Gupta and Ferguson 1992:8), proving that agency counts for something, that Yaqui identity is also shaped by the courage and determination of individuals.

In these stories space is not an inert background upon which history is enacted but rather a significant component in the construction of modern Yaqui selves. Occupied and mutable, spaces are "constituted out of social relations" (Massey 1994:2). Cultural geographers have extended traditional concepts of space and history by advocating the perception of time–space as a single entity (Friedland and Boden 1994; Harvey 1990; Massey 1994:2; Soja 1989). Edward Soja expands upon this idea in his argument for "a simultaneously historical and geographical materialism; a triple dialectic of space, time, and social being" (1989:12); he calls for a recognition that each of the three elements interacts in a dialectical creative tension with the other two at all times, that historical experience and space and social life are "mutually constructed" and productive (1996:72). Like the history Inez recounted and the brief accounts Enrique shared, Luz's "beautiful history" concerns the way both war and individual fortitude *constitute* specific spaces by means of human movement. Movement that socializes space in turn shapes Yaqui ethnic identity and generates the meanings that ultimately create a notion of "homeland."

Staying, Visiting, Making a Homeland

As predominantly small-scale farmers, the Yaquis of southern Sonora have been unable to produce crops in the volume necessary to compete in northern Mexico's globalizing marketplace. Due to a lack of the capital needed to operate their modernized farms and a spiraling cycle of debt and credit loss, a majority find themselves in the predicament of having to rent their land to non-Yaqui farmers. The loss of control over their own lands, coupled with the need for employment in a cash-based economy, has made long-distance movement once again a reality for Yaqui people—albeit this time to border cities and the promise of factory jobs, to the fields of large agribusinesses, and even across the international border. Such journeys are inevitably talked about and formulated into stories, yet the Yaquis I know also speak of this type of movement with a great deal of ambivalence.

Indeed, the terminology used by Yaquis when discussing journeys is revealing. Yaqui consultants used the Spanish word *viajar* (to travel) only when they were discussing *my* plans—for a visit to the museum in Hermosillo (Sonora's capital city), for a vacation to the National Fair in Aguascalientes, for a trip home to see my husband.[16] A review of the terms Yaquis utilize to indicate their own experiences of movement provides insight into lives circumscribed by economic need, shaped by intense attention to interpersonal relationships, and defined by a difficult history.

The three trips I made to Hermosillo during my field study were greeted by María and Lencha Bakasewa (elderly sisters who were the matriarchs of the family I knew best) with doubt and concern. My anticipation—of going out to eat and visiting the museums and the library at INAH—was matched by their skepticism.[17] Whom was I going to stay with? Who would accompany me? The women discussed my plans in detail and toyed with the idea of sending someone along to escort me, "to keep you from crying with loneliness," they explained, but no one from the family could spare the time away from work or children. Their unease did not correspond solely to my identity as a female or as a non-Mexican; similar concerns surfaced, for example, when Marcela Valencia's brother, a teacher, needed to go to Hermosillo on school business. The city of Hermosillo is a three-hour bus ride from Potam, but Marcela (the eldest sister in her family) and her mother both insisted that he return that same day, voicing worries about his "being lonely" and "getting lost." Marcela quelled my excitement for her brother's chance to see the city and its cathedrals for the first time with the admonition, "He cannot stay. We don't have people there."

As opposed to my own gravitation toward "travel," Yaquis were more likely to speak of their own journeys in terms of "visiting" or "staying" (with someone). It should be understood that for many Yaqui individuals movement is a part of religious practice as well as a social reality. Yaquis anticipate and enjoy annual pilgrimages to San Francisco's shrine in the town of Magdalena. In the autumn of 1997 Lencha and her husband took their grandchildren to the fiesta of San Francisco; they were astonished when I asked if they were going to stay in a hotel. Although their family is one of the few that have sufficient finances for a night in paid-for accommodations, Lencha explained that "Yaquis . . . *visit* other people" (meaning Yaqui people), that they would be sleeping in the home of a Yaqui acquaintance who had, over the years, become "like family." In a similar way, many Yaquis go to Arizona, "staying with" or "visiting" relatives and friends in order to assist on ritual occasions.

It is not surprising to learn that return to the communities along the Yaqui River, even in the present, is a positively valued practice. Many

Arizona Yaquis visit southern Sonora—a place they consider their ancestral homeland—with regularity. Some Arizona Yaquis make a pilgrimage during Holy Week to view an elaborate version of the ceremonies that they also perform. Others have traceable family ties in the Yaqui pueblos and come to attend the baptisms, first communions, and weddings of their godchildren as well as the funerals of relatives. Such visits by Arizona Yaquis are viewed by Sonoran Yaquis with a great deal of pride as a return to the homeland, the cradle of Yaqui culture and society. In addition, young people who spend months away from home working in factories along the Sonora–Arizona border often request time off in the spring to attend the annual pueblo fiestas. During this time of year they return in great numbers to their communities, where they participate in rituals, share special meals, enjoy the company of family, and look forward to social dances and time with friends.

"Staying," "visiting," and "return" are terms rooted in the historical realities and present-day financial struggles underlying Yaqui life. Deportation, taking refuge in the sierra, trekking to safety across the Arizona border, and the violent separation of families and communities at the beginning of the twentieth century—these were experiences that translated, for many Yaquis, into cultural survival as a conscious effort. It is from the perspective of economic need and historical experience, then, that we can understand these contemporary idioms of movement and their rootedness in relationality. Staying and visiting, forging networks of ritual kinship, and depending on each other in lean times are cultural practices that play a key role in the endurance of the Yaqui community and in the construction of Yaqui identity.[18]

Whether in narratives about war and deportation or in conversations about present-day needs, many Yaqui individuals portray distant travel outside of the Yaqui Zona Indígena as forced, coerced, or, at the very least, undesirable. An examination of stories of displacement and exile promotes a partial understanding of those attitudes as being embedded in historical experience. Yet movement is a multivocal concept (V. Turner 1969). The verbs used by Inez Leyva in her description of Yaqui deportation ("sent off," "traded," "sold," "tied," "tossed") provide a stark contrast to the verbs used to describe those forms of modern movement that are acceptable ("visiting," "staying"), words that portray belonging as opposed to alienation. These narratives also provide a basis for comprehending the indignation and the rage in Luz's voice as she spoke of her Yaqui children, "forced to wander about as *nomads*, once again."

While modern migration for employment is viewed as necessary and the birth of the Yaqui diaspora at the turn of the twentieth century from an experience of attempted genocide is remembered with horror, movement involving return (both in the past and present) is commemorated and praised. Indeed, movement itself, both as action and idiom, serves to circumscribe the homeland. Physically, Yaquis reasserted their claims to an aboriginal territory through journeys home after being exiled to places like Chihuahua, Valle Nacional, and Yucatán. The Sonoran Yaqui pueblos continue to be made into a homeland by visits from Arizona Yaquis and the return of sons and daughters working in distant cities. Akhil Gupta and James Ferguson write, "With meaning making understood as a practice, how are spatial meanings established? Who has the power to make places of spaces?" (1992:11). In answer to these questions I point to Yaqui narrative as a powerful tool. Discursively, Yaqui land as a homeland is reinscribed with every story about displacement, with every tale of triumphant return. Collectively, narratives of displacement and return serve as a key scenario (Ortner 1973)—a "model of" a people's endurance in the past and a "model for" their continuation *as a people* in the present.[19]

An examination of history in terms of "space" lays bare both social relations and power. A spatiohistorical account of the Yaqui deportation at the turn of the twentieth century gives us a better understanding of the convergence of factors and actors—nationalist ideology, Sonoran politicians, settler farmers, plantation bosses, U.S. manufacturers, and Yaqui resistance fighters—that ultimately resulted in Yaqui removal. A discussion of Yaqui movement across the space of the nation also highlights a distinct experience that even now inscribes Yaqui ethnicity: they identify strongly with a homeland made meaningful in part by a history of displacement. The Yaqui homeland is a place continually imagined and made "real"—situated and strengthened in its location—through narratives about movement. Such moving stories play a significant role in shaping who the Yaquis are today and how they envision their connection to home.

4
Traces of the Past
Haunting and Enchantment on the Yaqui Landscape

It was a still, cool evening in late May, and Regina Valencia and I stood in the crowd gathered for a religious fiesta. Regina was a local elementary school principal and keen observer of Yaqui verbal artistry, and I had interviewed her several days earlier about the Yaqui homeland and her understanding of its history and its meaning to the Yaqui people. Her eyes intent on the activity that surrounded us, Regina leaned into me and spoke in a low tone, "I remembered a story. About *yo hoara* [enchanted home]." I nodded, and she continued: "They say that there was a little boy who wanted to become a deer dancer, but he couldn't dance well. He went to an older man seeking help, and that man said, 'I am going to take you to a place where you will learn to dance.' And the two of them went walking. They came to a cave, and the old man told the boy, 'You are going to continue walking. And even though you might see frightening animals, snakes and other animals, don't look back and don't be afraid.' And so the boy continued on, and the old man remained behind. The boy encountered snakes . . . [and] other animals. But he was not afraid, and he didn't turn back. And even though snakes wrapped themselves around his legs, he wasn't afraid. And for that they gave him that gift. It is said that he danced very well. Beautifully. That it came from yo hoara."

"The cave was yo hoara?" I asked.

"Yes," she replied. "It is a story I remembered. . . . It was told to me in Yaqui, but I told it to you in Spanish. Yo hoara. That is what they say, that it is in caves, or even in dreams. There, one can obtain the ability to dance beautifully. Not just dancers . . . those who play the violin, drum, and other instruments. Those who make music—that they also receive their talent in this way."

The Yaqui pueblos and the network of farms and ranches associated with each pueblo are intensely lived-in spaces. The mesquite desert that descends from the rocky Sierra de Bacatete, surrounding the Yaqui towns and farmlands in a proliferation of gentle hills, is also part of the

Figure 3. Sierra de Bacatete

Yaqui cultural landscape. Places on the land, socialized through human activity and narrative, become entangled with cultural memory and play a significant role in the Yaqui ethnic imagination.

Many places on Yaqui terrain are identifiable by the experiences associated with them and by the stories told about them. Everybody knows that Chinese merchants used to live in Potam Viejo (Old Potam) just to the east of the canal and that one can still find fragments of colored glass or adobe bricks from their disintegrated houses and shops. Everybody knows that the Bacatete Mountains once provided refuge for Yaqui resistance fighters and that ritual specialists and traditional leaders make the pilgrimage every year to pray at General Tetabiate's tomb, which lies near the old Mexican army garrison at the place called Tetacombiate. Everybody knows the meandering curves of the Yaqui River, and most Yaqui families have their own memories of farms and ranches and the bounty it supported *antes*—in the past. And everybody knows stories about Kawi Omteme (in Spanish, Cerro Enojado, or Angry Mountain), the rocky imposing peak near Vicam Pueblo, and they say that Kawi Omteme is "enchanted," that gold can be found there.

The importance of place emerges in the course of conversations that carefully trace the everyday comings and goings of relatives, neighbors, and visitors. There are stories about places that exhibit magical qualities and locations that attract spectral inhabitants: the mountain near Vicam Pueblo that is known for the consequences of its anger and for the whimsical blessings it bestows; a sacred hill in the desert above Loma de Bacum, where the town's patron saint has been seen washing clothes by the river; ghosts that wander the streets of Potam; the weeping that is audible on the windswept plain in front of Rahum's church. I have heard ghost stories recounted by ordinary Yaquis (mothers, religious leaders, old men, teenagers, and kindergarten teachers), narratives that captivate rapt listeners.[1]

Many narratives frame the homeland as a terrain quite literally saturated with the past. As stories construct the past, they convey contemporary realities and attach meaning to places, and Yaqui ethnic identity is grounded in such discourses about place. Yaqui individuals identify specific locations on their land (certain caves, ridges, waterholes, and hills) as *yo hoaram* (enchanted homes), gateways to an esoteric and culturally valued knowledge. Yet other places (familiar village streets, windswept plazas, and various locations in the countryside) are known to be haunted, bearing witness to the destruction that Yaquis experienced in the past, to their violent displacement, or to present-day locally wrought brutalities. Vivid accounts of assault, ambush, and drug abuse intermingle with stories about suffering ghosts and familiar apparitions. In this chapter I attempt to understand the storied relationship between Yaqui memory, identity, and place. Contemporary Yaqui narratives draw the homeland as a space dually characterized by apprehension and belonging, a landscape that is both haunted and enchanted. I explore the tensions implicit in these narratives, arguing that they may be interpreted as complementary modes of spatialized comprehension—a "cognitive map" (Jameson 1991) of present-day experiences and anxieties set in a landscape layered with intense cultural meanings.

This Weeping Land

The Yaquis' connection to their homeland along the Yaqui River is evident in everyday references to the sacred Ocho Pueblos, in the stories of Yaqui exile and return at the turn of the twentieth century, and in continuing disputes about the southern border of the Zona Indígena. Yaqui individuals are also intimately connected with the homeland as a place where experiences become "fastened onto" (Stewart 1996:106) caves and ponds, low hills and sudden gullies. And an important clue to the attachment Yaquis feel toward their aboriginal landscape is encapsulated in the phrase "inim bwan bwía," this weeping land.

Edward Spicer writes that inim bwan bwía was "much used during the twentieth century in Maestros' sermons" (1980:312). According to Spicer, "This is probably a Yaqui version of the phrase in the Old Testament which has been translated in English as 'this vale of tears'" (1980:312). In my own research, inim bwan bwía has emerged as a multivocal and deeply meaningful concept. Pedro Molina, an intense, soft-spoken older man, once tried to convey the essence of the phrase to me during an interview. Eyes narrowed, he commanded my full attention as he explained, "To understand this, no? Inim bwan bwía. Here, in this land of ours, there was weeping. It was understood as *this* land of ours." Pedro pointed down with both index fingers and paused for several seconds as he emphasized the word "this." He continued, "They [the elders] spoke of it very delicately. Inim bwan bwía-po [here in this weeping land]—as if they loved the land a great deal. Yes. It was a land of much sacrifice. . . . Very cutting. Inim bwan bwía-po. Many say that one comes to this land only to suffer. This is what we understand."

Regina Valencia added another layer of meaning as she linked inim bwan bwía to service performed during the fiesta, the annual ceremony held by each pueblo in honor of the patron saint. Referring to the lengthy and detailed public counseling given to new *fiesteros* (hosts of the fiesta) by the *maestros* (Yaqui male religious authorities) on the fiesta's first night, Regina asked, "Haven't you heard them saying 'inim bwan bwía-po' in the sermon? . . . It is because, well, those who came before— our ancestors—said that those who made the fiesta did so in order to sustain the world. '*To sustain the world*,' that's what they said. It is a great responsibility, this obligation."

Yet narrative can also reveal a very subtle understanding of inim bwan bwía, inscribing a cultural memory of violence onto the Yaqui landscape itself. One story came unexpectedly on a chilly November evening in 1996, when I was roasting ears of corn with Marco Usacamea. I was asking Marco about the wars of the late nineteenth century and about Yaqui efforts to resist the occupation of their land by Yori settlers. Marco replied that he didn't know anything about "the war" except that there was "a place called Mazocoba" where many Yaquis were killed by

"Spanish soldiers."[2] Marco paused momentarily, tending to the corn browning over hot coals, and then he said that some ranchers who work in the *monte* (wilderness) surrounding the Yaqui pueblos have heard an anguished weeping coming from the earth. The sounds, he explained, are said to be those of Yaqui women chased down and shot at close range by soldiers, the screams of women still clutching children in their arms in the hope of protecting them, the cries of babies trying to suckle the breasts of their dead mothers.

When I first heard Marco's story, I took it as a wrenching allegory, a culturally produced moral discourse about the brutalities of war and the desperation of dispossession. Mentally, I tried to pinpoint the skirmish or the massacre to which he might be referring. Did his oblique narrative recall the year 1861, when a Mexican troop stationed near Torim Pueblo killed dozens of women and children? Was it a reference to the 1868 Bacum massacre, when 120 unarmed Yaqui prisoners were gunned down as they tried to escape the burning church in which they were being held?[3] Over time I have come to believe that the story's referent might be more general—that this narrative and others like it may index an accumulation of episodes of violent repression that occurred on and were centrally about the Yaqui homeland.

In Marco's narrative and in stories told by others, physical place acquires new significance as the homeland itself stands as an indictment of the atrocities of the past. Spicer may have heard biblical overtones in inim bwan bwía, translating it as "this vale of tears" (1980:312), but I find the second portion of his observation to be more insightful. He writes that the phrase "has, in Yaqui thought, connotations especially of the world of the secessionist towns when there was widespread suffering among Yaquis, and suggests the inhuman cruelties of deportation and the extreme deprivation suffered by those separated from their families in Sonora and Arizona following the dispersal" (Spicer 1980:312). This interpretation resonates with contemporary Yaqui discourses about land, history, and identity. At the same time, I would argue that we should not preclude the possibility of a more literal translation of the phrase: that inim bwan bwía is, for some, a tangible place and that the very act of walking through its hills has the potential to awaken a "political unconscious" (Jameson 1981). Sociologist Avery Gordon writes that haunting "is about reliving events in all their vividness, originality, and violence so as to overcome their pulsating and lingering effects" (1997:134). Sounds of weeping emanate from the Yaqui earth, echoing a past burdened with pain and hardship; at the same time, through its narrativization, such experience can be a transformative testimony to the survival of the Yaqui people.

The explanations and stories provided by Marco, Pedro, and Regina render inim bwan bwía as a richly multivocal concept. While the phrase clearly conveys a "memoryscape" (Shaw 2002) of suffering and violent experience, inim bwan bwía also expresses a certain preciousness and value, a sense of heavy responsibility, and a palpable attachment. Of course, "this weeping land" can be all these things simultaneously: a condensed moral code about obligation and the meaning of community, a physical repository of cultural memory, and a source of Yaqui identity.

Specters of Violence

Places on the land are central to Yaqui modes of historical reckoning. Yet "senses of place" (Feld and Basso 1996) also figure prominently in the process of meaning making in the present, enabling individuals to locate and perhaps to mentally contain incidents of violence perpetrated by Yaquis and non-Yaquis in the pueblos. Places have a specificity about them, a particularity that comes with being associated with certain happenings or social formations. But why do memories and stories become attached to places? Philosopher Edward Casey writes, "Human beings . . . are ineluctably place-bound. More even than earthlings, we are placelings, and our very perceptual apparatus, our sensing body, reflects the kinds of places we inhabit" (1996:19). Because we are embodied beings and because we know the world by sensing it, Casey argues, our sensation of existence itself is emplaced (1996:24). More than mere backdrop for human activity, place is a powerful actor in the construction of experience. This was certainly true of many of the narratives that I heard and recorded during my time with the Yaquis.[4] Indeed, Yaqui stories are replete with references to place.

I had always been warned about unruly *rateros* (young men turned small-time thieves) robbing stores for petty cash and accosting people on their way home from dances to demand a new pair of boots or a pretty gold bracelet. But when I returned to Potam for a visit in May 2003, I noticed an increase in the number and variety of these stories—a frantic proliferation of warnings, detailed accounts of shootings and stabbings, comments about the "cholos and drug addicts . . . over there in Santiamea" (the neighborhood occupying the southwestern corner of town) who sniff paint and do "crazy and irrational things."

Conducting fieldwork at the outer margins of the pueblo was no longer considered "safe," even during daylight hours. Places on the other side of town, once considered "far away" by concerned elderly informants (places where I had regularly visited and interviewed friends), were now "too far" to visit unaccompanied. Ana Ochoa cautioned, "You can't go about [alone] as you did before, Kristi!" She added that there are "now many *asaltantes* [assailants]" armed with pistols who attack innocent people even in broad daylight. Julia, the young wife of a rancher–turned–factory worker, complained that Potam is "much more dangerous, now," that there are too many drug addicts and just "bad people."[5] Whether or not they are "true" in a factual sense, these stories register a certain kind of truth (Shaw 2002:57–58), as they allude to something alarming and disconcerting about the contemporary experience of living in Potam.

When retelling these stories to me and to one another, narrators took great care to describe the exact location of each encounter. I had been to Potam just a year before, and since then a man in his early twenties had been murdered on the street in front of the bakery; an elderly woman had been attacked and killed at 2:00 in the afternoon as she skirted the northeastern edge of the *llano* (the open plain and ritual ground) in front of the church; a consultant's brother had been shot four times, twice through the torso, once in the shin, and once through the cheek, as he made his way down the street that runs parallel to the main road near the *cancha* (basketball court). "Do you know that little hill, that low incline behind the church?" Ana asked, locating her story about how two young males were enticed to "go out" with a friend and were brutally murdered, found at dawn the next morning by a rancher on horseback; the unlucky victims were lying on that little incline, one draped over the other. Place remains integral to understanding tragedy in a pueblo that has rapidly changed, that is "not like it used to be."

This attention to location in the discussion of violence is not entirely new; narrators recount tales of brutality and suffering as they seek to explain the presence of *muertos* (dead people) in predictable places. Late one night while standing next to Pedro Molina's pickup truck and watching fiesta activities in Rahum Pueblo, Pedro told me that one could occasionally hear weeping across the llano in front of Rahum's church. Later, in an interview I asked him to explain what he had meant that night. He replied, "Here, many have heard it. Many. Many have heard it. We too have heard weeping in Rahum."[6] He went on to set the scene. Years ago, after working on a construction project in Rahum, he and his two companions were at rest, drinking a beer,

> when we heard weeping, very sharp. We heard it coming from over there [pointing west]. And that other, the *güero* [light-complected man] heard it coming from near the church. And soon we heard it again. And, well, "Let's go!" . . . We took off! I don't know if it is the wind or what it is, but always one can hear that weeping. . . . A man passes by that place, a soldier, they say. There from the church . . . in Rahum. Every night, he walks. . . . He arrives from that side. A soldier. They killed him there a long time ago.

Pedro explained that his grandson is learning about this muerto in his elementary school classroom. "And well, this is the weeping. And many from here have heard it." He followed this comment with another story:

> And here, in this area [motions to the northwest], about one kilometer or two from here, weeping was heard as well. But this is crying, like she is crying to you. This señora who cries, her name is Rosa. They accused her of using sorcery, like they used in the past. And this señora, . . . it was a Wednesday. There they burned her with green firewood because she was an evil sorceress, they say. These are beliefs of the people. Poor thing, they killed her there. I didn't see it.

I asked Pedro when this happened, and he said, "Well, I believe it was in the twenties [1920s], around then. . . . And there, one can hear weeping. Crying. As if someone is hurting her. Every Wednesday."

And then there is the "white ghost," well known in Potam, a "soul in pain" who wears a white dress, covers her head with a veil, and moves through the night "with her feet above the ground, as if she were flying." Ana explained that the ghost "likes to go" down the road that leads to the water tower in Potam's Tinaco neighborhood, and maestro Raúl and his companions once spotted her where others have also witnessed her visits on the road next to Potam's primary school, the one shaded by towering eucalyptus trees.

Although sighting a ghost might be unsettling, not all such encounters are terrifying. Often, family muertos, affectionately referred to as *muertitos* (little dead ones), are fondly remembered. Their visits are anticipated every November 1 on the Day of the Dead. People joke about being spooked by these encounters: a boy's deceased grandmother slaps his behind in a dark corner of the yard, causing him to cry and making his aunts reel with laughter; a strange presence tugs on the toes of a teenager staying the night at his cousin's house; a muerto, "just passing" through a friend's house, moves a baby walker across a kitchen floor "out of his way."

But along with stories about visits from familiar muertos, there are times when the appearance of a ghost is interpreted as a bad omen, a portent of misfortune, or a sign of evil. Indeed, if specific places on the land attest to a violent past, it is arguable that ghosts themselves figure in the comprehension of a menacing present. Only three days before one ominous encounter, Ana had been telling me about her 17-year-old daughter's recent experiences with break-ins. Twice men had jumped the back fence in broad daylight when she was home alone. Frightened, Margarita had locked herself inside the house and waited for her family to come home. On the second occasion her young friends found a man hiding in the kitchen. Then one morning when I awoke and came outside, Ana proclaimed, "I didn't sleep well last night. I was afraid." When I asked her what happened, she explained, "I saw someone. The form of a man. Tall. He stood next to my cot, and then went that way." She explained that the form had moved toward the back corner of the lot, behind the kitchen, and she emphasized that this was the same place where the two men had jumped the fence, frightening her daughter. "At first I thought it was a man, but the gate was closed and the dogs didn't bark." Ana added, "I think it was a muerto." There was a note of relief in her voice, almost as if to imply that the presence was *only* a muerto and not a live intruder, thus making the incident less threatening.

Ana repeated the story to family and friends throughout the day. Her older sister Cecilia made Ana smile as she joked that perhaps it was their brother-in-law or her husband's cousin (both deceased) paying a visit. Narrative became a tool for sense making (Bruner 1991); as they retold and discussed the details of the encounter, Ana and her interlocutors grappled with the variety of possible meanings conveyed by the sign of the apparition. I listened to them as they worked toward interpretation and wondered whether Ana's experience itself wasn't also another form of meaning making. These days, among *poteños* (residents of Potam) I know, there is clearly a heightened level of anxiety about midday household break-ins and gunshots heard in the night, about being attacked on the way home from a festival, about increased drug use and the restlessness of youth on a reserve where all of the "good jobs" are both far away and insecure. Perhaps this generalized apprehension about a situation perceived to be spinning out of control becomes manageable when embodied in the ghost. As alarming incidents of violence and encounters with ambiguous apparitions are rearticulated in stories, they are both concretized and tied to place. The emplacement of violence is a mode of knowledge—the narrative containment of and a form of power over danger and uncertainty.

Enchanted Landscape

While the Yaqui land bears the trace of a violent past and a menacing present, it is equally characterized as a precious place, identifiable as uniquely Yaqui because of the continued presence of the ancestral Surem within the landscape itself. Outside of the pueblos proper, while walking through the dense mesquite bush toward the Yaqui River or going to visit a *comadre* (comother, the godmother to one's child) at a nearby *ranchito* (little ranch), one comes suddenly upon fences and homes, bicycles and animal corrals, carrizo ramadas, canals, and worn footpaths. The Yaqui countryside is cluttered with the effects of contemporary life. Even so, the landscape of the homeland is a place saturated with the past. Origin accounts like the one shared by Ramón Hernández assure us that the Surem, the diminutive ancestors of the Yaqui people who fled before the whites arrived, were not extinguished. Rather, they continue to exist in a world parallel to the visible one. As Ramón explained, some of the Surem "wrapped up a piece of the Yaqui River" and journeyed north. Others descended into the earth beneath the rocky surface of the Yaqui landscape. When questioned about the identity of the Surem, Josefina Vila responded:

> Well, those were, were the *first* ones . . . from the Surem it is said that we are descended. . . . When the Spaniards arrived, they [the Surem] were frightened. They left. They went in, I believe, down into the earth. Yes, they went down into the earth. Why? Because they were frightened by the Spaniards, when other people came. But they were the first ones to live here.

During an interview with 51-year-old Dolores Espinosa Nuñez I heard another version of the history of the ancestors. In her understated manner Dolores admitted that she had heard of the Surem. "My grandfather told us that they were people, like we are. And then later, . . . when they [the missionaries] were going about baptizing the people, many of them refused to be baptized. And they hid themselves. And they went down. Beneath the earth."

The "first ones" may have been physically different from modern human beings, but, as Dolores said, "they were people, like we are": they cooked for themselves; they used bows and arrows; and they were familiar with Kawi Omteme, the river, the coast, and other places on the Yaqui landscape. The Surem may have vacated the physical surface of the Yaqui homeland when they retreated into the earth, but they left behind them evidence of their existence. When Josefina told me about the Surem, she described them as being "smaller," just shy of a meter tall. "Small," she insisted. "Little people. They had tiny metates, tiny like toys." Josefina's uncle was a woodcutter, a man who was familiar with the monte surrounding the Yaqui towns. She explained, "When my uncle was living, he knew many things. He cut firewood out there . . . loads of firewood. Out there he found some metates, some *tiny* metates like this, with three little feet, yes. [Josefina held her index finger several centimeters from her thumb to indicate the minuscule size of the grinding stones.] Later, he found a little *olla* [pot] they had left."

Recall that Ramón Hernández himself discovered physical signs of Surem presence: "And a long time ago, while walking about on the lands, I found a little metate like this. [He held his hands up in front of him, spreading them about 30 centimeters apart.] . . . It is still out there. They were very short people, like this, the Surem. Hmm. And supposedly, they even say, hmm, the ancestors . . . that these people surely did exist."

Even today, the Surem can be glimpsed in visions or "out of the corners of [one's] eyes" (Molina and Kaczkurkin quoted in Schechner 1997:183), and they can be encountered unexpectedly in the desert or in caves (Evers and Molina 1993:41; Painter 1986:19). Several individuals informed me that the Surem were converted into snakes, ants, and other dangerous subterranean creatures because they rejected baptism and the Christian faith. Others shared stories about being frightened or disconcerted by the sudden appearance of a miniature person next to their horse in a darkened alleyway or along a path through the monte; these beings beckoned them to follow, and they surely must have been Surem. Some Yaquis believe that these immortal beings are powerful to the extent that they can endanger the lives of ordinary mortals (see Evers and Molina 1993:41).

Yet it is from the Surem that those Yaquis who are brave and open—*pascolas* (ritual clowns), *curanderos* (male and female healers), and deer dancers and their musicians—derive certain "spiritual" capacities (Painter 1986:16). "The enchanted people, those who went away to preserve the Yaquis' aboriginal relation to the world" (Evers and Molina 1993:38), embody origins and the memory of a time before the arrival of whites, and they give certain gifts of power to modern Yaquis. Therefore, the ancestors are also perceived in a positive way by many who know about them.

Whatever the opinion of the nature of the Surem (whether inherently good and enchanted or defiant and bothersome), narratives about these little people *locate* Yaqui ancestry, assigning it a definite place. The fact that the Surem continue to exist beneath the surface of the Yaqui homeland anchors the Yaqui people to their territory. Yaquis establish primordial rights to their homeland as a physical place by virtue of the immanence of their ancestors. The copresence of the Surem, whose tools of domesticity litter the hills, attests to Yaqui autochthony, thereby validating Yaqui identity as incontrovertibly indigenous.

Testimony to the significance of the land to Yaqui identity occurs in uncountable ways. The Ocho Pueblos, established in the early seventeenth century under Jesuit direction, have become a symbol of Yaqui identity, central to the ideological construction of their homeland. According to Yaqui myth, each of the Ocho Pueblos was founded by "a Yaqui prophet [who] performed ceremonial labor (tekípanoa) at the town site, thus designating the place as sacred" (Spicer 1980:171). Spicer argues that the Ocho Pueblos became a concept, in and of itself, "the image of ideal human . . . relations, towards which Yaquis were oriented" (1980:308). He writes that the Eight Towns, taken as a unit,

> gave orientation for Yaquis in a spiritual and sacred space, that is, located them in relation to the supernaturals and in relation to one another in the service and under the authority of the supernaturals. Corresponding to this spiritual space there was of course ordinary space in which towns were constructed and people had to manage their lives. Always, for those who were aware, the management of the business of life, of living together as Yaquis, could be referred to the system of meanings linked with the Eight Towns symbol. . . . This system, or rather subsystem, of symbols was therefore a source of [a] sense of common identity among Yaquis. As such it was a basis for nonidentification with Yoris and others. [Spicer 1980:309]

In everyday conversations, when Yaqui individuals talk about the Ocho Pueblos, they are not merely speaking about eight physical towns; they are also presenting their collective ethnic "face" to the rest of the world. As a symbol, the Ocho Pueblos is polysemous; it means many things all at once—the people's solidarity (Spicer 1980:310), the survival of war and the encroachment of outsiders, the moral system of ceremonial labor that binds community members to one another and to God, and the sacred mandate through which God granted this land to the Yaqui tribe.

Yet while the homeland in its entirety is constructed as a meaningful place (through the immanence of the Yaquis' Surem ancestors, by the fact that the ground is steeped in the blood of a difficult history, by the symbolic construction of the Ocho Pueblos as divinely sanctioned unity), specific places on that landscape also become critical in the process of Yaqui identification with the land. Here, I am referring to yo hoaram, those enchanted places on the landscape where brave and perceptive Yaquis can access esoteric knowledge and musical ability—identifiable locations that serve as access points to a unique cultural heritage.

On that same sunny May afternoon that Pedro Molina explained to me the meaning of inim bwan bwía, he also shared several stories about the enchanted places he knew on Yaqui land. One of those stories was about an experience Pedro had when he was much younger:

> Where we used to go for firewood there is a big ridge—long—and there. . . . It had noise, like the dancing of the deer, the pascola, the drum, songs. At night is when it can be heard. Yo hoara, they call it. Enchanted. And there, many went there, there, in order to dance better. To become enchanted. And so, then, a pascola or a deer dancer went there to play. And in this way they were enchanted.

Surprisingly, the stories I heard about charmed locations—the one shared by Regina Valencia about the little boy and the enchanted cave and the story told by Pedro Molina about the enchanted ridge—did not result from a question about yo hoaram. Rather, these narratives were forthcoming when I asked Regina and Pedro about Yaqui understandings of the *yo anía*. Described by Spicer as "'the ancient and honorable realm' . . . the domain or world of respected powers" (1980:64), yo anía is a Yaqui term that can be translated as "enchanted world" or "ancient world" (see Evers and Molina 1993:62–64; Spicer 1980:64). Evers and Molina explain that the yo anía is "an ancient world, a mythic place outside historic time and space, yet it can be present in the most immediate way" (1993:62). The yo anía is the place where the immortal Surem are thought to dwell, and, according to Spicer, "it is from the immortals that the special power for dancing and making the music appropriate for the Pascola, the Deer, the Matupari (raccoon), the Nahi (dragonfly), and other animal dances is channeled to men" (1980:67).

When I asked about the yo anía, both Regina and Pedro chose instead to tell me stories about yo hoaram, the enchanted homes on the Yaqui landscape. I do not know whether their answers were a deliberate evasion or a careful reinterpretation of my query, but the concept of yo hoaram—sites that can be experienced, discovered, identified—is very distinct from the more nebulous notion of yo anía, an enchanted world inhabited by ancestral Yaquis.

According to Evers and Molina, the Yaqui term *yo* "is not easily translated." It means old, not merely "'old' but the oldest old, the ancient, the primordial" (Evers and Molina 1993:62). At the same time, the term *yo* also means "enchanted," which is how it was glossed by my informants. In turn, the word *hoara* in the Yaqui language means "home." Hoara should not be equated with the generalized notion of homeland in the sense of a territory remembered and constructed as "home" in the wake of late-nineteenth-century exile and return.[7] Rather, yo hoara refers to certain hills and caves, ridges and earthen depressions—in other words, natural geophysical features within the traditional boundaries of the homeland. Yo hoara connotes a sense of particularity.

As opposed to the yo anía, an enchanted ancient world or realm, yo hoaram are specific identifiable places on the land, the "homes" in which enchanted beings dwell. Equally, they are perceived as portals through which seekers might be blessed with a special gift, a talent beyond the ordinary. As Pedro continued his narrative, he eagerly identified specific places: "And there. Many went there in order to dance better. To become enchanted." He waved out to the desert with his hand, explaining, "And out there is another place. Sadly, the water dried up. Now there is nothing there. This is called Baasiuti. Baasiuti: [the place of] divided water. And out there was another." With his finger Pedro indicated direction:

> And over there, there's another. And there was another [enchanted place] in Kében. Kébenia, they call it. Kébenia. And out there, there is another. My grandmother's sister used to tell me. Angelina was the old woman's name. She died when she was 115 years old. She used to talk about when there was . . . there was a pool of water. There, they could hear the playing, at times . . . those things [*teneboim*, cocoon rattles] worn by the deer.

She used to take care of the goats there. She told me about that. That they [certain individuals] became enchanted [near that pool]. One señor became enchanted there. He was a drummer. . . . There is, too, this . . . Harón Kawi. Enchanted peak. And in the sierra, too, there are many *encantos* [enchantments].

Pedro seemed impatient to list place after place for me, pointing in the direction of every enchantment, each with its own specific location. "I only know the ones around here," he smiled. "There are many others."

The Experience of Place

Phenomenologist Edward Casey (1996) contends that just as places themselves are sensed and experienced, all sensory experience is also emplaced. It can then be argued that social realities, the diverse ways in which human beings perceive and order their experiences, are also inseparable from place. Among the Yaquis, narratives of haunting and enchantment are not merely about history and encounters with ghosts and ancestors in a multiply layered world; they are fundamentally about place—about the Yaqui homeland as an entity and about natural landmarks and special locations on the homeland. These stories are about the ways that these places embody memory; they are about identification with a particular landscape.

Yaqui land bears traces of violent experience. Fears about a troubling present and a chaotic future, embodied in ghostly apparitions, become understandable and possibly even controllable through emplacement, dialogue, and storytelling. The Yaqui homeland is a place where the phrase "this weeping land" conveys the sense that pain is intimately tied to identity, where the land itself bears witness to human suffering. Haunting creates for Yaquis what Avery Gordon (after Cixous and Clément 1986) calls "the 'imaginary zone . . . every culture has . . . for what it excludes,' for what is personally, historically, and sociologically unspeakable" (Gordon 1997:178). Gordon explains: "Being haunted draws us affectively, sometimes against our will and always a bit magically, into the structure of feeling of a reality we come to experience, not as cold knowledge, but as a transformative recognition" (1997:8). As the desert weeps, memory is firmly emplaced, and a visceral awareness of the past becomes a powerful vehicle for making meaning.

The Yaqui landscape is associated with uncountable individual experiences, with a certain history of human occupation and use. Ancestral

Surem continue to exist just below the surface, substantiating the Yaqui claim to the land as fundamentally theirs. Histories of the Surem, like accounts of a weeping wilderness, reveal the Yaqui homeland as a place with "rememories that you can bump into, even if they did not happen to you personally" (Gordon 1997:197), a place "in which 'history has physically merged into the setting'" (Benjamin 1977:177, quoted in Stewart 1996:90). Finally, the Yaqui landscape is a blessed space, brimming with enchanted places. The land holds promise of a sacred knowledge, a "way of knowing" inaccessible through ordinary means. As hauntings and encounters link experiences of the past to specific locations on the Yaqui landscape and provide a means of coping with the present, as enchanted sites provide access to ancient ancestral worlds and to a wealth of cultural knowledge, teaching Yaquis *how to be Yaqui*, Yaqui social reality, cultural memory, and even identity itself are unwaveringly emplaced.

II

The Articulation of Gender and Ethnicity

5
Women Embodying Yaquiness
The Struggle for—and with—Difference

The first part of this book has been an exploration of the ways in which space, place, and history converge in the constitution and negotiation of Yaqui ethnicity, shaping the ways in which the "present" itself is understood and lived by Yaqui individuals. Our examination of the Talking Tree story has illuminated Yaqui understandings of their own ethnogenesis as an experience rooted in a particular space that is bounded, centered, and replete with still-identifiable places and as a process that occurred in relation to impending European invasion. Our study of personal memories has revealed the impact of forced movement—the displacement of Yaquis from their aboriginal territory in the late nineteenth and early twentieth centuries—upon the Yaqui ethnic imagination and the significance of this history of exile and return in the discursive construction of the Yaqui homeland. We have explored Yaqui stories describing chance encounters with ghosts and haunted locations, places that imbue the landscape with a deep history and allow alternative understandings of a complex present. We have been privy to other stories disclosing the existence of hidden enchanted places on the Yaqui landscape—treasured portals to a realm of specialized cultural knowledge. We have, in sum, focused on the roles played by space, place, and history in the production of cultural identity.

Yet from another perspective, part I also centers on the discursive constitution of Yaqui ethnicity. Indeed, Yaqui identities are made, at least in part, as they are articulated or expressed (Hall in Grossberg 1996:141) through historical narrative, myth, memory, and everyday conversation. Still, as Stuart Hall notes, articulation has a double meaning, as in the conjoining of two or more separable parts (Grossberg 1996:141). It is "articulation" in this second sense that part II explores, because, for Yaqui women, female-gendered identities overlap with Yaqui ethnicity in very powerful ways.

When I first moved to Potam, I had hoped to study women's experiences and understandings of femaleness. I wanted to look at women's

self-representations and how gendered identity and status were negotiated. Yet the Yaqui women I came to know almost invariably positioned
themselves *first* as Yaquis. It was difficult for me to engage women in
conversations about themselves exclusively *as women*; Yaquiness continually entered the equation. Consultants preferred to talk about what
"Yaqui women" do and believe, how "Yaqui women" behave, and how
"Yaqui women" are different from Yori women. Many female consultants avoided talking about "women" in a general sense, that is, without
first qualifying that gender category as Yaqui or Yori.

What forces converge to create such an ethnicized sensibility of gendered identity? Hall states that the "elements" of any articulated unity
"can be re-articulated in different ways because they have no necessary
'belongingness'" (Grossberg 1996:141). Using the frequent articulation of
political ideology and religion as an example, he notes that "religion has no
necessary political connotation. . . . I don't mean religion is free-floating.
It exists historically in a particular formation. . . . Nevertheless, it has no
necessary, intrinsic, transhistorical belongingness. Its meaning—political
and ideological—comes precisely from its position within a formation"
(Hall in Grossberg 1996:142).

While Hall's theory addresses the articulation of ideological elements
within specific modes of discourse, his idea can be usefully extended to
enhance our understanding of identity. We can argue that the connections that articulate different facets of one's identity are also not pre-
determined; rather, they are products of a very particular cultural and
historical milieu. Gender does not have to be conceptualized in terms
of ethnicity, but the fact that it so often is, for Yaqui women, is telling.
It leads me to believe that a history of antagonism between the Yaquis
as a group and those who sought to deport them, assimilate them, even
eliminate their cultural identity, as well as the present-day experiences
of discrimination and economic marginalization—in essence, the experience of identifying and being identified as a Yaqui—contribute to
the configuration of many other parts of a Yaqui individual's identity.
The impact of the Yaqui spatiohistorical and highly "located" experience of their own ethnicity may be so strong that stepping outside of
that identity—or submerging that facet of identity in order to highlight
another—is either undesirable or difficult to imagine. Chantal Mouffe
alludes to this idea in her assertion that a subject, a self, a "social agent"
is a "plurality" and that "this plurality does not involve the *coexistence*,
one by one, of a plurality of subject positions but rather the constant

subversion and overdetermination of one by the others" (1992:372). Yaqui gendered realities are forged in a milieu in which ethnicity (itself thoroughly emplaced and often understood in spatial terms) seems to be especially meaningful, and Yaqui women's gendered identities—albeit negotiated, contested, and constantly shifting—also shape (and are undeniably shaped by) ethnic identity.

One of the clearest memories I have from my time in Potam was formed in the moments following mass on a Thursday in October 1996. Marcela and I pick our way through the crowded and uneven cemetery surrounding Potam's church, visiting the graves of her grandparents and of a cousin killed the previous year in an automobile accident. We cross the sandy expanse of the llano and sit down to drink icy Cokes outside the clapboard sandwich shop at the end of Potam's *calle principal* (main street). The pueblo bubbles with late-afternoon activity. An old school bus painted red and white, many of its metal-rimmed windows permanently stuck in the open or closed position, pulls up, grinding and sputtering to a halt, and teenagers in school uniforms disembark. Men, their eyes shaded by straw sombreros, ride past on heavy black single-speed bicycles. One older man pedals his bike slowly, his wife on the back. She holds her patent leather–clad feet parallel to the ground in order to balance herself and a bag of groceries. Her gray hair is caught up in a bun, her slender neck adorned with strings of faceted plastic beads in marine blue, ruby red, and gold. She wears a white cotton skirt decorated at its edge with a profusion of the bright, coarsely embroidered flowers that are one of several distinctive sartorial markers of Yaqui identity. Marcela nods toward the couple, remarking that many people dress up when they journey from ranches and farms out in the countryside for a day of shopping in the pueblo.

This image—of a woman on the back of a bicycle wearing what Yaquis and others identify as "traditional" dress—is remarkable, but not because it is uncommon. In the nearby city of Obregón Yaqui women are highly visible as they shop in the stores and markets, as they crowd taco stands on busy street corners, and as they wait with bags at the bus terminal. These women are frequently identified as Yaqui by Obregón's Mexican residents because of what they wear (wide, colorful skirts, shawls, and hammered gold earrings) and because of the way they conduct and hold themselves.

This chapter opens our discussion of the articulation of women's gender and ethnicity with an exploration of ethnic embodiment. Clearly, dress is a form of communication, and some Yaqui women choose to wear their ethnicity for all to see. One of the most significant features of Yaqui ethnic dress is the embroidery—the colorful flowers that embellish women's skirts, blouses, and handkerchiefs. Such flower imagery resonates with, even puts on display, one of the key symbols of Yaqui culture. Ethnicity and women's gender are also articulated in another highly embodied experience—giving birth. Birthing is at base a gendered act, but Yaqui women's narratives also explicitly link ethnicity to birthing behaviors and attitudes. When telling stories about giving birth, Yaqui women emphasize their ability (unique in their eyes) to "endure" discomfort and suffering. Yaqui mothers liberally employ this cultural discourse of endurance, thereby valorizing their own suffering as women while at the same time drawing an unambiguous distinction between themselves and non-Yaqui women. Yet the embodiment of ethnicity takes numerous forms. In the chapter's final pages I examine the ways in which ethnic identity impacts and impinges upon women's economic lives and material choices. Yaqui women bear the burdens and reap the benefits of their ethnic identity as they face the challenges of everyday material life in a desert pueblo. How does being Yaqui and living on an indigenous reserve in northern Mexico affect the "structure of possibility" (Stern 1995:331) for these women, and, importantly, how do they respond? I consider the stories of two women, each of whom, for unique reasons, could be identified as embodying a truly "Yaqui" experience.

The World of Flowers: Gender, Dress, and Yaqui Identity

Michael Taussig reminds us that "alterity is every inch a relationship" (1993:130). Difference may be relational, but to be meaningful it must also be recognizable, and the clothed body is frequently one of the first indicators of ethnic distinction (Eicher 1995; Weismantel 2001). Taussig's work with the Cuna of Panama demonstrates that alterity is often gendered. He writes, "It is the Cuna women, not the men, who bear the mark of tradition—the nose rings, the vivid and strikingly beautiful appliquéd *mola* blouses and head coverings. In the visual scheme of things it is not the men but the Indian women who are alter" (Taussig 1993:130). Similarly, among contemporary Yaquis, women are more likely than their male counterparts to don ethnic dress.

Items of everyday apparel—the skirts, trousers, jeans, blouses, and T-shirts often referred to as "Western" clothing but perhaps more appropriately termed "cosmopolitan" or "world fashion" (Eicher and Sumberg 1995:296)—are affordable and widely available from a village seamstress or in the city's shops. Yaqui men are most often seen wearing jeans, button-down shirts, cowboy hats, and boots or sandals. Although Yaqui women's fashion repertoire varies widely in form, from business suits to jeans, from church dresses gathered at the waist to miniskirts, many Yaqui women choose to dress the "Yaqui way" because it signifies something about them and their identity.

"Traditional" apparel for Yaqui females is usually handmade, and when a woman needs a new outfit, she brings meters of material to one of the many seamstresses in the pueblo. The typical outfit consists of a wide, calf-length skirt made of brightly colored satin and trimmed with white lace and a button-up short-sleeved blouse, worn untucked. A rebozo is used as a head covering or is draped over the shoulders, and footwear consists of plastic flip-flops, leather sandals, or low-heeled slip-ons. Most Yaqui women have a pair of thin, half-moon-shaped gold-plated earrings, purchased in the city or from local hawkers, and a few older women wear *mapoam*, long strings of tiny beads in purple, black, gold, or red wrapped many times to fit tightly around the wrist.

It is the *sea hiki* clothing, however—the white cotton skirts, slips, blouses, and handkerchiefs embroidered with yarn in large fuchsia, magenta, Kelly green, aqua, and orange flowers—that is especially meaningful to Yaqui women. Embroidery is primarily a woman's art; many young girls learn to embroider from their mothers and female relatives, and women who are adept at embossing cloth with fine, even stitches can sell their handiwork for hundreds of pesos. Clothing decorated with sea hiki (embroidered flowers) is sought-after during the Yaqui ceremonial high season, beginning with Lent in February and ending in early summer with the last of the pueblos' saint's day fiestas.

In the Yaqui language, *sea* (a variation of *sewa*) means "flower," but the word is widely used and conjures many other images associated with Yaqui culture and belief. Flower symbolism permeates nearly every Yaqui religious ceremony, from the red ribbons called "flowers" that adorn the antlers of the deer dancer and the flower imagery that permeates Yaqui deer songs (Evers and Molina 1993), to the colorful flowers painted on the headdress of the Matachín dancer and the feathered "flower" plumes he carries in his hand. According to Yaqui legend, the blood that spilled from the side of Jesus's body when he was crucified was transformed into flowers upon reaching the ground (Painter 1986:100).

The word "sea" recalls Sea Hamut, the wise Flower Woman who traveled from her seaside home to interpret the strange humming sounds emanating from the Talking Tree and who forewarned the Surem of the coming of the whites. In the interpenetrating worlds of Yaqui cosmology, sea is associated with the *sea anía*, the "flower world." Rooted in ancient times, the flower world is still considered by some to exist in a present parallel dimension, becoming visible in the springtime, when the desert is in bloom. Evers and Molina write, "Located in the east, in a place 'beneath the dawn,' the sea anía, flower world, is described as a perfected mirror image of all the beauty of the natural world of the Sonoran desert" (1993:47). The sea anía is permeated with the supernatural and is believed to be the home of sacred brother deer (Evers and Molina 1993:47). The word "sea" can conjure images of the *sea taka* (flower body), an inborn gift, a special power that can be used for evil or for good (Evers and Molina 1993:53; Painter 1986:11–13). Those blessed with sea taka can perceive another level of reality through their dreams and visions; they can heal others and ward off evil (Painter 1986:13–15).

A Yaqui consultant once described the sea hiki on women's clothing as "fantasy flowers." Skirts and blouses splashed with sea hiki symbolically map the flower world onto the female body. Sea hiki summons an image of everything that is good and associated with Christ and the enchanted deer. It recalls the power inherent in the sea anía; it reminds us of Sea Hamut and of the powers given to one who has the "flower body." Yaqui embroidered apparel references complex notions of power and cosmology, a deep history of belief. To outsiders sea hiki bespeaks ethnic alterity, but to insiders it calls forth a key symbol specific to Yaquiness itself.

Birth, Bravery, and the Construction of an Ethnicized Gender

Ethnic clothing is not the only way Yaqui identity is linked to gender. In their stories about labor, delivery, and the endurance of pain, Yaqui women point to the ways in which they reproduce and reinforce cultural identity through the uniquely female act of giving birth. The high status of motherhood in Yaqui culture is evident upon an examination of women's personal narratives. Yaqui women become producers of family and of society by giving birth, and in their talk these women call attention to their own unique female biology, valorizing it and making themselves powerful by means of it. As Yaqui women articulate their gendered identities, both to me and to each other, the birthing process itself emerges not only as a way to differentiate Yaqui women from Yaqui men but also as a point of pride and ethnic distinction.

Yaqui women utilize stories of birthing and endurance to inscribe boundaries between themselves and those women who are cultural outsiders. This discursive tactic is noticeable in the many birthing narratives that I collected while I was in Potam, where there seems to be a consensus that Yaqui women are "strong," able to "give birth *en un ratito* [in a short amount of time], *sin problemas* [without problems]." In contrast, Mexican and American women "hardly know how to give birth anymore," and Yori women are "*bien chillonas* [real screamers]."

The house I lived in with Ana and Marco was less than 50 meters from the home of one of Potam's midwives, Marta Moreno. I had visited Marta's home many times to hear about her work and the births she had attended and to review the delivery statistics she had carefully compiled in her six years as a *partera* (midwife). I had been inside Marta's delivery suite, a tiny, one-room, dirt-floored waddle-and-daub structure with cleanly whitewashed walls and a small burlap cot next to the door. I had seen the jars of bright orange antiseptic, her stethoscope and blood pressure kit, the bandages and soft cloths, all lined up neatly on a shelf next to the shortened, elevated delivery table.

One evening, shortly after I came to live with Ana and Marco, I wondered aloud about the noises of childbirth I imagined must emanate from Marta's place. Sound travels well in the quiet pueblo, especially after dark: fragments of conversation from people riding by on bicycles can be distinguished; music filters through the bush from the radios being played on ranches out near the canal; laughter, gunshots, barking dogs, rattling bicycles, even the thumping beat from a dance in Vicam Pueblo (ten kilometers away) are all audible in the still night air. Surely, I reasoned, we would occasionally hear women suffering from the pain of childbirth at Marta's nearby home. I asked Ana, "Do you ever hear cries from women in labor over at doña Marta's house?"

Ana looked surprised. "No," she replied. "Why, have you?"

"No, but I just thought, you know, since it is so close, that you might hear something when a woman is delivering."

Ana chuckled. "Yaqui women don't cry out during delivery. *Ellas lo aguantan* [They endure it]. Where you live, do women make noise?"

"Yes," I nodded. "Some scream, even curse because of the pain."

Ana laughed. "Yes, they say that Yori women are more scandalous. Some even cry at times! But Yaqui women, no. They just endure it. Sometimes they complain, but very quietly, very slowly."

Narratives of suffering and the ability to endure inform the constitution of Yaqui gendered identities—specifically, concepts of femaleness. When sharing their life stories, Yaqui women enumerated the obstacles they had overcome as well as the problems they continue to face; I heard countless tales of alcoholism and husbands' infidelities, of domestic violence and the struggle to carve out a life in the impoverished Zona Indígena. Yaqui women employed this notion of endurance to distinguish their experience from that of Yaqui men. Time and again I was told by female informants that women have more "courage," more "valor" than men, that women do not hesitate to confront a frightening situation if their children are in jeopardy. As Ana Ochoa put it, "It is said . . . that women always endure more. Women endure everything better than men do. That is what they say here."

While this concept of "enduring" hardship contributes to constructions of gender within Yaqui culture, it is also a theme that permeates everyday Yaqui life, articulating a very specific historical, political, and cultural experience. The Spanish verb *aguantar* (to endure, to bear) is employed by Yaquis in casual conversations, historical narratives, arguments, and life stories to delineate ethnic boundaries. While it is a commonly used idiom throughout greater Mexico, endurance is frequently appropriated by Yaquis to designate the quality of their own cultural practices and experiences. Evidence of a sharply honed consciousness of the prevalence of struggle and opposition in Yaqui experience is reflected in individuals' narratives of the past, as the paired themes of suffering and endurance surface time and again. Yaquis see themselves as having endured tremendous hardships. The wars of the nineteenth century, forced removal from their homeland, enslavement in Yucatán, violence, and attempted genocide are offered as examples of the trials that Yaquis have endured. These stories of suffering are coupled with affirmations of endurance. Narratives depicting journeys of return to the homeland abound, illustrating a will to return from exile and the triumph ("with God's help") over cultural obliteration.

The importance of "enduring" becomes abundantly evident in Yaqui ritual life, as an ability to endure the arduous rituals at the core of this group's elaborate ceremonial complex becomes a marker of the quality of one's Yaquiness. Spicer wrote, "There is an explicit recognition among Yaquis that . . . their religious life is more demanding than that of other peoples, and . . . that this characteristic Yaqui way expresses the highest moral worth" (1980:312). Yaquis practice a thoroughly indigenized Catholicism. The historical suffering of the Yaqui people resonates strongly with the agony of Christ, his persecution and crucifixion. When a Yaqui child falls ill, parents make a vow, promising that child to God or the saints in exchange for his or her survival. Those who are healed contribute years of ritual service. For instance, in the Yaqui pueblos hundreds of men, having been promised to the Chapayeka ceremonial society, carry out their duties during Lent and Easter. They are the masked dancers representing the soldiers of the Pharisees, evil ones in pursuit of Christ. During the Lenten season it is the Chapayekas who assume control of the pueblo. Their duties are numerous and difficult and include constant vigilance of the pueblo's streets, the observation of absolute silence when the mask is donned, hours of dancing and marching in the hot sun, sleepless nights, sexual prohibitions, and strictures against drinking.

The Chapayeka society is just one of dozens. Yaqui maestros and *cantoras* (female singers, ritual specialists) are dedicated to lifelong service. During the ceremonial high season maestros and cantoras go without sleep for days at a time; they must be ready at a moment's notice to lead a wedding or offer prayers at a vigil. Yaquis insist that one must fulfill ritual duties with vigor and enthusiasm. For them, the endurance of some degree of suffering during ceremonies is associated with ethnic identity and cultural pride. As a Yaqui maestro once explained, "There is nothing more beautiful than one's own culture. To know how to pray, to know the prayers, well, . . . that is beautiful. Beautiful, but . . . *muy pesado* [very heavy or difficult]."

Endurance appears to be a significant component informing a poetics of Yaqui ethnicity, a sort of expressive form or style, an aesthetic logic that permeates significant cultural practices (see Flores 1995; Herzfeld 1985; Limón 1994). Demonstrating the ability to endure is an important way of being both Yaqui and a woman. Bearing in mind the historical, political, and social experiences of the Yaqui people over the course of the past four centuries, it is not difficult to understand why Yaqui women then employ narratives of endurance (in this case, a specific ability to endure the birthing process) in order to differentiate themselves from mestizos.

Stories of bravery in childbirth proliferate among women in Yaqui communities. A good example of this type of women's talk occurred one hot afternoon in September 1997 while I was visiting Carlota Kus in her home on Potam's west side. The temperature was over 105 degrees Fahrenheit, and she and I were sitting in the shade of the ramada attached to her brick house, enjoying the tamarind juice *helados* (popsicles) that she kept in her freezer to sell, when Carlota's neighbor Amalia Jusacamea came over to purchase a bottle of Pepsi for her family's lunch. I had met Amalia, an outspoken older Yaqui woman, on several occasions. She sat down with us, declaring that she had not seen me for a while, and promptly asked, "When are you going to have a baby?" Without waiting for my reply, she declared, "There is nothing to be afraid of. It is over very quickly, and when you see the baby you will want another one."

The three of us sat and chatted for some time. Our conversation wandered from the topic of Carlota's toothache to the subject of a funeral I had attended the previous week and then back to childbirth as Amalia abruptly exclaimed that her daughter had given birth to a baby girl on Sunday. Marta Moreno had attended the delivery. I asked if the young woman had "cried" (a common and culturally appropriate question), and Amalia proudly stated that her daughter is ashamed to cry and carry on. She recalled, "When I arrived there, Marta told me, 'Your daughter is *bien macha* [really tough]!' '*Que bueno* [That's good],' I said, 'que bueno.'"

Amalia then began to recount her own memories of birthing. She had 12 children, two pairs of whom were twins. She told me that she preferred to give birth at home alone or with the occasional help of other female relatives and that she would call for the partera only afterward for help in cutting the umbilical cord. She launched enthusiastically into a story about the birth of her first child:

> With Juanita, I had arisen early in the morning, at dawn. And I built the fire and put the water on for coffee, and I began to feel strange. "I am going to give birth," I thought. And so, very quickly, I threw down a *petate* [mat], and I spread a sheet on top of it, just like that. And here [indicating her lower abdomen with her hand] I felt very heavy. "Ooooh! The baby is coming!" I said to myself. And I squatted down like this, and Juanita was born right then. And then when the baby cried, my in-laws woke up and hurried out to see.

Yaquiness is often measured by degree and by the essence of one's behavior. Individuals who exhibit *mucha vergüenza* (a great deal of embarrassment or shame) around non-Yaquis—who hide when outsiders come to visit, who refrain from conversation and shield their faces—are considered by those around them to be *si hiaki* (very Yaqui). Amalia's story, told with great relish, not only demonstrates her own investment in the discourses describing birthing as an act of bravery but also highlights the way in which the notion of vergüenza is bound up with the concept of endurance. Amalia maintained that she never wanted the assistance of a doctor because she would be embarrassed to have him see her exposed. She refused to cry out when giving birth, she explained, because it also embarrasses her to act like that. In other words, her shame was not merely tied to bodily exposure and a sense of modesty; the inability to endure pain would also have been a source of shame. Amalia's narrative establishes the quality of both her womanhood and her ethnicity. It is just one of many discrete speech events contributing to a larger discourse within which notions of ethnic and gendered identity are strongly articulated.

Women, Work, and Yaqui Identity

Ethnicity can be communicated through women's clothing and inscribed in narratives about "endurance" and birth, but how does identity affect women's economic realities? How does identity impact the laboring body? Does a woman's identity as a Yaqui shape the type of work that is available to her? Does it influence the way she chooses (or is compelled) to spend her day? To these last questions I would answer an unequivocal "yes." Here I step back from those (often consciously made) ethnic "assertions" apparent in the clothed body and in narratives about birth to consider the subtle ways in which Yaquiness is engrained in the challenges women face and in the tactics they employ in order to ensure their families' economic survival. Yaqui ethnicity impacts a woman's material reality and therefore shapes how she perceives herself and how others see her. Here I examine the work histories and family circumstances of two Yaqui women, Cecilia Ochoa Bakasewa and Lorenia Choki Buitimea. Their stories, although admittedly compressed and focused, are intended to provide a snapshot of the contours of daily life and the economic possibilities available to Yaqui women and their families in the late twentieth century. I select their stories not because they represent *the* Yaqui woman in any absolute or essential way but because the stories of Cecilia Ochoa and Lorenia Choki provide a partial yet revealing glimpse of the experience of being a Yaqui woman.

Cecilia

The sun hung low, shimmering orange in the May evening sky as I entered Cecilia Ochoa's extended family compound. Her cousin's husband, Antonio, greeted me as usual with a handshake. That night Antonio's mother-in-law was hosting a prayer ceremony to San Isidro, the patron saint of farmers. I accepted their invitation to stay for the prayers and for the dinner to be served afterward. "Is Cecilia here?" I inquired.

"No, Kristi," Antonio replied with a definitive shake of his head. "Fíjate que se fue al maíz. Temprano se fue!" [Look, she went to the cornfields. She left early!] May is one of the times that maize is harvested in the Yaqui River valley, and Cecilia had seized the opportunity, as do many, to glean what she could in order to earn some money. Cecilia loves household ceremonies, and I knew she would be disappointed if she missed the *rezo* (prayer session). I watched for her the rest of the evening while I helped Antonio with his English and throughout the prayers and the dinner. Finally, an old white pickup truck pulled up to the fence, its back end full of women. Cecilia heaved four large sacks of maize onto the ground and climbed over the tailgate as her son Ricardo hurried over to help her haul the bags into the yard. She wore a man's long-sleeved work shirt over her blouse to prevent the sun from burning her arms, and underneath her skirt a pair of trousers protected her legs from the abrasive leaves of the dry cornstalks. Her black hair, stringy and dusty, hung limply behind two small clips. She looked tired.

Cecilia bathed and changed her clothes. When I walked over to greet her, she was eating her bowl of menudo alone in the dark at the well-worn table under her mother's outdoor cooking shelter.[1] In the bluish light from the street lamp I glimpsed the flash of her beguiling smile, and she quickly pulled a burlap cot to my side "so you don't get tired standing." She told me excitedly that she was able to fill four sacks with corncobs, which she estimated to weigh between 60 and 80 kilograms. She would be able to sell these at one peso per kilogram—a very good day's work.[2]

Like many Yaqui women, Cecilia prioritizes her family and her involvement in local religious practices. Although she does not hold an official position in any of the formal ceremonial societies that elaborate the expression of Yaqui Catholicism, Cecilia gives herself willingly to the tasks of devotion. Throughout 1997 and 1998 she traveled weekly to the pueblo of Rahum to kneel and help carry the saint for the *konti* (ceremonial procession).[3] During Cuaresma (Lent) she goes early to church to sweep the sanctuary in preparation for processions, and she spends hours cooking the many dishes to be offered on the Day of the Dead and for the numerous household rezos held throughout the year. The large amount of time and labor Cecilia dedicates to the logistical support of ritual activities in Potam and in nearby Rahum Pueblo is typical among women who identify as Yaqui. Cecilia sees devotional labor as part of her identity and as vital to the community's social health.

One of four sisters, Cecilia was 37 years old when I came to Potam. The hard work that defines her life has contoured the muscles in her broad back and caused her fingers to callus, and her face bears the stains of an unrelenting desert sun. Yet none of this diminishes her striking beauty. Cecilia wears a dark skirt that falls just below the knee and a waist-length, untucked, button-up blouse. On her feet she wears plastic flip-flops, and one can hear her coming from a distance. She walks quickly, her cobalt blue rebozo fluttering behind her—too fast, "very un-Yaqui," her sisters tease. By far, Cecilia's favorite piece of clothing is the white cotton slip that peeks out from beneath the hem of her dark skirt, embroidered with sea hiki flowers in bright shades of purple, yellow, fluorescent orange, and pink.

Cecilia was born and raised in Potam. Her father, wiry and gaunt, now given to teasing his many grandchildren, had owned a small herd of cattle when she was a young girl that he eventually lost to debt. Because her mother helped her father on the ranch, which was located in the countryside, Cecilia lived with her paternal grandmother during the school year; her sisters lived with their maternal grandmother and her second husband. After completing junior high school Cecilia enrolled in secretarial classes in Ciudad Obregón, but she had to quit before the end of her first year.[4] "I left because there was no money for transportation [to and from Obregón] and all the rest of it. At that time, my papá . . . used to go on 15-day or month-long drinking binges . . . and he didn't work." She related this information without bitterness, and I wondered aloud, Did it make her angry? "No. What was I to do? *Ni modo* [No matter]," she said. At the age of 16 Cecilia began staying at home to help her mother with the housework, leaving behind her education and any chance for a well-paying job.

She and Carlos met at a dance in Potam. He was a year younger, and they began to date. When Cecilia turned 20 he asked her to marry him. She expresses pride in the fact that they were married "properly," that they had a traditional Yaqui ceremony as well as a Catholic church wedding. "Yes, we were married *con tamales* [with tamales]," she explained, "but we could not afford pascolas." To many Yaquis, pascolas personify tradition. They are present at virtually all major Yaqui public ceremonies and at many private ones as well. Pascolas dance during pueblo religious fiestas and during Semana Santa (Holy Week), and they honor the deceased at a *novenario* (ceremony marking the passage of the ninth day after a death) and at a *cabo de año* (ceremony marking the end of a year of mourning). When the family can afford it and if the bride and groom are so inclined, pascolas are hired to dance at the wedding—one dressed as a "bride" and the other as a "groom"—to please the crowd with their ribald joking and their intricate dances and to tease and embarrass the couple. Cecilia's reference to marriage "with tamales," then, is an understated way to say that her wedding was conducted in the traditional Yaqui manner, even though the families could not afford to hire pascolas. A "Yaqui wedding" or a wedding "Yaqui style," as it is commonly called, is an important way to signify identity. Although very few couples have Yaqui weddings anymore, such ceremonies are still esteemed as a core tradition, identifying the couple as "true Yaquis."

Cecilia described the preparations for her Yaqui wedding in detail: on the day of the wedding, her mother and her sisters spent hours assembling and tying the ends of oily, meat-filled tamales, which were then piled into special carrizo baskets. Late that July afternoon Cecilia, dressed in a white sea hiki blouse and skirt, walked through the streets of Potam with her mother, her grandmothers, and her *madrina* (her godmother, who is a wedding sponsor) to the groom's home. There the family presented the bride, and the groom's parents accepted her along with the family's gift of tamales. Cecilia and Carlos sat side by side on a woven mat in front of the wooden house cross, where the Yaqui maestro advised them always to demonstrate respect in their marriage and never to abandon one another.[5] The ceremony was sealed with a dinner and the exchange of *bolo*, tin pails filled to the brim with chile (thin sliced beef in the deep red chile pasillo sauce), *wakabaki* (beef bone soup with garbanzos, green beans, maize, and carrots), and piles of fresh flour tortillas.[6]

Cecilia and Carlos were married in a manner favored by Yaqui tradition, and in many ways their life together exemplifies the struggles faced by young Yaqui couples because of their identity and because of the fact that they live on an indigenous reserve, a place that is replete with cultural meaning and history but that has little infrastructure and few prospects for employment and that is unattractive to outside investment. Cecilia and Carlos have four children who were between 5 and 16 years of age at the time I conducted my research. Carlos had left school after the fourth grade to join his father and brothers in their work as fishermen in the nearby town of Lobos, where they work, three to a *panga* (canoe), casting their nets for shrimp in the Bahía de Lobos.[7] As an adult Carlos joined the Yaqui fishing cooperative, but the work is seasonal—the shrimp harvest lasts from September to November, and without the set of traps required to catch crabs or the crates for oyster cultivation, Carlos spends the months between December and August in Potam, trying to pick up odd jobs. When I first met Carlos in the autumn of 1996, I asked him about his work. Carlos told me about how the motor in his panga had failed, about his repeated trips to Guaymas to fill out paperwork with the cooperative, and about the frustration of having to wait for the motor to be repaired while the harvesting season slipped away.

I asked Cecilia what Carlos does during the rest of the year. She responded, "He works at whatever he can, watering in the fields, at times he weeds, sometimes he goes to the sea to look for work." Several years back Carlos joined a farming cooperative, and the tribe allocated him nine hectares of land to the southwest of Potam, near the river. "But he rents it out because he cannot get credit with the bank," she explained. "He still owes them money. They gave him credit once, but the crop failed; they got virtually nothing out of it, and since then he has been in debt."

Cecilia spoke with animation about Carlos's ritual service, the fulfillment of a vow he made several years ago to serve as a Chapayeka if God would heal him of an illness that had befallen him. *Mandas* (promises to God or the saints) are typically made for a period of three years, but Carlos, who views the performance of the Lenten duties of a Chapayeka as service to God and to the community, has extended his manda and continues his role.[8]

"What was the most difficult time in your life?" I asked Cecilia in early October 1997.

She replied, "Well, right now, because all of my children are in school, and at times there is not even enough money for them to take the bus.[9] Sometimes Carlos has no work. . . . We never know when the money is going to come." During the lengthy periods that Carlos is unemployed, Cecilia improvises ways to help provide for her family. Aside from the household duties that remain a part of her daily routine—the piles of laundry soiled by children who play and sweat in dusty streets, the task of cooking three meals a day over an open fire, the trash and debris to be swept out of the yard—Cecilia has pieced together an income from a variety of jobs. "I used to sell in Obregón," she explained. "Before Lucy [her youngest child] was born I used to go everyday to sell pinole, panelas, tamales. But when Lucy was born I stopped because it was a struggle to go every day with a little one."[10] Cecilia knows that she could get work as a domestic in the houses of the upper middle class in Obregón, but that does not appeal to her "because some of the women there scold a lot." She had planned to work the squash harvest in the fields of the huge commercial farms near Empalme, a Mexican town lying just outside the boundary of the Yaqui Zona Indígena, but she argued that the pay, at that time a mere 30 pesos per day, was not worth the predawn to late-afternoon workday. "How am I to give the children their lunch, get them ready for school in the morning?" she asked.

In Potam Cecilia's options are limited. Her younger sister, a school-teacher with a steady salary and mother to a newborn infant, had recently begun to sell candies, flour, beans, and an assortment of other fresh and dry goods from her kitchen. When she asked for help, Cecilia jumped at the chance. Working for her sister, she would not have to leave Potam at all, would have help feeding her children, could spend a portion of her day doing her own family's laundry, and could monitor the comings and goings of her older children to her satisfaction. For 20 pesos a day Cecilia tended the store, vending coffee, onions, sardines, *machaca* (shredded dried beef), milk, cheese, toothpaste, and lipstick to an inter-mittent stream of customers. She cared for her sister's four-month-old daughter and did other chores around her sister's house as well: washing and hanging laundry, sweeping and wetting down the patio to dampen wind-generated dust swirls, cooking the midday meal for her and her sister's children.[11] At home Cecilia fried *duritos* (chips) and sealed them into small plastic baggies to sell in the store. She roasted corn over the fire to make pinole; she made tamales and sent her children out to sell them for two pesos apiece. At harvest time she went to glean from the corn and wheat fields.

Cecilia envisions a bright future for her children—high school diplomas followed by stable jobs and lasting marriages. She wants fat grand-babies to hold, pinch, and tickle. She would like her children to remain on the Yaqui Reserve, but that hope is coupled with uncertainty. In 1997, with her son Ricardo on the verge of graduating from junior high school, she feared that she would lack sufficient funds for school fees and bus fare for both Ricardo and a daughter who was already attending high school in Vicam. Cecilia considered the possibilities aloud: perhaps her husband would find steady work over the summer; maybe she could patch together a few more odd jobs or call in some favors owed her by comadres, family members, and friends.

During the time I lived in Potam, Cecilia's labor (the work she did for her sister, the foods she cooked and sold in the pueblo, and the money she earned from gleaning local fields) was an irreplaceable asset to her family's financial survival. Yet, even when women's labor becomes the primary source of income, women's work is still represented as being supplementary to men's. Discourses about the lack of opportunities for men proliferate in the Yaqui pueblos. When I first arrived in the Yaqui communities, an acquaintance complained that there was "almost no work" around Potam itself; if a Yaqui man could not find work in the fields, he would be unemployed. The reality of the situation in the Yaqui Zona Indígena is that gendered occupations and roles combine with a historical destabilization of subsistence agriculture ("men's work") and a relative lack of local infrastructure, transforming the traditional bread-winners into the ones who are out of work.

Cecilia's story demonstrates that women's strategies for survival in Sonora's Yaqui communities are often an extension of the types of work they do at home. Whether embroidering clothing to sell during the holidays, making tamales to vend door to door, going out to glean the fields after the corn or wheat harvest, selling *pico de gallo* (fruit salad drenched in chile and lime) at school events, laundering and cleaning for wealthier families, or operating a makeshift *dulcería* (candy store) from her kitchen, a Yaqui woman's informal sector labors ensure the economic viability of her family and blur the distinction between public and private. These tactical economic interventions are both shaped and constrained by an undeniable positionality, a very particular experience of history, class, and ethnicity.[12] Such work is largely stopgap, tempo-rary, and unpredictable, and, since most of the time it occurs within the confines of an already beleaguered Indian reserve, it cannot be viewed as anything close to sustainable.

Even though salaried work and jobs that pay an hourly wage are dif-ficult to come by, an increasing number of Yaqui women have entered the ranks of those with salaried jobs, those who work five or six days a week with regular hours, those who must temporarily leave home and children to the care of an older daughter, a sister, or a trusted relative. The types of work that Yaqui women typically succeed in obtaining are varied. Jobs range from relatively well paid to poorly compensated. For some jobs a high school degree or teaching certificate is a necessity, while other types of work require no formal education. Some jobs allow women to work half-days in Potam, while others necessitate a lengthy commute within the Zona Indígena or relocation to a different city. In general, opportunities for employment in Potam are limited; there are no large factories or business subsidiaries in the Yaqui Zona Indígena, and smaller businesses in Potam (such as grocery stores and dry goods vendors) are typically owned by non-Yaquis who tend to hire non-Yaqui friends and relatives to work for them. I know of no Yaqui men or women who traveled regularly to nearby Ciudad Obregón for work, nor was there any sort of Yaqui community established in Obregón. Competition for jobs at the big Gamesa and Sabritas factories in that city is fierce, and since many Yaquis lack the necessary education, a network of other Yaquis to depend on for connections and a sense of stability, daily bus fare, and at times even personal documentation such as a birth certificate, most of them find that such jobs are too frequently beyond the realm of reasonable possibility.

At times, groups of (usually younger and single) Yaqui women and men obtain work picking tomatoes, squash, melons, or chiles on the large commercial farms located just north of the Zona Indígena near the city of Guaymas. Foremen arrange for buses to pick up day laborers in Potam before dawn, and they return in midafternoon. This is hard seasonal work, and in 1997 the pay was minimal, at only 30 pesos (about 4 dollars) per day. As in Cecilia Ochoa's case, such work is almost impossible for mothers with small children at home.

The majority of Yaqui career women I know work as teachers or administrative secretaries in the pueblos' schools and in the tribal offices. Many of the teachers at the kindergarten, elementary, and junior secondary level are Yaqui women who have earned either a bilingual or a regular teaching certificate, and there are some who have successfully completed a course of study at the nearby normal school, earning the equivalent of an associate degree in education. There are also those individuals, like Lorenia Choki Buitimea, who journey to border cities in the hope of obtaining better-paid jobs with full benefits in *maquiladoras* (assembly plants).[13]

Lorenia

When I met Lorenia in late October 1996, she was a 22-year-old single mother of two who had spent time working in a maquiladora in Nogales, Sonora, a city on the border with Arizona where there is a small but well-established Yaqui community.[14] Lorenia was born in Potam, one of six children. She attended all six years of primary school in the pueblo and had just begun her first year of junior high school when her parents decided to move to a ranch in a nearby village. Her family had no land, and her father worked as a field hand, an agricultural wage laborer. As there was no junior high school in the village and since her parents would not permit her to stay in Potam with other relatives, Lorenia stopped going to school and decided not to finish her secondary education even when her family moved back to Potam two years later.

When she was 19, Lorenia traveled to Nogales, where one of her sisters lived, in order to look for a job. There was nothing available in Potam, she complained, only work in the fields. After just one week Lorenia was hired by a maquiladora, where she worked for three and a half years, assembling bobbins for fans. Lorenia remembers long work days that started at 7:00 a.m. and ended at 5:00 p.m., with 20 minutes for breakfast, 30 minutes for lunch, and a 10-minute break in the afternoon. She earned 40 pesos a day. Lorenia recalls that factory work was difficult because of the constant noise, which used to give her headaches, and because "you have to be there, that's all, working without getting up, without talking or anything else. [If we talked] they reported us."

Lorenia lived in a large women's dormitory on the plant's premises. In the dormitory the women all slept in bunk beds in one large room; there was a kitchen in which each person could cook for herself, and there was a 9:00 weeknight curfew that was extended to 2:00 a.m. on weekends. Lorenia moved out of the dorm after four months. Some things had been stolen from her locker, but she confided that the real reason she left was because she was afraid (as were others) that someone was practicing black magic. Some of the women saw things during the night—"*sombras* [shadows]," "*bultos* [figures]," shapes in the dark, "*cosas bien raras* [very strange things]." Lorenia felt she had no choice but to move back into her sister's home, which was located farther away from the plant.

Like many young women who flock to Nogales from the rural areas of Mexico, Lorenia savored her income and her newfound freedom. She dressed up and went out with her girlfriends on weekends, and this is how she met her first *esposo* (husband). She smiled: "I met him. We became engaged, and in that way we began. I became pregnant . . . and we got together. We lived together, but I didn't like it because he was very jealous. He didn't let me go out or [talk to] my friends, no one." The couple rented a house, and she gave birth to a baby girl. But Lorenia did not stay with her baby's father for very long. "Now when I had my daughter I left him because I didn't want to endure it. At times he wanted to hit me! Yes! He hit me one time, but I never put up with that. . . . I told him I was going to go, and I left! I left that house."

She moved in with some girlfriends. While continuing to work at the maquiladora, she paid 50 pesos per week for childcare because the plant's daycare center was full. "Many people have such difficulties with their children, working and caring for their children." Lorenia became pregnant again two years later in Nogales by a Yaqui from Potam who was serving in the Mexican army. They had met through some friends; she thought it remarkable that he wanted to be with her, a single mother. When it came time for her son to be born, she returned to Potam, moved in with her mother, and worked cleaning house and providing childcare for her friend Teresa, a teacher.

Lorenia's identity profile (young, single, indigenous, female, and from a rural area) is typical of those who seek work in the border maquiladoras. While there are surely many reasons Nogales (and not nearby Obregón) has become a magnet for Yaqui young adults, two of the most significant may have to do with ethnicity and community. Maquiladoras typically hire indigenous individuals willing to work for less, whereas most of the factories in Obregón hire better-educated mestizos.[15] In addition, Yaquis may choose to go to Nogales because there is already a well-established network of Yaqui families there; as I emphasized in chapter 3, Yaquis feel comfortable where they have "people"—other Yaqui people.

While Lorenia would be the first one to point out all of the drawbacks of working in a maquiladora (the relatively low salary, the regimented working conditions, the necessity of living far from her natal home in Potam), she is proud of the fact that she had been able to support herself, her children, and her mother and sister on that income. The last time I saw Lorenia was at Potam's fiesta of Santísima Trinidad in the spring of 1997; she had long since quit caring for Teresa's children, claiming that she could not feed her family on the wages Teresa could afford to pay. She was planning to return to Nogales the following day.

Postscript

Since my initial fieldwork in 1996–97 I have returned to Sonora several times. On these visits I have been struck by the remarkable consistency and continuity in the rhythms of daily life in Potam. Men continue to struggle with unemployment. Roads remain unpaved, and the water purification project begun some years ago sits unfinished. Annual fiestas and the Lenten and Easter Week ceremonies persist, demanding of ritual hosts a large amount of time and labor and drawing huge crowds from the pueblos and beyond. The crackling loudspeaker of the produce seller still announces the availability of avocados and tomatoes, bananas, mangos, garlic, and chiles. Women still work from early morning to midafternoon, washing clothes and cooking, conducting their required social calls at dusk. Potam looks, smells, and feels the same. Yet the economic circumstances of some people's lives have changed somewhat—there are new opportunities for work close to the Zona Indígena that, while not transforming life on the reserve, have bettered the fortunes of some individuals and families.[16]

The location of maquiladoras is no longer limited to the border zone. The signing of NAFTA (North American Free Trade Agreement) in 1994 cleared the way for maquiladoras (also referred to as *maquilas*) to move farther south into Mexico. Notably, prior to a visit I made to the Zona Indígena in 2002, several new maquilas had opened in nearby Empalme, a town located just outside the northern border of the Yaqui Reserve. While these maquilas draw workers from across Sonora as well as from other parts of Mexico, the Yaqui Zona Indígena is a ready source of (predominantly young) men and women eager for the chance to work.

Just how many Yaquis have taken advantage of this unforeseen opportunity can be read as an index of the lack of available well-paying, dependable, nonseasonal jobs in the Yaqui communities. Every day Empalme's maquilas send eight buses (each with 45–50 seats) to Potam. By 5:30 in the morning these buses, full of workers, have departed for Empalme. Buses are sent to other Yaqui pueblos as well—to Huirivis and Vicam, Rahum and Bacum; typically, they also fill to capacity.

Even though some maquilas have shifted south from the U.S.–Mexico border region, they remain export oriented, labor intensive, and assembly focused. One of Empalme's maquilas produces parts for automobile electric windows. Another manufactures parts for air bags. Workers may leave one job for another for a range of reasons: they may be in search of better pay or benefits, different hours, or a better work environment, or they may leave due to personal circumstances. But there is also a great deal of unpredictability in maquila work. Factories close and relocate, a parent company may lay off workers following a dip in the market, individual workers may be fired for any number of infractions. Julia, a young Yaqui woman from Potam, worked in a factory that assembled golf bags, while her husband, Guillermo, worked in a different Empalme maquila. Julia and Guillermo wanted to start a family, but she had not been able to carry a baby to term. When Julia became pregnant once again, they made the decision that she should quit—that they would rely on his salary. Shortly thereafter, Guillermo was laid off too, his plant slated to close.

Juan, a Yaqui man in his early twenties, described his daily routine, typical of other Yaqui maquila workers. He arises around 4:30 a.m. in order to be on time for the bus. When he arrives in Empalme, the plant is open, and work begins at 6:40 a.m. His day is spent standing or sitting in front of his place on the line. He is given one 15-minute break in the morning and 30 minutes for lunch. The normal workday ends at 4:30 p.m., and buses take workers back to Potam. Most of Juan's counterparts work six days per week, but he has arranged to work overtime so that he can take computer classes on Saturdays. The late bus from Empalme arrives in Potam at 6:00 p.m.

The hours are long, but Juan and his Yaqui coworkers are able to stay in the pueblos, living at home with their families. Maquila work is hard, often tedious, and highly regulated and monitored. There are few opportunities for advancement and no guarantee that the plant one labors in today will be there tomorrow. Yet we must remember that unemployment on the Yaqui reserve is at crisis levels. Maquilas provide medical benefits and a dependable wage. Indeed, these are some of the best-paying jobs available to Yaquis who would like to remain on the reserve.

While the working lives of some Yaqui women and men have changed as maquila plants have moved within reach of the Zona Indígena, other Yaquis continue the work they were doing when I lived in the pueblos. Marcela Valencia, Ana Ochoa, and Marco Usacamea are still employed as primary school teachers in and around Potam. After having served for many years as the *directora* (principal) of a local elementary school, Regina Valencia went back to teaching in a village closer to home. Still single and independent, she enjoys the new house she built in her parents' compound, and she values living with family in the Yaqui community in which she grew up. Carlota Kus still lives on the west side of Potam, selling *dulces* (candies), sodas, and homemade popsicles from her window. When I went to her home, Carlota proudly presented her first granddaughter, then just a few days old. Carlota's husband, Claudio, once a productive farmer and fisherman, had taken ill: cancer had reduced his body to a mere shadow of its former robust form. In the winter of 2004 I received word that Claudio had died.

With her oldest daughter and son both in college and her two elementary school–age daughters being looked after by her sister, Cecilia Ochoa was finally free to seek work. Since 2003 both she and Carlos have worked as seasonal laborers in agribusiness-owned fields near Empalme. Like other women field hands Cecilia dons long pants, a skirt, a long-sleeved shirt, and a baseball hat to protect herself from the intense spring sun. She and Carlos rise at 4:00 a.m., prepare lunch for themselves, and catch the bus to Empalme. There they weed and harvest fields of cherry tomatoes, melons, or squash—the work is seasonal. When "working the tomatoes," Cecilia is paid 13 pesos per box, and she claims that she can harvest eight boxes per day for a total of 104 pesos (just over U.S. $10.00). She and Carlos work seven hours a day, six days a week.

When work is available, roughly 200 people from Potam journey to Empalme's sweltering fields. As is the case with nearby maquilas, agribusiness laborers hail from most of the Yaqui pueblos as well as from the nearby fishing village of Guásimas. The work is hard; exhaustion and aching muscles are normal. Laborers receive social security and health benefits during the period they are working, but harvest seasons are short, and the work never promises to be anything other than temporary. Cecilia and Carlos have been able to keep their oldest children in college, pay for school uniforms and fees for the younger children, and keep food on the table. Field labor—the repetitive bending and pulling and lifting done in the sweltering Sonoran sun on someone else's land under the watchful eyes of a harvest manager—is punishingly hard; it slowly destroys the body and taxes the spirit. Yet despite these difficulties, Cecilia expresses thankfulness that both she and Carlos are finally working.

Living Identity

The stories in this chapter demonstrate how identity is simultaneously performed and materially bound. As Yaqui women emphasize endurance in childbirth narratives, they negotiate concepts of femaleness (as opposed to maleness) and inscribe an ethnic boundary between Yaquis and Yoris. Similarly, female gender and ethnicity are put on display as Yaqui women don the embroidered clothing that both signifies indigenous identity and symbolically references the Yaqui flower world. In these and myriad other ways ethnicity and gender are coproduced in everyday practice. One is not merely a woman but always a Yaqui woman; here, gender is constantly mediated, even overdetermined (Mouffe 1992), by ethnicity. More to the point, we must acknowledge that gender and ethnicity are mutually configuring (Alonso 1995:77). Yaqui ethnicity is gendered, just as gender is ethnicized.

In the Zona Indígena the economic and social marginalization arising from a history of conquest and ethnic conflict powerfully impacts the material realities confronted by Yaqui women. Yaqui ethnicity and the implications that accompany this identity and its complex history can be "read" in the details of Cecilia's and Lorenia's stories. For both women identity produces possibility and circumscribes choice. As a Yaqui woman who wants to continue to live in Potam close to her family and at the heart of her people's homeland, Cecilia has few employment options. We find her, like so many other Yaqui women, "making do" (Certeau 1984) at home and in the informal economy—selling home-cooked goods door to door, gleaning the fields after the harvest, getting by any way she can. At the same time, Yaqui ethnicity compels Cecilia's support of and eager participation in the pueblo's annual ceremonial calendar. From her own Yaqui wedding to the rezos sponsored by her household, "Yaqui tradition" is a point of pride for Cecilia and a practice from which she derives great personal satisfaction.

Saddled with this same difficult history and its contemporary legacy of racism, mistrust, and economic deprivation, Lorenia embodies ethnicity in a different way. She became one among a multitude of indigenous women who flocked to the Sonora–Arizona border in the late twentieth century in search of the job security and biweekly paycheck promised by assembly plant work. Like many of her indigenous counterparts in the maquiladoras, Lorenia experienced a personal freedom not normally available to a Yaqui woman living in a small pueblo. At the same time she longed for home, experienced racial tensions, and encountered the long hours and physical hardship implicit in the assembly plant environment. Both Cecilia and Lorenia express great pride in being Yaqui, fully aware that Yaquiness itself has shaped their past and will undoubtedly affect their futures.

6
Domesticating Ethnicity
Women's Altars, Household Ceremonies, and Spaces of Refuge

If ethnic identity can be displayed on the female body and inscribed in everyday narratives, if ethnicity can impact and circumscribe the economic possibilities for working women and men, then it should not be surprising to find that there are specific social spaces that seem to reinforce or nurture the articulation of Yaqui ethnicity and women's gender. In many societies both past and present, home space has been associated with women's labor, reproduction, and identity (Massey 1994; Moore 1988; Pellow 2003; Rosaldo 1974). This is equally true for the Yaquis, to whom home is the idealized location of a woman's productive activity and social life. Created and maintained by women, "homeplace" (hooks 1990:41–49) is arguably the primary locus of women's power in Yaqui society.

But for Yaquis, home is not solely a place where women's gender is constituted. It is where family and culture are first reproduced. It is also a key site in the production and expression of Yaqui identity. While nearly all Yaqui life-cycle rituals—a girl's *quinceañera* (fifteenth birthday and coming-of-age celebration), a couple's wedding celebration, the rites of infant baptism, and the novenario and cabo de año for the dead—have a church component, a significant portion of each ritual (notably, the component that is identified as uniquely ethnic) takes place within the confines of Yaqui domestic space. Home is where Yaquis reestablish ties to their ancestors during the Days of the Dead and reaffirm personal relationships with the saints who protect them. For Yaquis, the home compound is the physical locus of the household, the group of people in an extended family who dwell together in the space of the domicile, sharing economic resources, food, and ritual time. And many Yaquis share Luz García's sentiment that the household, *la familia* (the family), is the kernel of Yaqui society, "the foundation of social organization."[1]

Home, then, is one of the most important sites wherein women's gendered identity and Yaqui ethnicity are conjoined. Like all place making, this process is circular. Women socialize the space in which they live, making home into a place of utility and belonging. In so doing, women simultaneously reproduce Yaqui ethnicity in ways that are both novel and significant. Homeplace, in turn, binds the very identities associated with it—in this case, ethnic identity—more strongly to the women who dwell there.[2] What are Yaqui houses like, and how, exactly, are household spaces socialized into homeplaces?

In Potam, as in most other Yaqui towns and villages in this southern Sonoran river valley, family residences are thickly "occupied" places (Stewart 1996:41). Packed-dirt patios, swept clean and sprinkled liberally with cooling water, form the heart of Yaqui home spaces. On a late afternoon one is likely to find family members chatting quietly under the shade of a fluttery-leafed pitahaya tree, a secondary school student doing her math homework, an aunt combing the tangles out of her niece's freshly washed hair, and small boys chasing hens through the yard, stopping only to beg a few pesos from their grandmother to buy homemade duritos, tamarind candies, or chile-crusted mango lollipops. Home spaces teem with the sounds of barking dogs and the lively accordion of a local *ranchera* band getting some airtime on the radio.[3] Pale blue parakeets chatter and chirp from a cage suspended in the breeze, and water trickles into an open cistern as someone scrubs school uniforms on a washboard. The smell of mesquite smoke from a low-burning fire warming water for coffee or afternoon baths mingles with the cloying scent of green hay and horses damp with sweat.

A Yaqui residence might just as easily be occupied by a single nuclear family and their visiting nephew as by an older couple, their teenaged sons, and their married daughter and her family. Household composition is fluid and shifting, and families share kitchen utensils and cooking pots, bedrooms and living space.[4] Whatever their composition, Yaqui families live in what might best be described as compounds—two or three dwelling structures built around a central, ramada-covered kitchen adjacent to a patio area.[5] Most houses are made of carrizo cane cut by local men who know how to weave it, green and pliable, between mesquite framing posts and over heavy cottonwood beams. Those families with adequate financial resources might build a two- or three-room adobe house with real glass windows, a metal roof, and a cement floor.

The spaces inside these houses are cluttered and personal. Clothing spills out from an overfull armoire. Dressers are piled with deodorants, bottles of inexpensive perfume, combs, cans of hairspray, paper roses, and stuffed animals won at a carnival. On the walls hang old calendars naming the saints' days of years past. Framed graduation and baptism pictures share space with the portrait of a daughter on her quinceañera and a cracked red hula hoop. A well-worn saddle balances atop a box full of clothes waiting to be laundered. Jars of sea salt and Dolca coffee sit side by side on an oilcloth-covered kitchen table, and spiders share a dark corner with a tiny altar. Things still in use or things that might be used again—plastic grocery bags, the keys to a truck, the sharp knife that flays beef and opens cans—are tucked up into carrizo rafters. These spaces feel lived-in, familiar, rooted in the needs of children and elderly people and the intimacy of family.

Although intensely private, Yaqui homes are not isolated from public activity. Rather, the relationships underpinning the elaborate system of Yaqui ceremonial societies stem from the ties extended between family members, friends, and ritual kin. (These ritual relationships will be discussed in the following chapter.) At certain times during the year ritual practices and traditions draw the pueblo directly into Yaqui home spaces. The Yaqui home is fashioned into a homeplace through human activity—the presence and movement of bodies, the construction of altars, and the ordinary labors of making repairs, cooking, and cleaning.[6] A compound or house becomes a homeplace as it is practiced (Certeau 1984:130); the spaces within a house, socialized and sacralized in large part by women's labor, constitute that homeplace, making it knowable, meaningful, and important. Not only are home spaces practiced, they are also essentially practical, embedded within and created from layer upon layer of social relations (Massey 1994; Soja 1996). Houses may be constructed by men, but they are purposefully, vigilantly, and lovingly socialized by women.

This chapter examines women's material production and sacralization of home spaces. I consider how the Yaqui home—a place where altars are constructed to personal saints, a focal point of women's sociability and economic cooperation, a venue for ceremonies considered central to Yaqui culture and tradition—becomes a source of female authority, an unexpected space of women's agency, and a key site in the production and maintenance of Yaqui ethnicity.

The Topography of Motherhood

There is a strong matrifocal (mother-centered) tendency in Yaqui communities, and the ideologies of motherhood articulate strongly with the social space of the home. But because such meaning systems cultivate both the empowerment and disempowerment of Yaqui women, home can also be a complex place, one that accommodates and generates contradiction.

Anthropologist Jane Holden Kelley, who conducted research in Potam during the 1970s, writes that the Yaquis with whom she worked considered domestic space to be the proper location of women's productive and reproductive activities, and she describes a marked social control of women's movements by male family members, especially husbands and fathers. Although Kelley had traveled to Potam in order to collect women's life histories, she found that she was almost unfailingly directed to an elder male authority when she inquired about Yaqui culture, history, or religion. The culture she encountered was one in which there was a pronounced sexual division of labor, with childcare and responsibility for managing the household assigned to women, one in which the movements of household members were directed by a male patriarch. She writes, "Women and children [in Sonora] were more dependent on men for permission to leave the house and for transportation [than their Arizona counterparts]" (Kelley 1978:22). She also notes the application of unspoken rules regarding sexual propriety: "Beyond near relatives, older people, and children, it is generally improper for males to call upon or formally visit females or vice versa" (Kelley 1978:57).

In contemporary Yaqui communities there persists a strongly gender-associated division of labor as well as a real concern with maintaining the appearance of propriety in situations of intergendered sociability. Women speak of jealous husbands and tend not to form close friendships with men unless they are relatives or *compadres* (coparent, godfather to one's child). Just as Kelley observed nearly 30 years ago, the Yaqui home continues to be a female-gendered domain, the most appropriate locus of activity for industrious wives, devoted mothers, and circumspect young women. I have overheard working mothers being criticized by their sisters and cousins, friends and fathers for not attending to household chores, for neglecting to monitor the whereabouts of a teenaged daughter who is sure to be "wandering about carefree" and unchaperoned. While Yaqui women tease one another about being home before their husbands arrive and joke about finishing chores and having the afternoon meal ready on time, it is my sense that their playfulness often belies real expectations, obligations, and, at times, unpleasant consequences.

In spite of those discourses that would circumscribe female activity to the domestic sphere, the Yaqui women I know never portrayed themselves to me as confined or stuck at home. Regardless of the persistence of ideologies that would control female sexuality by limiting the location of women's activity, Yaqui women in fact exercise a great deal of freedom of movement and association. Married women arrange and take pleasure in their own social calendars, generally maintaining a separate social life from their spouses. Husbands and wives may attend the same celebrations, but they most often do so with different groups of people: men go about with brothers and compadres; women attend with relatives and close female friends. Groups of women stroll about the pueblo together, laughing, talking, and enjoying quinceañera parties, weddings, and religious fiestas. Women embark on all-day shopping trips to the city, walk long distances to visit friends, and spend countless hours cooking, chatting, washing laundry, and relaxing in the homes of family members. Contrary to Kelley's observation that poteñas were "dependent on men for permission to leave the house" (1978:22), over two decades later I noticed no such dependency. Granted, there is still the expectation that women—whether or not they work outside of the home—will complete their chores, raise the children, and prepare meals in a timely manner. This is the *doble jornada* (double workday), the combined burden of wage labor and housework borne by women in Mexico and many other parts of the world that continues to be a reality with a real impact on women's lives (Fernández-Kelly 1983; Gutmann 1996:150, 275). Nevertheless, Yaqui women come and go as they please. I never witnessed or heard of women asking permission to go out for necessities or for a visit or to participate in a social event. In those few families with vehicles it is usually the husband who drives, who owns the vehicle, and who ultimately has more access to its use, but wives demonstrate no shame or hesitation in asking for a ride to town or transportation for themselves and *compañeras* (companions) to a fiesta in a neighboring community. Women whose families do not have vehicles simply take the bus or hitchhike when they need to go somewhere.

It is through everyday practices that the ideologies of honor and shame, machismo, and the cult of motherhood are transformed into characterizations of women's and men's "natural" dispositions.[7] Of course, such ideologies are cultural and historical constructions that, through practical enactment, assume the appearance of common sense and generality when in actuality they serve the interests of a discrete group. This discursive process of naturalization depoliticizes gender roles, inhibiting critical reflection or questioning (Barthes 1972, 1977; Fiske 1990:90). How does one reconcile the realities of social control over women's reproduction and the unspoken restrictions placed upon intergendered association with women's relative freedom of movement and the authority they exercise in the household? How does one begin to understand that the respect accorded to women for running an efficient home, for hosting ceremonies, and for assuring the health and development of their children equals or even exceeds that gained by women who work outside the home? How does one interpret women's narratives that extol decidedly traditional values of domesticity? An answer to some of these questions may be found by examining the association of mothering with homeplace and by exploring the relationships that obtain between domestic space, ritual power, and women's ceremonial labor.

Motherhood is celebrated as a feminine ideal in Mexican popular thought, and it is regarded by Yaquis as one of the most important roles for a woman. In Potam the cult of motherhood flourishes.[8] Women are often perceived by Yaquis as being naturally predisposed to the role of nurturer, and their identity is more strongly bound to the ideals and practices of motherhood than Yaqui men's identity is to fatherhood. People are greatly concerned not to forget Mother's Day; by comparison, Father's Day is a minor consideration. Religious icons connoting an ideal, impossible motherhood that combines sexual purity with unparalleled self-sacrifice are ubiquitous. Heavy framed renderings of the Virgin of Guadalupe—frequently described by Yaquis as the most compassionate and accessible of the *santos* (saints)—adorn the walls of nearly every household; and Itom Ae (Our Mother), a small image of the Virgin Mary dressed in a light blue mantle, presides over important ceremonies.[9]

When asked, most Yaquis identify the eldest male as "head of household." However, many individuals, especially women, accord older women in the family substantial prestige. There are many instances when the eldest woman becomes de facto head of the family. This tendency toward matrifocality, an "underreported phenomenon" throughout Mexico, according to Gutmann (1996:256), indicates something significant about the practices and perceptions of motherhood in Yaqui communities. Yaqui mothers may act as heads of household for a number of reasons. For instance, economic circumstances may necessitate a husband's long-term absence. Some men spend the autumn and winter months of the shrimp harvest working in Lobos with brothers and male cousins; others labor for weeks at a time on farms and ranches; still others venture as far as the maquiladoras on the U.S.–Mexico border in search of work. At times, wives are abandoned by their husbands, and there are those families in which male alcoholism exacts a heavy toll, the loss of wage jobs, herds of cattle, and even plots of land being attributed to the fact that a man "liked to drink."[10] In such situations and in many families wherein fathers and husbands are present, women take on (or share) the responsibility for leadership; they become keepers and administrators of the family's money, organizers of social and ritual events, advisors, and primary breadwinners.

Regina Valencia emphasized the need to honor women, to recognize them for their central role in their families and in the community. She spoke of the way in which older women are regarded as adept managers and knowledgeable advisors: "Here, in large families, the woman is *la que manda* [the one who leads, the one in charge]. . . . They always ask her for her opinion . . . an older woman. The oldest one." Not everyone would agree that the eldest female is the most influential member of an extended family, but the matrifocal orientation manifest in Regina's assertion is not uncommon. Women constantly refer to their mothers and grandmothers as authorities when it comes to family matters, questions of ritual propriety, health concerns, and matters of personal comportment and belief.[11]

Matrifocal ideologies and practices reinforce the identification of domestic space as female gendered. Men and women alike refer to their natal homes not as the father's or family's home but always clearly as "la casa de mi mamá" [my mother's house]. Yaquis associate the household compound with what is important about a woman's authority and knowledge, and it forms the nucleus of many women's economic and social lives. Yaqui mothers and daughters typically have close relationships of mutual interdependence. They see one another as allies and confidantes. Women's mothers' homes are readily identified as spaces of comfort and security; when necessary, they become grown daughters' spaces of refuge from alcoholism, economic distress, domestic violence, or a husband's infidelities. While married women take different tactical approaches to such dilemmas, in times of trouble many gather up their children (and sometimes their husbands) and return home—to their mothers' homes—to live.

Interior Supplications

At once representative of a certain hierarchy, emblematic of traditional notions of women's domestic duty, the control of women's sexuality, and male authority, the home also becomes a space of refuge and comfort for Yaqui women, a site of female knowledge and power.[12] Yaqui women create homeplace through a variety of practical labors. They cook an uncountable number of meals—thick red chile, tangy menudo, freshly made tortillas, and plain salted beans. They wage a daily battle with dust, constantly wiping chairs and tables and wringing gray-brown water from wet cloths. In the early afternoon they sweep up crumpled papers, the stale edges of tortillas, and red cellophane candy wrappers left by children in an effort to make the patio a pleasant place for visiting and working.

The flowering basil planted in the garden, the dried seeds of a *chile pasillo* cast onto a rooftop, the presence of numerous crosses (a sturdy wooden cross in the center of the patio, the wispy, ephemeral crosses made by binding grasses and leaves and flowers with wire, the tiny carrizo crosses from Palm Sunday tacked to a wall or nailed to a doorjamb) are the material practices that protect the home and signify a Christian identity. And many women seek blessings or good fortune through other means of sacralizing home space: in a hidden corner or an unused room behind the kitchen, inside the front door or on a shelf in a store or business, they construct altars and light candles to the saints.

Ana Ochoa's altar is nestled between a storage container and the service counter of the small dry goods shop attached to the front of her home. There is a jar of fresh-cut basil, a clear glass of holy water, and pictures of San Judas Tadeo, the Virgin of Guadalupe, and La Mano Poderosa (The Powerful Hand).[13] Ana lights a candle to her saints on the evenings she is home. She had once kept the altar in the room behind her kitchen, but she added to it and moved it when she built her shop. In contrast to Ana's altar (small and concealed), Catalina Gomez's altar is prominently displayed inside the door to her two-room cedar plank house. Its high table features a large framed picture of the Virgin of Guadalupe, a small statue of San Judas Tadeo, a tiny Niño Dios, and a candle. Homemade flowers crafted from bright red, yellow, blue, and pink crepe paper are tacked to the wall behind the saints, and the entire ensemble is framed with sparkling blue and gold tinsel. Catalina stands next to her altar and smiles broadly as I snap a picture. She tells me that she has just moved the altar indoors; she prefers to have it outside but doesn't want "her" (the Virgin of Guadalupe) to get wet in the winter storms.

Lucía Bajeka's altar is even more ornate than Catalina's, and it serves purposes in addition to the display and veneration of saints. As a curandera, Lucía conducts her consultations in front of the altar. Both she and her granddaughter Julia also serve as *kiyostes* for the church. Yaqui kiyostes (*kiyohteim*) are ritual specialists who care for the female images used in rituals and processions. As Potam's head kiyoste, Lucía keeps the image of Itom Ae on her altar at home. She makes new clothing for this Virgin Mary, she cleans and washes her clothing when necessary, and she is responsible for bringing her to the church for all major ceremonies. Julia shows me her grandmother's altar. At its center Itom Ae stands about half a meter tall on a sturdy wooden platform. Her black eyes stare out from underneath her veil and aluminum crown, and around her neck are several necklaces, plastic beads covered with metallic red and gold paint. Julia gently touches Itom Ae as she tells me that this Virgin's feast day is in August and that she helped her grandmother make her lace-trimmed aqua dress—stiff, shiny satin under several layers of organza. Various pictures of different Virgins and saints adorn the wall behind the altar: the Virgin of Guadalupe with her deep blue mantle, supported by cherubs; San Judas Tadeo in his pastoral setting; a metallic etching that Julia identifies as "the Virgen del Carmen, Virgin of the Sea." On the altar next to Itom Ae sit two porcelain images of Baby Jesus (El Niño Dios), a statue of the Sacred Heart, two half-burned candles, a small bottle of holy water, some basil, and three unbroken eggs for curing.

To some Yaquis building an altar is not viewed as necessary or even a good idea. The practice seems old-fashioned, even unorthodox—the material culture of an outmoded folk Catholicism. When I asked one woman whether or not she had an altar in her home, she answered with a sharp "No." Without hesitation she added, "Because I have faith in the Lord." Among the Yaqui, altar building tends to be woman's work. While there is variation in the way altars are built and contestation over the question of whether or not their construction is an appropriate religious practice, a great number of women view the altar as an important part of the home and as integral to their expression of belief. Altars can be aesthetically pleasing, and most women are proud of the devotional labor that they invest in their creations. By constructing altars, women prepare an honored space for the saints who bring blessings to their families and homes.

Setting a Table for the Dead

Although the Yaqui people are best known to non-Yaqui Sonorans for their elaborate public ceremonies (the performance of the Passion at Easter, the sacred dances and large ceremonial processions throughout Lent and Holy Week, and the annual fiesta hosted in each pueblo to venerate the patron saint), the household ceremonies that fill the spaces of time in between these large events are also significant, and they are remarkable for their sheer number and frequency. Ceremonies conducted in the domestic domain include food offerings and prayers for children who have passed away on the Día de los Angelitos (Day of the Little Angels), celebrated by Yaquis in late September; rezos held on designated feast days for various saints such as the Virgin of Guadalupe and San Ignacio; and the counseling sermons and rituals accompanying a traditional wedding. Most of the ceremonies necessitated by the passage of a deceased person into the afterlife also take place in the household space, including the prayers offered daily through the novenario, the monthly rezo for the soul of the deceased, and the cabo de año, at which time mourning is lifted from the family during a three-day religious celebration simply referred to as "fiesta."[14]

The organization of household ceremonies involves careful planning (weeks in advance, if possible), many hours of labor, and substantial expense. Many of the ceremonies that take place in the home involve a large cast of indigenous ritual specialists—maestros and cantoras who chant prayers in Latin, Matachín dancers, and pascola clowns and deer dancers who entertain the crowd and dance throughout the night. Through its historical persistence, its age-old identification with Yaqui tradition, and its thoroughly syncretic character, home-centered ceremonialism sets Yaquis apart from other norteños and serves as an important avenue of ethnic assertion in contemporary Sonora. Moreover, since it is most often ordinary women who construct the altars, cook the food, and transform household space into a site for sacred activity, women become key actors in the production of Yaqui ethnicity itself.

One of the most important of these household ceremonies occurs every November 1 as women arise before dawn to begin setting a table for the dead. This is Todos Santos (All Saints' Day), the eve of Mexico's Día de los Difuntos (Day of the Dead), when the *aniimam* (souls of the dead)—ancestors and relatives who have more recently passed away—visit the households of their descendents in order to commune with the living. The atmosphere is lively and festive as preparations are made. All day long food is cooked and set out on specially prepared *mesitas* (little tables), where the dead gather to partake of the food's essence. At the end of the day maestros and cantoras conduct prayers for the dead, and finally family members join in the feast.

Preparations for this meal with the dead begin in the last days of October as men construct the table on which the food will be placed. This mesita is called a *tapesti* in the Yaqui language. Standing just under two meters tall, these delicate tables are made from the straight branches of specially cut batamote, a type of wood indigenous to the area. Branches are whittled smooth and lashed together to make a flat surface, then set on spindly mesquite legs. The tapesti sits in the center of the family's patio in front of the house cross. Beneath the tapesti burns one small candle. Once the table is laden with food, it is then called a *tapanko*. Women are the ones who effect this transformation. Early in the morning a woman covers her tapesti with cloths that are store bought or specially embroidered in the bright pink, magenta, fluorescent green, and blue flowers characteristic of Yaqui sea hiki. First, an earthenware jar of water is placed on the altar, followed by steaming cups of coffee and *pan dulce* (sugared rolls). Fruit is offered next; oranges, grapefruits, apples, sugarcane, mangos, and bananas spill over the edges of a large basket. The house quickly becomes a busy place: men fetch firewood and bring fresh milk and cheese from nearby ranches; sisters, aunts, cousins, and nieces come and go, helping the hostess prepare the many complicated dishes she will need to cook; and older children are sent time and again to the store or to neighbors' houses for needed ingredients. Women pat out dozens of flour tortillas; pots bubble with spicy *frijoles puercos* (beans made with *chorizo* [pork sausage] and cheese), chile, and traditional wakabaki. Women try hard to include some of the favorite foods of the person or persons being honored. In some families this means obtaining hard-to-get seeds of *bledo* (wild grasses) in order to make thick golden *atole de bledo* (grass-seed porridge). In other families it means purchasing fresh mussels or oysters, baking cornbread, or sautéing shrimp with jalapeños and onions.

A day spent preparing food for the mesita is hard work, but it is also a festive time of reflection and conviviality. Men share a cold beer with

Figure 4. Early morning *tapanko*, Potam, Sonora

compadres or relatives, and children chase one another around the yard, excitedly waiting to eat. Women drink copious amounts of coffee and catch up on the news about family and friends. In the privacy of their kitchens, out of the earshot of men, older women tell licentious jokes and embarrass young girls with questions about their boyfriends. Setting mesitas for the dead is a demonstration of love and respect, and, as Spicer notes, the Yaqui "feeling toward the aniimam is warm and intimate, devoid of horror" (1954:124). There is a belief that the dead can help the living, and generous offerings of food on the Day of the Dead are believed to generate "good will" among visiting souls (Spicer 1980:347). People joke about the presence of the dead. Muertitos are fondly remembered, and there is laughter about the grandmother who "will feel full" after consuming all of the rolls and coffee put on the table for her, about the pack of cigarettes for an aunt who "liked to smoke," about the orange-flavored sodas, marshmallows, and candies for a great-uncle who had a sweet tooth.

In the late afternoon and early evening, when the cooking is finished, families gather around their mesitas to wait. Groups of maestros and cantoras can be heard in the distance as they travel from house to house, singing their prayers for the dead. The rich smell of incense wafts through the night air, and people pull on jackets and shawls against the cold and huddle around glowing coals from the fire. When the maestros and cantoras finally arrive, they kneel in front of the tapanko. The maestro lifts the book of the dead (a tiny black book also called the *Aniimam*) from its place on the altar, and the ritual specialists begin their *alabanzas* (praise hymns). The cantoras' voices converge in a piercing harmony as the maestros recite the name and ritual role, if appropriate, of each ancestor.[15] The conclusion of the prayers is marked by the lighting of a firework. There is a brief moment of silence, and then the hosts rise and begin distributing food from the tapanko into bags for the maestros and cantoras. Piles and piles of food are given away, and the family feasts on ample leftovers as the ritual specialists disappear into the dark night.

On November 2, the Día de los Difuntos (also known as Fieles Difuntos, or All Souls' Day), Yaquis go to the *panteón* (cemetery) in order to clean and decorate the graves of their muertos. This is the public portion of the holiday, and there is a festive atmosphere in the cemetery: Matachines dance at the church; vendors sell hot dogs, hotcakes, punch, tacos, and balloons; and families sweep gravesites and paint wooden grave markers. Graves are adorned with homemade paper flower wreaths

Figure 5. Decorating graves at the cemetery in Potam for All Souls' Day

called *coronas* and are covered with fresh flowers—deep purple *mano de pantera* (cockscomb), bright lilies, and orange marigolds. Thousands upon thousands of glittering candles—large pillar candles, tiny white candlesticks, and votive candles—light up the church with a soft glow and warm our ankles as we walk through the graveyard. A procession is made around the cemetery, and the maestros and cantoras sing for all of the souls present.

Historically, Mexicans celebrated both the private aspect of the Days of the Dead (the welcoming of the dead to the home with an offering of food and drink) and its public expression (the cleaning and decoration of graves in the cemetery).[16] Writing about colonial Mexico, Linda Curcio-Nagy explains:

> The private aspects of the festival are more closely linked to traditional native views regarding the continuation of kinship relations after death. The natives believe that dead relatives continue to protect them and to serve in essence as intermediaries between the spirit world and the living. The public aspects of the celebration—a night vigil in the cemetery, high mass in the church, and decoration of the grave site to honor the dead—all stem from medieval Mediterranean Catholic tradition. [2000:162]

In northern Mexico many non-Indians still attend mass and clean the graves of their loved ones as a show of respect, but they do not build mesitas in their homes. Among the Yaquis the household feast and the prayers for the dead remain significant cultural practices. As such, Yaqui Days of the Dead traditions serve to further differentiate Yaquis from their mestizo neighbors.[17] On the eve of Día de los Difuntos the Yaqui home becomes a space that is vital to the ritual, generational, and ethnic life of the community. Commensality nourishes community; by setting elaborate mesitas in their homes, Yaqui women engender a community of the living and the dead, joining together past and present kin, a family reunion on a grand scale.

Spatial Communication

Yaqui women's labor and agency are inextricably bound to the production of homeplace. While it is vital to acknowledge and expose the gender ideologies that assign or even relegate women to domestic space, it is even more important to celebrate how women transform the patios and rooms of their homes into spaces of communion and intergenerational continuity. Through everyday lived experiences and deliberate practices such as altar building and ceremonial hosting as well as cooking, cleaning, and maintaining a desired aesthetic, women socialize houses into homeplaces. Yaqui women "remap the space they occupy" through ritual practice (Flores forthcoming:216), making it both central and sacred and in the process empowering themselves, their children, and their communities.

Home is the site in which women's gender and Yaqui identity are most strongly conjoined. As amply illustrated in various Yaqui stories—about exile and return to the homeland, about the yo hoaram that speckle the desert landscape with portals to a sacred cultural knowledge, and about the haunted places that anchor memories of violence in the space of the pueblo—narratives can construct place. Not only that, narratives can also bind culturally produced places to identities, namely, ethnic identities.

But to understand the ties between homeplace and Yaqui identity we need to go a step farther. As Margaret Rodman writes, "Places not only feature in inhabitants' (and geographers') narratives, they are narratives in their own right" (2003:206). Here Rodman has identified a highly significant form of communication. I contend that Yaqui homeplaces—in the very ways in which they are arranged, occupied, bounded, and adorned—can and do "narrate" a number of things, including family responsibility and centeredness, and relations with the saints, as well as the inhabitants' ethnicity. What I suggest, then, is that we can interpret Yaqui women's place making in the home as a mode of spatial communication—to Yaqui selves and non-Yaqui others—about women's agency in the production of identity and about the continued centrality of ethnic identity in contemporary Yaqui life.

7
Material Relations
Reciprocity, Devotional Labor, and
Practical Community

Among contemporary Yaquis reciprocity, relationality, and ritual labor are deeply implicated in the production of ethnicity. In the following pages I examine the deceptively simple gifting practices that foster inter-familial bonds and fortify Yaqui communities. This complex system of exchange and mutual obligation is important because Yaqui ethnic iden-tities are never created, negotiated, or performed in a vacuum. Indeed, Yaqui selves are always beings in relation—to other Yaquis, to non-Yaqui indigenous peoples, to the mainstream Mexican population, and to the saints and holy figures that bless Yaqui homes and families. Gifting prac-tices form the material foundation for the annual pueblo fiestas, a set of ceremonies that are central to the intensification of Yaqui cultural iden-tity. An elaborate network of kin and ritual kin relationships, paired with a formalized system of reciprocity, underpins the Yaqui fiesta complex. The fiesta, in turn, sustains the critical relationship between the pueblo and its patron saint, encourages the preservation of indigenous forms of knowledge, and puts cultural identity on public display. This chapter explores the relationship between women's devotional labor, cultural celebrations such as the fiesta and the Virgin of Guadalupe's feast day, and the practicalities of reciprocal obligation. Whether participating in a fiesta, hosting a household ritual, or simply sweeping the church before a ceremony or mass, *tekípanoa* (devotional labor) is perceived as a "gift" (Flores 1994), presented as a sign of faithfulness to God. In public fiestas and in smaller domestic ceremonies this gender-inflected labor creates a culturally appropriate space in which the ideals and values viewed as central to Yaqui identity can be played out.

In Yaqui pueblos reciprocity and interpersonal relationships contribute immeasurably to the creation of an economically and socially sustainable community and, at the same time, to the constitution of a set of cultural values identified with "Yaquiness" itself. On a September afternoon in 1997 Ana and I sat in quiet companionship; I typed my field notes from the morning, and she rinsed the breakfast dishes in preparation for the afternoon meal. An elderly woman whom I did not recognize appeared at the gate, dressed in traditional Yaqui clothing. She removed the rebozo that protected her head from the sun and called out a greeting in Yaqui. We returned her greeting, Ana waved her into the patio and offered her a seat, and I ducked inside the kitchen to get some refreshments for the guest. After serving coffee and cookies I continued my work at another table. Ana and the woman chatted in Yaqui. Their conversation about family news and health was polite and punctuated by long periods of silence. Now and again I glanced up from my work to see the visitor sitting with her hands folded in her lap, her gaze fixed upon some point in the distance. Ana did the same. After about 30 minutes of this talk the woman leaned back and slowly extracted a small plastic baggie from the pocket of her skirt. Ana raised her eyebrows in polite interest as the woman handed her a pair of gold-plated earrings. Ana then went into her kitchen, returning after a moment with 100 pesos.[1] The woman folded the money into her pocket, thanked Ana, and departed.

When the woman was out of sight, Ana came over to explain. "That señora came to *empeñar* [pawn]," said Ana. She was a distant relation who had visited with the hope of exchanging her earrings, which Ana estimated as being worth 600 pesos, for a temporary loan. "People think we are rich because both of us work," Ana sighed. The woman needed money badly enough to risk losing what was likely her only pair of earrings. Ana considered the possibilities aloud: perhaps she couldn't afford the medicine required by a sick grandchild; perhaps she needed to visit the doctor in town; perhaps she simply needed to buy groceries for the week.

The two women had agreed upon a deadline for the repayment of the money. An unpaid bill results in the borrower forfeiting the pawned item, and this happens often. Ana and her husband, both teachers with modest salaries, support their extended families in a myriad tangible ways. From their small store they frequently give groceries on credit to neighbors and friends, and, when asked to lend money, they give what they can. It is considered unsociable, even un-Yaqui, to say no to someone in need.

Among the Yaquis it is said that babies who make their hands into fists in their sleep grow up to be stingy adults, never giving to others. It is said that *gente buena* (good people) are of generous spirit and that one should neither desire nor await the return of a favor or gift. The majority of Potam's Yaquis struggle on a daily basis to make ends meet and to support their families. For those men who are unemployed, who work as seasonal laborers picking tomatoes or tending cattle, or who dig latrines or cut firewood and for those women who glean the fields after the April harvest, who send their children to sell tamales door to door, or who endure the daily predawn journey to Lobos to work with the fishermen, survival in lean times is often contingent upon an intricate economy of gifting and reciprocity. Any examination of the many ways Yaqui women and men "make do" (Certeau 1984:29) cannot neglect to take into account the systems of exchange that bind them into an inter-dependent community.

Reciprocity and Relationality

The principal networks of reciprocal obligation in Sonora's Yaqui communities build outward from the family; that is, family members are beholden to one another to the greatest degree. Responsibilities to family are followed by duties to one's compadres and after that by obligations to nonritually related friends. Those individuals with modest but steady salaries—teachers, secretaries, tribal administrators, and store owners—face real claims made upon them by their extended families for help with the purchase of food, the replacement of a propane tank for a stove, unexpected medical costs, school tuition, the purchase of school uniforms, or bus money. Here expectation and obligation go hand in hand: those who "have money" should notice when a family member or a friend is in need, and they should give without being asked. Those who are fortunate enough to have full-time employment or a household store are approached on a fairly regular basis by financially stressed neighbors, distant cousins, and ritual kin hoping to obtain a bag of groceries on credit or to hock a treasured pair of earrings or a gold watch in exchange for a short-term loan. Such informal exchange networks may ensure a family's economic survival.

Many diverse forms of reciprocity permeate everyday life in the Yaqui pueblos. From the silent, subtle, everyday exchange of objects, food, and labor to the grand, highly formalized gifting system set into motion at fiesta time, reciprocity and the complex interpersonal connections that are solidified by these practices form the underpinnings of Yaqui society. Minor exchanges may occur with extreme regularity: some are spontaneous, while others are planned, and material items are not the only entities exchanged. Food is exchanged for food, but food is also exchanged for labor, labor is exchanged for tools or cookware, clothing, or money, and objects or money are given in return for food. These exchanges are rarely discussed. However, when they are mentioned, reciprocal exchanges are never spoken of as buying or trading. Rather, the Spanish verb *regalar* (to give as a gift) is used, conveying a sense of gifting or fulfilling a request. And while no one verbalizes their detailed knowledge of who has given or received and in what quantity, people do keep track. They know when they owe and when they can count on return.

Every adult has ties, strengthened and intensified by reciprocity, to other adult members of the family, neighbors, compadres, and work associates. Family assumes priority, but the ties of ritual kinship are also strong. The Yaquis adopted the system of godparenthood introduced by Jesuit missionaries in the early 1600s (Spicer 1980:22), altering and significantly expanding it (Spicer 1954:60, 1980:23). This complex of relationships, known as the *compadrazgo* system, has been modified to such an extent that today the unique variations in the way they establish and practice godparenthood are considered by Yaquis to be a distinctive marker of their own group identity. The compadrazgo complex binds an *ahijado* (godchild) to his or her *madrina* (godmother) and *padrino* (godfather), making the child's *padrinos* (godparents) compadres to the child's mother and father. This is a formal relation that is deeply meaningful to the individuals concerned, and it is at once ceremonial and economic, interpersonal and interfamilial. The Yaqui godparent–coparent relationship is established most prevalently upon the occasion of a child's baptism into the Catholic Church, as parents select godparents to sponsor their children. The bond shared by these *compadres de pila* (baptismal coparents) and the child's parents is considered the strongest possible tie one can have to another human being outside of family. Godparents participate in the baptismal ceremony, purchase a gown and shoes for the infant, and enter into an enduring relationship of obligation and mutual respect with both child and parents. After the rite of baptism a celebratory meal is prepared, parents and godparents are counseled by a Yaqui maestro, and the relationship is confirmed as parents present their new compadres with the traditional gift of bolo (three new galvanized tin pails brimming with food, a new carrizo basket full of tortillas, and several embroidered napkins).[2]

In addition to baptismal sponsorship there are many other occasions upon which the ties of compadrazgo are forged. Both bride and groom require padrinos on their wedding day: the sponsors help purchase the clothing or shoes, accompany the bride to the church (or, less commonly, to the groom's home if a traditional wedding is being performed), and participate as witnesses to the rite of marriage. Family members seek godparents to prepare the deceased for burial. Padrinos bear witness to confirmations and first communions and the dedication of a child to a saint. To celebrate her quinceañera a girl may have several sets of godparents, those who present her at the quinceañera mass and others to contribute to the dinner, purchase the cake, or sponsor the dance. An individual may serve as godparent for the same godchild on more than one occasion; for example, parents may ask a daughter's baptismal padrinos to be the godparents upon her quinceañera or her wedding day, reinforcing the ties established when the young woman was an infant. More frequently, however, new padrinos are selected for nearly every life-crisis event of an individual, greatly extending his or her family's web of ritual kin connections.[3]

Yaquis assert ethnic identity by pointing to the ways Yaqui-style compadrazgo differs from that of non-Yaquis. There are distinct, culturally articulated ideals toward which "real Yaquis" are expected to strive. Yaqui tradition dictates, for instance, that exactly three consecutive children within a family should have one baptismal godparent in common. As Graciela Ortega explained, Yaqui godparents "baptize three," while "Yoris only baptize one." Carlota Kus associates this practice with the sanctity of the number three, calling it the "three blessings of God . . . [the] baptism, the confirmation, and the first communion." She emphasizes that holding to the custom of baptizing three in one family forges the strongest possible bond between godparents and parents, making them "true compadres."

The relationship between a godparent and his or her godchild as well as with his or her compadre or comadre is one of both endearment and respect.[4] The element of formality is another aspect of compadrazgo that continually surfaces in Yaqui discursive reinscription of ethic boundaries. It is widely held that husbands and wives should "never baptize together." Regina Valencia explained: "Here in the tribe it is not well perceived if the husband is the compadre of his own wife. That is, . . . a couple . . . should not be compadres because they should have respect for one another." Husbands and wives have argued and have had sexual relations—they know one another too intimately to maintain the distance that this specific form of respect demands.

Despite the Yaqui practice of limiting the number of baptismal god-parents within one family, there are many other occasions upon which compadrazgo ties are established. Aside from baptisms, first commu-nions, confirmations, burials, dedications to the saints, weddings, and quinceañeras, there are numerous Yaqui religious societies into which individuals are inducted, each one requiring ritual sponsors. During Lent adult males being initiated into the Chapayeka society and small chil-dren performing the role of *angelito* (little angel, or protector of Christ) require padrinos. Godparents sponsor adult males upon their initiation as maestros or Matachín dancers. Men and women who serve together as fiesteros often consider themselves compadres, and at times this rela-tion of mutual respect and trust extends, as parents of those serving as fiesteros also consider one another compadres. Of course, as with any interpersonal relationship, ties to ritual kin vary in intensity; in the eyes of participants, some relationships end up being much more valuable than others. But in terms of sheer quantity alone, the network of ritual kin surrounding each individual is remarkable if not astounding.

The broad array of ritual kin connections forged by nearly every individual in Yaqui society affects the continuous intertwining of a very public ritual system with private lives and family decisions. But these voluntary ties bind families together in many other significant ways. For economically vulnerable families, the compadrazgo complex is a spe-cial mode of relationality that figures prominently as a tactical resource during times of financial distress. The repetitive reciprocal gestures of respect and obligation, the everyday exchanges between Yaqui ritual kin, demonstrate not only a mode of economic coping but also the undeni-able articulation of religious practice and gendered relationships with class and ethnic identities.

This interpenetration of identities and expectations became evident on the day I was invited to accompany Marcela Valencia and her fam-ily to her brother-in-law's cattle ranch on the Yaqui River. Marcela's husband, Alejandro, wanted to cut several bundles of mesquite to raise money to pay for a computer course for their daughter. Although Ale-jandro was there to work, the day was a relaxing outing for the rest of us. Marcela and I played *lotería* (a game similar to bingo) with the children. We tidied up around the ranch, picked limes from fruit trees near the river, and readied the picnic dinner. We stayed until sunset, when Ale-jandro's brothers brought the cattle home for the night. As we returned to Potam, the back of the borrowed pickup truck laden with mesquite,

Alejandro and Marcela quietly discussed the possibility that Alejandro's comadre, a non-Yaqui storekeeper who lived on the other side of town, might agree to purchase some of the wood. We drove to the comadre's home and were invited to pull into her fenced yard so that no one would steal Alejandro's wood supply. As I jumped down from the cab I noticed firewood piled up to a meter high along one wall in the backyard. We were welcomed into the spacious adobe home for coffee, pan dulce, and conversation. After a short while the subject of the freshly cut mesquite was broached. At first the family protested that they did not need any wood, saying it was too bad that Alejandro had made the trip. But in the end they agreed to take two large bundles—more than half of the mesquite in the back of the truck. They paid Alejandro, and we went on our way. Our next stop was at the home of Marcela's comadre, Laura, whose family endured chronic financial trouble. Alejandro pulled up in front of the two-room house Laura shared with her husband and eight children and called out cheerfully to her as he began unloading limb after limb of mesquite onto the darkening street. Laura and her oldest daughter quickly came to lend a hand, surprised and smiling. After we hauled the wood into their yard we headed home. When we were alone Marcela told me that Alejandro is a very good man, always looking after her comadre. The afternoon's events provided a valuable lesson for me about gifting versus selling, about the careful calculation of favors owed and relative wealth. I saw enacted the obligation of a wealthier comadre to accept (and pay for) a load of mesquite that she did not actually need and may not have really wanted and the responsibility to give to someone in need without being asked.

In her foreword to the 1990 edition of Marcel Mauss's *The Gift* Mary Douglas writes, "A gift that does nothing to enhance solidarity is a contradiction" (1990:vii). Indeed, according to Mauss's (1990) theory, the gift establishes a relation, and every gift requires return. This is certainly the case in southern Sonora's Yaqui communities, where relationality and reciprocity not only are part of the everyday but also form the very basis of the annual fiesta.

Ties that Bind: The Fiesta System and Its Relational Networks

Every year each of the most prominent Yaqui pueblos sponsors a fiesta to honor the town's patron saint.[5] The fiesta season runs from late spring to midsummer. A fiesta typically lasts four days, during which time the saints are honored with prayer vigils and ritual processions called kontis. Every pueblo's fiesta is a dual celebration. Two ramadas are constructed, one for the red side and the other for the blue. While this color-coded division was once employed by Jesuit missionaries in a didactic drama symbolizing Spain's fifteenth-century struggle between the Moors (red) and the Christians (blue), many Yaquis now have the understanding that, as Regina explained, "the blue represents the good, and the red represents the bad."

The crowds of people that attend a fiesta are entertained as they watch the deer dancer, laugh at the pascolas' jokes, and enjoy the small fireworks called *cohetes* that explode from towering scaffolds known as *castillos* (castles) erected especially for the occasion. At least one of the nights of the fiesta features a social dance, and there is an abundance of good food. Fiesta hosts work hard to keep the ritual specialists (cantoras, maestros, Matachín dancers, pascola dancers, deer singers, and the deer dancer) and their families, town officials, and guests satiated with chile stew, wakabaki, *atole*, piles of fresh tortillas, and plenty of coffee. While the conflict between Moors and Christians may no longer be an explicit part of popular interpretations of the fiesta, the event still has an air of good-natured competition. During the long nights of the fiesta attendees try to visit both the red and blue ramadas to see who has more food, better dancers, and a more spectacular fireworks display.

The principal organizers of the fiesta are the fiesteros, 4 men and 4 women for each side, a total of 16 individuals. These 16 sponsors, each with his or her own contingent of *moros* (helpers), spend the year preceding the fiesta making preparations. With the exception of the Lenten season, they meet every Sunday at the church to venerate the saint, hold a small konti, collect dues, discuss the order of events, and allocate tasks. Each of the men (the fiesteros) selects a female (a fiestera) as a partner. Fiesteras officially serve as compañeras to fiesteros. Fiesteras are not secondary characters but true partners in this elaborate production. For the entire year leading up to the fiesta these men and women faithfully attend the Sunday veneration, kneeling for long periods of time while prayers are offered to the saints and processing under the hot midday sun. The women contribute just as much money to the fiesta fund as their male counterparts, and they do not shy away from assuming roles of leadership during the organizational process.

The fiestero's term of service is one year, and those who become fiesteros are considered for that year to be part of the five *ya'uram*, the

interlocking leadership complex that composes the civil–religious government of each of the Yaqui Ocho Pueblos (Spicer 1954, 1980).[6] While
their political influence on town policy is limited (Spicer 1980:187), fiesteros are nonetheless accorded great respect.[7] Long after they finish their
duties they are remembered by fellow Yaquis for this role; having served
as a fiestero or fiestera becomes an enduring marker of one's personal
identity. This status may be connected with the importance of the fiesta
to the life of the pueblo.

Although men and women work as partners in the production of
the fiesta, the event itself is characterized by a decidedly gendered division of labor. This complementary division of labor corresponds closely
to the allocation of space, particularly within the fiesta's ramadas. The
ramadas constructed by the red and the blue fiesteros may differ slightly
in layout, but overall they have the same form. The ramada is divided
into rooms. The open side facing the church is divided in half; on the
left is the altar, in front of which the maestros and their accompanying
cantoras kneel throughout the long hours of the night to pray, and on
the right is the space in which the deer singers, deer dancer, and pascolas
perform. There are many times when the prayers and the ritual dancing
occur simultaneously. The area immediately in front of this portion of
the ramada is periodically occupied by the Matachín troupe. There, to
the music of violins and guitars, these men who dedicate themselves to
the Virgin Mary make the shuffling, complicated steps of their dance
look effortless as they twirl in slow circles, weaving intricate patterns
around one another. This church-facing portion of the ramada is occupied by male and female ritual specialists, and men, women, and children are welcome to watch and enjoy the performances. However, as the
four-day fiesta winds to a close this becomes an increasingly male space,
as men crowd in close, joking with the pascolas and sharing bottles of
tequila and beer in a spirit of relaxed conviviality.

Adjacent to the church-facing ramada opening there is a large enclosed
room where the fiesteros keep their supplies—50-kilogram sacks of
flour piled to the ceiling, legs and sides of beef hanging from the rafters,
boxes full of freshly baked bread, bags of roasted hand-ground coffee,
pinto beans, garbanzo beans, sugar, cinnamon, dried chiles, lard, plastic
spoons, and Styrofoam cups. This is the room in which the fiesteros' families, typically their mothers, sisters, wives, and younger children, rest and
visit and dispense food to the kitchen when needed. Immediately behind
this supply room, mirroring and diagonal to the church-facing dance

space, is the kitchen area. The kitchen faces the pueblo, and it is where all of the food is prepared and served throughout the fiesta. Men help lift cauldrons, carry firewood, deliver supplies, and occasionally sit in the dining area, but this is fundamentally a female-gendered space. Here the assistants of the fiesteras labor for long hours cooking chile, wakabaki, and cinnamon-flavored atole. At any given time there are more than 20 women working in the kitchen. They talk and joke with one another, exchanging news and gossip as they pat out the huge fiesta tortillas; they toss the dough into the air, stretching it until it is paper thin and perfectly round. The kitchen becomes a veritable stage for the performance of women's ritual labor as men, other women, and children waiting to be served look on, commenting favorably on the richness of the chile or a particular woman's technique in the art of tossing tortillas.

Just as pueblo fiestas provide an opportunity for the construction and representation of gendered identity, so are fiesta-related activities heavily imbued with ethnic meaning. The weekly konti attended by the fiesteros is a solidification of the Yaquis' connection to their land. Every Sunday the fiesteros meet at the church to pray and kneel in front of the saint. Along with the maestros, cantoras, governors, and various members of the military society, the fiesteros perform this konti, which enacts a symbolic "surrounding" (Spicer 1980:99). Walking in a counterclockwise direction, they process behind images of the Virgin and the pueblo's patron saint, stopping to genuflect at each of four crosses located in the church's cemetery (Spicer 1980:173–174). It is Spicer's hypothesis that these crosses, said to "represent Saints Matthew, Mark, Luke, and John," are also "given the meaning of the 'four corners of the world'" (1980:173). He argues that this Catholic ceremony acquired a new meaning sometime in the nineteenth century, when the dispute over the Yaqui homeland reached its peak, writing, "the land meaning of the crosses . . . is consistent with the growing concern over boundaries and land encroachment" (Spicer 1980:174). The ceremony, he explains, "is an affirmation of Yaqui stewardship, in the name of God, of their Yaqui traditional territory. Visiting these 'four corners' each Sunday by all the active religious and secular organizations of the town symbolizes the circuit of the Yaqui traditional territory by the angels and prophets at the time the boundary was defined and made sacred" (Spicer 1980:173–174).

These are the rituals that solidify the relations between Yaqui people, their homeland, and their sacred pueblos. Furthermore, the fiesta celebration itself is a grand public display of all that is good about Yaqui culture. Despite the financial difficulties that beset every Yaqui community and touch the lives of the majority of Yaqui individuals, the fiesta system continues to thrive and to attract devoted participants and enthusiastic spectators. The konti ceremonies that accomplish a "weekly visit to and surrounding of the four corners of the Yaqui world" (Spicer 1954:139) also momentarily move the Yaqui people from the margins of the nation to a symbolic center. The sheer volume of traditional food available at the fiesta is a utopian enactment of abundance in an otherwise economically distressed community—a performance of possibility. Women's ritual labor in the fiesta ramada, based on cooperation and reciprocal gifting, embodies that unalienated, socially centered aspect of work that recedes in a world oriented to capitalist markets and wage labor. Young people who have migrated north to work in the maquiladoras in the Arizona–Sonora border towns take leaves of absence or even quit their jobs to come home for the fiesta. The fiesta can be interpreted as an oppositional utopian moment, an affirmation and repositioning of Yaqui community where survival supersedes the pressure to assimilate, where emplacement stands as an answer to historic efforts to displace, even eradicate, the Yaqui people.

One of the most remarkable aspects of fiesta giving is the way in which fiesteros are chosen and the vast webs of reciprocity subsequently set into motion. The relationship of the fiesteros to one another and to the fiesta itself becomes obvious on the night they are selected for this role. In the month preceding the fiesta the current fiesteros meet in secret in order to select their successors. On the designated date they go in the dark of night to knock on the doors of the new fiesteros. When the selected person steps out, a red flag is waved over him or her, and three fireworks are set off. Much laughter and teasing of the newly elected ensue, as the job of the fiestero is both an honor and an unenviable burden. The new fiestero is given a small box of fiesta supplies to distribute among the four moros that he or she will choose.

The language that describes this process of the induction of new fiesteros is particularly instructive, for it reveals the attitudes of relationality and profound obligation that underpin the fiesta system. When a person is selected as fiestero, it is said that he or she has been *amarrado* (tied) to the role. On the night of selection one is pressed into service, literally "bound" to the fiesta and all of the responsibilities it entails: the economic burden, the necessity to contribute fiesta funds every week, the tremendous commitment of time, and the reality of having to organize a team of assistants. The newly elected fiestero not only is tied to the fiesta but is immediately connected to the seven other fiesteros on his or her side, people with whom that fiestero will be intimately associated, for, ultimately, the perceived success or failure of the fiesta rests on their ability to cooperate and to marshal the resources of the pueblo. So it is not surprising that as the time of selection draws near people joke about hiding or running away; they tease one another, saying, "Te van a amarrar!" (They're going to tie you!). Everyone is nervous about the possibility of being bound to the fiesta.

The new fiesteros immediately set about constructing a tight web of obligation with those they know best in the community, as the supplies required to feed all of the ritual actors as well as the hundreds of guests who attend the fiesta are always acquired through an intricate system of reciprocal ties. Such links are initiated in the spring at the end of that year's fiesta celebration, when leftover food stocks are distributed to the 16 new fiesteros. Each one is given a small portion of staples—a sack of flour, several kilograms of beans, bags of sugar, coffee, and chiles, cartons of cigarettes, firecrackers, and so on. In turn, the fiestero divides these goods into smaller portions, gifting a share to "as many people as possible," thereby extending and building the network of people on which he or she will rely the following year. Fiesteros give to aunts and uncles and to distant cousins, to sisters and brothers, comadres, padrinos, nieces, friends, and coworkers. Those who receive from the fiesteros may also divide their portion, giving to their relatives and friends, further continuing and broadening the web.

The following spring, when it comes time for the fiesta, everyone who received a gift of food is under obligation to return that amount or greater to the fiesteros. These returned gifts are used to supply the fiesta. Regina Valencia was a fiestera for Rahum's fiesta of Corpus Christi in 1997, and she described to me the involved process of proliferation:

> When I received the fiesta there, when the old fiesteros exited, they delivered all that was left over. Like a sack of flour, a sack of sugar, beans, lard, chiles, garbanzos, everything that was left over, they delivered it all to me. And I distributed it to *everyone I could*, as far as I could stretch it, so that this food would return back to me. They have to give back; for example, if I hand out ten kilos of flour, if the person likes, he can give me a sack, or the same, or a bit more. And if I give out [tin] pails, they also have to give me pails. Or baskets, or petates.

Although the amount of return stipulated is more flexible today than it was in the past, the ideal is still to give back double or as much as ten times the amount received. While many individuals actually reciprocate with the same item they were gifted the year before, some prefer to give money, allowing the fiestera herself to purchase whatever supplies she might be lacking. In any case, the gift demands return. As Regina explained, "There are people who don't ever give back. But they also say that when these people die, they carry this [burden] over their shoulders. . . . Parents always say that when the fiesta arrives, if [someone] gives you something, you must give back. Food or money. Alms."

When I was conducting fieldwork, acquaintances consistently teased me that as an honorary member of the Yaqui community I, too, might be selected as a fiestera and that I would have to kneel in front of the saint every week and scrape money together for an entire year to pay my fiesta dues: "Te van a amarrar, Kristi!" my companions would laugh.

Sitting on a sack of flour inside the fiesteros' supply room at 2:30 in the morning on the first day of the Corpus Christi fiesta in 1997, I discovered that "tying," this system of binding relations, encompassed anyone it wanted. I had been chatting quietly with Marisela, the wife of one of the fiesteros, as I tried to wake myself up and gather enough energy to go back out to the ramada, where crowds were gathering for the pascola and deer dances. Regina had her pile of supplies just across the room, and her mother, Dolores, approached, carrying a steaming bowl of beef *caldo* (soup) and a small plastic bag with six pieces of bread. I thanked her for the food and had begun to eat when Marisela shouted gleefully, "Kristi! Kristi! You have been given bread; now you are tied! Next year you will come here to the blue ramada and you will bring your mountain of supplies and you will sit here for three days without sleeping!"

Pretending not to understand, I said, "But the bread was only a gift."

Marisela's reply was swift: "Ah, but Kristi, *that is how it is done!*" And laughter rang out all around me. In the Yaqui system all gifts demand reciprocity. By accepting a gift—and it is taboo to refuse—one becomes part of the system that enables the fiesta to continue year after year.

Tekípanoa: The Labor of Devotion

In the Yaqui language the word *tekípanoa* means "to work or labor." Originally derived from Aztec (Nahuatl), the term was introduced by the Jesuits to articulate their concept of "planned activity for productive purposes and could be applied ... to the work of farming and herding for the missionaries" (Spicer 1980:66). While the word *tekípanoa* can be used in a general sense, signifying ordinary productive labor, it is employed most often when speaking of ritual. Indeed, ceremonial labor, labor given with vigor, a "good heart" (Painter 1986), and a desire to fulfill one's duty to God or the saints, is the highest form of tekípanoa (Spicer 1954:177). Such obligations to the supernatural arise when an individual makes a manda, a promise of service to the Virgin or to a saint in exchange for divine assistance. These promises are the foundation of the perpetuation of the entire Yaqui ceremonial system.

Tekípanoa is carried out in innumerable ways by people acting both in highly formalized roles and as individual supplicants. As Spicer reminds us, the men who are members of the Chapayeka, Pilate, and caballero societies perform tekípanoa every Lent as they reenact the Passion of Christ. The maestros who offer prayers and sermons year-round at every public and household ceremony are working to fulfill their obligations to the saints and other holy figures. Members of the Matachín society perform tekípanoa to the Virgin Mary as they dance through the night at wakes and fiestas. The ways in which tekípanoa or ceremonial labor may be manifested are virtually uncountable.[8]

Tekípanoa may be an expansive category in Yaqui culture, but it is also highly compartmentalized by gender. Only men and boys belong to all the Lenten ritual societies, from the caballeros and Chapayekas to the Judas society; ceremonial performers such as the Matachines and the deer dancers are always male; the pueblo governors, members of the military society, and the maestros are male as well. Women can be cantoras (female singers who assist the maestros), *kiyostes* (women who care for female images and the altar), *tenanchim* (bearers of female images), *alpesim* (female flag bearers), and fiesteras. With the exception of the women who hold these formal ritual roles (and their numbers are very few compared to the heavily populated male ritual societies), men form the majority and most visible aspects of the Yaqui ceremonial system.[9] Women's ritual activities are, for the most part, informal and behind the scenes. Yet they are plentiful: it is women who dress the saints and sweep the church before religious processions; it is women who usually construct household altars and who cook and serve the food so vital to both fiesta and household rituals. Women's tekípanoa may be less visible than the work done in male ceremonial societies; nevertheless, their ritual labor is considered highly important, even critical, to the well-being of the community. And one of the most interesting and overlooked aspects of women's ritual participation is the tekípanoa that occurs in the planning and hosting of domestic ceremonies.

The time and care Yaqui women invest in the arrangement of household ceremonies become apparent when we examine one such event, a family's rezo, or prayer ritual, held to honor the Virgin of Guadalupe. The Virgin of Guadalupe's feast day is celebrated on December 12. It commemorates her appearance to Mexican Indian Juan Diego on a hill near Mexico City in the sixteenth century. Since the Virgin of Guadalupe is, arguably, the most prominent figure in Mexican Catholic spiritual life, this is an important day throughout Mexico, and it is no less significant to the Yaquis. Yaqui families in Potam host household rituals venerating the Virgin, usually in fulfillment of a manda. Ana Ochoa, her mother, and her aunt are typical in this regard. Although they spend time at one another's house on a near daily basis, each woman separately organizes and hosts a rezo in her home on December 12. Several years ago Ana had suffered with kidney problems; she was gravely ill, unable to get out of bed, and it was believed that she might die. Ana's aunt Lencha and Ana's mother, María, both made prayerful promises to the Virgin of Guadalupe, who is considered one of the most powerful and compassionate of the holy figures. Ana recovered from her illness, and every year all three women fulfill their mandas by constructing home altars for the Virgin and by inviting the maestros and cantoras to come and pray.

In 1996 Lencha was the first member of the extended family to host a rezo. On the morning of December 11 she and her grown daughter Rosa María began preparing for the ritual specialists and guests who would arrive for evening prayers. While Lencha set about cleaning the tripe, the main ingredient in the menudo she was planning to serve, Rosa constructed the altar. Under their protective ramada abutting the adobe wall of her mother's house she re-created in miniature the *cerro* (hill) on which the Virgin of Guadalupe first made her appearance. She piled large stones into a meter-high mound and then whitewashed the entire pile. Rosa made a backdrop by hanging a new floral-print tablecloth from the ceiling of the ramada; the cloth draped down the wall to the top of the hill of stones. She then brought out two large framed portraits of the Virgin of Guadalupe and secured them on top of the rock *cerrito* (little hill). She seemed to be enjoying herself as she adorned the stones with homemade crepe paper roses and irises in bright colors. Rosa had

Figure 6. "Welcome" *cerrito* for the Virgin of Guadalupe

recently been to the city of Guaymas, and she had purchased six special iris stems cleverly fashioned from dried corn husks, dyed in rich hues of scarlet, fuchsia, and plum, which she placed in parallel rows underneath each of the portraits of the Virgin. I helped Rosa string green, silver, and blue tinsel above the pictures. At one point she ducked into her house and then emerged with two smaller portraits of the Virgin, which she added to her altar. Ana arrived with five votive candles, which the women lit and placed among the stones. When Rosa María's husband came home from work in the early afternoon, he set to work with the help of his two nieces suspending banners of brightly colored *papel picado* (cut paper) from a line draped between the posts of the ramada.

Once she was finished with the altar, Rosa got out a large pot, built a fire, and made cinnamon hot chocolate from fresh cow's milk. In their kitchen ramada her mother, Lencha, continued to cook the menudo. When I entered the room, I found Lencha busy in front of a large cauldron bubbling with garbanzos, green chiles, garlic, and glistening white, freshly cleaned tripe. Lencha set aside the onions and cilantro she was chopping for the garnish, exclaiming that I must feel hungry. Before I could object, she threw two ocean fish into a frying pan and served them to me with lime, salt, chiles, and corn tortillas. Lencha and Rosa had spent the previous day making *buñuelos* (crispy flour fritters), and I watched as Lencha deftly drizzled them with thinned, carmelized honey.

When the maestros, the cantoras, and the various children and relatives accompanying them arrived late that afternoon, Rosa, Lencha, and the other women of the household were still busy at work in the kitchen. Chairs and benches were pulled around as the ritual specialists kneeled on carrizo mats in front of the altar and began to sing their prayers in Latin. Lencha and Rosa sat down for only a few minutes; they spent most of their time finishing the cooking. About 45 minutes later the prayers were over, and the ritual singers were invited to sit at the table, where they were served steaming bowls of menudo, cups of coffee, buñuelos, and hot chocolate. After finishing their meal the specialists were given large plastic containers full of menudo and bags of buñuelos to take along with them as they went to conduct prayers for another family.

The following day the same sequence was repeated at Ana's home. Ana's daughter Loreta and her cousin decorated their whitewashed stone cerrito with balloons, paper flowers, and Christmas lights. The yard was thoroughly swept and watered down. Ana's comadre, Dolores, arrived in the early afternoon and went straight to work cutting several pounds of beef and dozens of potatoes for chile. The women also made macaroni salad and frijoles puercos to serve with the chile. At 4:00 Ana's sisters and her best friend arrived with an army of children, and the household became a flurry of activity. We set about making tortillas; Dolores told me that we were to use ten kilograms of flour. As we patted out, pulled on, and draped the enlarged fiesta-style tortillas over the rounded *comal* (the metal plate or disc on which tortillas are cooked), Ana's sister Cecilia let out a gasp, "They are coming already!" Ana heard this and came running out of the house. The cantoras had arrived two hours earlier than anticipated, and the maestros were not far behind. The food was not ready, and we were less than halfway through our bag of flour.

When the maestros arrived, they and the cantoras settled down on the mat in front of the cerrito and commenced their harmonized recitations. Just after the prayers began two of the seven cantoras stood up and walked over to the kitchen fire. They pulled up their sleeves and began patting out tortillas. During the ritual a few people sat and watched the prayers. The cantoras and other women at the fire talked and laughed as they made tortillas and tended the beans and chile. Children kicked a soccer ball around the yard, and the women working in the kitchen alternately spoke about the prayers, pueblo news, and the latest developments in their favorite *telenovela* (television soap opera).

We finished cooking the food and folding the tortillas just in time, and as the maestros ended their chants we carried a wooden table outside and placed a clean tablecloth on it. The ritual specialists were served plates heaped with chile, salad, beans, and tortillas. Plastic plates full of steaming leftovers were piled into bags and given to the maestros and cantoras to take home. At every rezo, after the specialists and their children have finished eating, tradition holds that they fold up the tablecloth at both ends. This is the sign that the host family and the women who prepared the meal should gather round the table. The head maestro gives a formal speech of gratitude in the Yaqui language, followed by a hearty *chiokoe utte'esia* (thank you) for the meal, and the troupe heads off to another house.

While men assist with some of the preparations for household ceremonies (constructing altar tables, hauling firewood, fetching supplies), women's work and presence are often the most notable in domestic ritual space. When Cecilia Ochoa's mother-in-law died, it was Cecilia and her sisters-in-law who organized and hosted the monthly rosary. Her husband, Carlos, and his father attended, but it was the women who prepared the small meal, cleaned the yard, arranged for the rosary singers (who also happened to be women), and constructed the altar, and it was primarily women who formed the audience, bearing witness to a significant family event. During an interview about women's roles in Yaqui ceremonies Regina Valencia once looked at me incredulously as if to say, "Hadn't I noticed?" "When there is something that needs to be done for a fiesta or in the house or something, it is always the woman. . . . It is always the woman in the kitchen or with the children, yes . . . the woman." Although Regina's claim may be somewhat of an overstatement, from my own observations it is not far from the mark. Women are integral to both household ceremonies and pueblo rituals; they are involved from start to finish—from the making of a manda, to the planning, organization, and preparation for a domestic ritual, to the cleanup.

Events like these demonstrate the significance of women's labor to household ceremonies and point to the centrality of women themselves as ritual actors, as performers of tekípanoa. Yaqui household rituals dissolve any dualistic notion of a performance's "frontstage" and "backstage" (see MacCannell 1973; Scott 1985).[10] In Yaqui domestic ceremonies the area of food preparation, what might ordinarily be classified as happening backstage, is not only visible but in many ways is on par with what happens frontstage. During the rezo in honor of the Virgin of Guadalupe the spaces of the kitchen where women are busily preparing food, the raised hearth where tortillas are made, and the ramada under which the meal is served interpenetrate with the spaces of the altar, the petate on which the ritual specialists kneel to offer their prayers, and the surround occupied by witnesses to the ceremony, family members, and visitors. The spaces of worship and preparation, the social and the spiritual, are fluid, coalescing to create a relaxed, convivial atmosphere where children play, where cantoras chuckle and talk amongst themselves, where hosts move back and forth between the prayer mats and the kitchen, making certain that everything is ready for the meal. As they cook and make tortillas women quietly chat and joke. They do not feel compelled to sit and watch the prayers the entire time, and they do not perceive the ritual as residing solely in the performance of the prayers. When I lived in Potam, I met no one aside from the maestros themselves and some of the cantoras who could translate what was being sung in the Latin prayers. On one occasion, during a household rezo, I asked Ana's aunt Lencha, considered by her family members, comadres, and friends to be a very devout person and a source of knowledge about Yaqui religious traditions and ceremonial propriety, whether she understood the texts sung by the maestros and cantoras during their prayers. Lencha paused and, before answering, wrinkled her brow, as if perplexed at why I would pose such an utterly inane question. "Not really," she finally shrugged, and then she hurried back to the kitchen to begin filling bowls with stew for her guests.

In domestic ceremonies women's tekípanoa becomes part of the ritual's performance, an integral element in the veneration of the saint. The hosts, in the case of Ana's family, women fulfilling a manda to the Virgin of Guadalupe, construct the altar and prepare the food; the maestros and cantoras offer the prayers. Both aspects are necessary for a successful event. At no time was the fluid intermingling of the spaces of performance, the easy shifting between participatory roles, more apparent than when those two cantoras walked over to the fireplace, rolled up their sleeves, and without a word started making tortillas during Ana's rezo. As the cantoras moved with ease from the petate to the cooking area, that movement erased any supposed boundary between frontstage and backstage, indicating the importance of the dinner to the completion of the ceremony.[11] The significance of this meal is underlined again in a very formal way at the end of the ceremony, as the maestro recites a highly ritualized text simply called *las gracias* (the thanks), expressing gratitude to God and the hosts for food and acknowledging the women's labor as an essential part of the performance.

Success in hosting a rezo increases the family's and community's respect for a woman as she demonstrates her ability to fulfill her vow and to provide adequate and well-prepared food for her guests. In domestic rituals women become highly visible as key actors in Yaqui ceremonialism. The prominence and frequency of such rituals and their centrality to the religious life of the family highlight women's ritual agency in a way that large public rites such as Semana Santa do not. In this way tekípanoa contributes to a Yaqui woman's standing in the community, further defining the qualities of her gendered and ethnic identity.

The Practicality of Relationships

In contemporary Sonoran Yaqui communities domestic ceremonies and pueblo fiestas structure the performance of gendered labor, linking it to specific cultural meanings. As such, ceremonialism is highly valued by

Yaqui women as a marker of their own cultural identity. Household ceremonies and fiestas are perceived by women as a vehicle through which they create and reproduce Yaquiness. At the same time, the continued existence of ethnic tradition is contingent upon the maintenance of a series of deeply significant relationships. Yaqui individuals bind themselves to ritual kin and to God, the Virgin of Guadalupe, and various saints. Such relationships are established and nurtured through the performance of ritual labor in both formal and domestic settings and through complex webs of obligation and reciprocity.

In his *Theses on Feuerbach* of 1845 Marx wrote, "Social life is essentially *practical*. All mysteries which mislead theory into mysticism find their rational solution in human practice and in the comprehension of this practice" (1978:145). For the Yaquis with whom I have lived no statement could be truer. The relationships between ritual kin, among family members, and between friends are, at their core, practical, even highly material. These relationships are rooted in a sense of mutual obligation; they hinge upon the gifting and return of time, labor, and food, upon the willingness to hire someone in need or to loan money without hesitation. Reciprocity and relationality also form the basis of the veneration of the saints: used by fiesteros to amass the supplies and the labor needed for a successful fiesta, the elaborate system of gifting and return set into motion at the beginning of a new fiesta season spirals out to reach into every corner of the community. The fiesta feast, created through the cooperation of so many community members and "performed" by women, concretizes community and highlights relationality.

The materiality of relationships in Sonora's Yaqui communities is eminently apparent. From the welfare of the community itself to the health of individual family members, a state of continual well-being is predicated on a relation; the manda made to a saint when a child or loved one is ill and the honoring of that promise in a household ceremony become acts of reciprocity. Labor is conceptualized as tekípanoa, the ultimate gift and demonstration of devotion.[12]

In the Yaqui pueblos a willingness to give, to do favors without being asked, to share even the most meager of resources is considered an attribute of a true Yaqui. In the fiesta, where non-Yaquis see a waste of money and scarce resources, Yaquis celebrate a utopian moment of abundance and possibility. In everyday material exchanges between relatives and compadres, in the proliferation of borrowing, loaning, and sharing, where fiercely independent Sonoran mestizos see dependence on others, Yaquis sense both interdependence and community, a network of relationships that provides a safety net in an insecure world. For Yaquis this system of gifting and reciprocity, of mutual obligation and the labors of devotion, is perceived as a moral economy (Scott 1976) that not only enables one to live but also provides a model for how to live *as a Yaqui* in the present.

8
Lutu'uria
Truth and the Terrain of Identity

Yaqui ethnic identity is undeniably tied to certain culturally approved modes of behavior, to specific expectations about the ways in which Yaquis should be responsive to and responsible for one another. For Yaquis living in the Sonoran pueblos the demonstration of devotion remains one of the most powerful means of cultural–ethnic identification. Yet among the Yaquis I know devotion is more than just the fulfillment of religious duty. Devotion radiates outward from this intensive engagement in ritual labor so that, in a very fundamental sense, giving oneself in service to others is a critical part of "being Yaqui."

Nowhere is this ethic of devotion clearer than in the meanings that coalesce around the Yaqui word *lutu'uria*. Let me begin with a brief illustration. It was autumn 1997, and for about a year I had been living with Ana and Marco, their two teenage children, and their infant daughter, Lila. Raúl, a relative whom Marco called "uncle" as a demonstration of respect, was also a regular presence in the household. In his late forties and unmarried, Raúl made ends meet, as do so many Yaqui men, by taking odd jobs, doing construction projects for friends, cutting and hauling mesquite firewood from the surrounding desert, and tending cattle on his cousin's ranch. He was also well known and respected as a maestro, an indigenous priest who sang prayers for the dead, led Easter ceremonies, conducted traditional weddings, participated in pueblo governance, and could impress an audience with his fluid and competent oratorical style. Raúl had been working, off and on, at Ana and Marco's home since the previous spring. Under the guise of family reciprocity—three square meals a day, as much coffee as he could drink, and new clothing—Raúl had been adding a room to the wattle-and-daub structure that served as the compound's winter kitchen and storage area; it also, temporarily, was my bedroom.

It was a steamy September afternoon. Coated with a layer of fine dust, I dragged myself home from a long day of interviewing and visiting in Mérida, the neighborhood on the far western edge of Potam. Raúl was the only one in the compound when I arrived. In an effort to prop up a thatched shade over the kitchen doorway, he was struggling to wedge a post underneath a heavy ceiling beam. Hearing the dogs bark, Raúl turned toward me, sweating profusely. With a knowing twinkle in his eye and a long, low sigh that seemed the epitome of exhaustion, Raúl exclaimed, "Lutu'uria!" With that he gave a chuckle, wiped his brow with his unbuttoned shirtsleeve, and turned back to his work.

In the Yaqui language lutu'uria is the fulfillment of social responsibility either through the performance of ritual duty or through ordinary labor in service of others. Yet, significantly, lutu'uria is also the gloss for "truth" in the Yaqui language. As defined in one Yaqui–English dictionary, lutu'uria is "truth (especially as evidenced by one's actions and by fulfilling commitments)" (Molina, Shaul, and Valenzuela 1999:88). Spicer writes, "A value-orientation of great importance exists in Yaqui society focused around the proper observance of all such obligations. The individual who actively recognizes such obligations and submits himself throughout his life to fulfilling them is said to have lutu'uria, to have demonstrated this highest of all human qualities" (1980:85).

An examination of the use of the term *lutu'uria* in Yaqui discourse reveals "labor in service of others" and "truth" to be intimately related concepts. When one speaks of truth as lutu'uria in the Yaqui language, a sense of duty or willing service is implied. Spicer argues that "lutu'uria does not refer to abstract truth or falsity of a statement; it refers always to activities and their consistency with obligations to others. It means essentially 'to be true to all those towards whom one has obligations'; it is wider than just ritual obligations and includes social obligations as well" (1980:95). As one older Yaqui man explained, lutu'uria is "the truth. Certain. Lutu'uria, well, is truth . . . that one is going to do some work." This connection, coupled with Raúl's comment on that hot September afternoon, opens a dialogue with Yaqui understandings: labor as intersubjectivity, relationality as truth.

Layer upon layer, reciprocity, social obligation, and cooperative labor permeate the experience of living in Potam pueblo. As we have seen in previous chapters, the economic stability of families and the continued vibrance of community ceremonialism depend on these factors. A brother-in-law may be asked to help with household repairs; one sister spends an entire day cooking, helping another sister prepare for a rezo; family members stay up all night long during a fiesta in order to dispense food supplies; women stand next to the comal at a ritual, patting out tortillas until their shoulders ache; an uncle patches the cracks and crumbling corners of a nephew's adobe oven. Such acts exemplify the reciprocal gifting of labor (Flores 1994) expected in a Yaqui community. These exchanges, unremarkable to cultural insiders because of their sheer multiplicity and the frequency with which they occur, are couched in an idiom that connects mutual assistance to the concept of sacred obligation. As it binds notions of service, labor, and responsibility to the supernatural world and the social body, lutu'uria is one of the clearest expressions of relationality in Yaqui culture, a palpable demonstration of the materiality of intersubjectivity.

An understanding of the concept of lutu'uria throws into relief my own experience as a fieldworker among the Yaquis, causing me to reflect on the relationship between an ethnographer and the people with whom she lives. My own active participation in various aspects of Yaqui daily life, which I initially perceived as experiential learning—participant observation at its most basic—continually garnered exclamations of praise from Yaquis with whom I associated and led to my acceptance at ritual events, even by complete strangers. I have come to believe that my Yaqui companions' attention to my admittedly inept attempts to help at ceremonies and around the house revealed an interest that was not only personal but also culturally informed. Understanding the Yaqui valuation of service as lutu'uria situates Yaqui consultants' preoccupation with my participation in both mundane tasks and in ritually essential labor in terms of a discourse that demands involvement, awards praise, and equates physical work with emotional investment.

Whether I was making tortillas, cleaning chiles, sweeping the church before mass, kneeling to venerate a saint through long and repetitious prayers, or carrying the Virgin during a procession, my presence and the extent of my (mostly behind the scenes) involvement in Yaqui ritual life were always topics of considerable discussion and were favorably commented upon as somehow making me a member of the community. Of course, such experiences will no doubt resonate strongly with anyone who has conducted long-term fieldwork. Informants are proud of us as we become even minimally competent in the performance of those essential tasks that play a substantial role in their everyday lives. Yet in the Yaqui case the cultural discourse surrounding the concept of lutu'uria makes possible an additional layer of meaning and connection.

My own experience helping at a konti is instructive. Midway through my field study Ana was selected to be a fiestera for Rahum, a neighboring pueblo. Within days Ana had appointed her moros in preparation for what was to be a yearlong obligation to attend the konti every week to venerate the pueblo saint. That first Sunday Ana, her moros, her sister Cecilia, Cecilia's youngest child, and I all piled into Marco's pickup truck and headed to the konti. When we arrived in Rahum, the maestros were already singing their prayers. With their heads bowed and with small flagged batons grasped tightly in their hands, the fiesteros and fiesteras quickly formed two lines before the altar, kneeling on the hard cement of the church floor. Spicer's description conveys a sense of the difficulties endured by the fiesteros in fulfilling this responsibility:

> The duties of the Pakhome [fiesteros] in their weekly devotions, which require the longest sustained kneeling postures on the concrete of the church floors and the gravel of the cemeteries, burning hot in the summer and icy cold in the winter, are frequently spoken of as the most exacting of all duties and therefore as the most to be commended when properly fulfilled on all occasions. There is an explicit recognition among Yaquis that, on the one hand, their religious life is more demanding than that of other peoples, and, on the other, that this characteristic Yaqui way expresses the highest moral worth. [1980:312]

Although prayers frequently last between one and two hours, fiesteros never bear the burden of their responsibility alone. There is constant movement and a quiet shuffling of feet as every few minutes, with a simple tap on the shoulder, a helper, family member, friend, or compadre replaces the one kneeling. In a scene that would seem choreographed were it not for the occasional giggle or the whispers of instruction to those volunteering for the first time, the Yaqui ethic of mutual obligation and service to one another is unmistakably evident.

When I felt it was my turn, I nervously slipped my shoes from my feet. I genuflected to the altar and knelt down on the cold cement floor to relieve Cecilia. After receiving her flag I crossed myself again. Head bowed, I knelt in line, listening to the reverberation of Latin prayers and the soft click of rosary beads, the piney smell of incense hanging in the air. In less than five minutes one of Ana's moros placed her hand on my shoulder, ready to take my place. The veneration was followed by a procession through the Stations of the Cross in the churchyard surrounding the cemetery and finally by a long meeting during which the fiesteros began to plan for the culminating event of the year—the fiesta that was to be held the following spring.

When we returned to Ana's natal household later that afternoon, I was surprised by the amount of attention my actions had garnered. As we entered the compound Ana announced, "Kristi helped us to kneel!"

"And she carried the Virgin, too," Cecilia piped up.

"You carried the Virgin?" smiled their cousin Rosa.

"She beat you!" Cecilia chided her oldest daughter. Everyone beamed at me, and conversation about how I had helped continued throughout the day.

After that, whenever I attended a ritual or a feast or when I tagged along on social visits with Ana or her sisters, my Yaqui companions would be asked if I had helped Ana with her fiesta duties. "Did Kristi help cook for the fiesta?" "Did she walk the konti?" "Did Kristi make tortillas?" I received similar feedback on uncountable occasions when I accompanied Ana or other relatives to the household of distant relatives and ritual kin in order to attend wakes and quinceañeras. These social calls followed a predictable pattern. Ana would introduce me as a visiting anthropologist. I would be offered something to drink and a chair close to where the women were gathered, and they would politely go on about their business, speaking to one another in Yaqui and Spanish and preparing the evening's meal. The first few times Ana had to nudge me—"Show them!" Work would temporarily come to a halt, and all eyes would be trained on me as I self-consciously stood up, grabbed a ball of dough, and quickly pinched down the edges before patting it gently from hand to hand until it grew and stretched into the shape of a tortilla, ready to be tossed onto the comal.

"She knows how to make tortillas," one of the women would inevitably exclaim under her breath.

"Yes, she knows" or "She really knows how to work," Ana would smile. And conversation would then open up to include me, most often focusing on what I had learned to do while living in Potam.

In an article published in *American Anthropologist* in 1993 Kirin Narayan compellingly argues that we should avoid a monolithic classification of native anthropologists as "authentic" insiders and nonnative anthropologists as "objective" outsiders. Narayan opens her essay with the questions: "How 'native' is a native anthropologist? How 'foreign' is an anthropologist from abroad?" (1993:671). She calls upon researchers to refrain from overly simplified, dualistic assumptions, asking instead that we examine the "multiple" and fluctuating "loci along which we are aligned with or set apart from those whom we study" (Narayan 1993:671). By encouraging my practical involvement in everyday life and during ritual events, I believe that Ana and her relatives were doing something much more than merely gaining a helping hand or teaching a visiting anthropologist how things are properly done in a Yaqui community. Through a combination of their actions and local understandings of the meanings and expectations connected with the concept of lutu'uria, they transformed my status.

Yaquis' insistence on my material involvement incorporated me into their lives not as a guest but as fictive kin. One incident, involving the hospitality of Ana's sisters and the ambiguous status of a cousin's wife, sheds light on this transformation. On this particular occasion I was seated in the kitchen eating supper with Ana's sisters Cecilia and Perla. The children, who had already been fed, were darting in and out of the room, alternately sitting on our laps and grabbing scraps from the table. Cecilia had placed a steaming bowl of beans and a small plate of tortillas on another table that was situated within a few meters of where we sat. She called repeatedly in the direction of the bedroom, trying to coax her cousin's new wife to come out and be seated for her evening meal. This young woman and her husband lived in a distant village, and they rarely visited Potam. Although the cousin had grown up around Cecilia and Perla, his wife was as yet a little-known entity, and now she had been left with his relatives for the day—too distant to be family, yet too related to be a guest, she had remained in the bedroom watching television for most of the day. She hesitated for quite a while before coming out and then ate quietly; she promptly returned to the bedroom. Cecilia turned to me, raising her eyebrows. "She is embarrassed to eat."

I asked why she should be embarrassed. After all, I quipped, I was not even remotely related to them, and nevertheless here I was, unabashedly partaking of the family meal. Perla corrected me in her tenderly under-stated way: "Yes, but you are our sister." In a Yaqui home guests are cor-dially welcomed and offered a seat while the hostess disappears to prepare food and drink. Guests are served, sometimes finishing an entire meal in solitude before conversation begins. It is expected that guests will neither refuse hospitality nor help with the cooking. As an honorary sister I no longer needed to have a special reason to visit Cecilia and Perla's home. I had prepared meals for them and had shared hours in front of the wash-tub and the oven with them. I had served food to *their* guests and had cleaned up with them after parties. It was understood that I did not have to ask for food, nor would it be appropriate for me to feel embarrassed about accepting it. I had the right to hospitality but would never again be served separately as a guest. Rather, I was to eat with the family, in back rooms and kitchens, *after* the guests had eaten. Their allowing—even expecting—my practical involvement in their lives opened many doors for me, granting me access not only to information and ethnographic understanding but to lasting comfortable relationships, richly infused with humor and affection. This was their gift to me.

Narayan's contention that "sympathies and ties developed through engaged coexistence may subsume difference within relations of reciprocity" (1993:682) rings true when I reflect on my own experience in Potam. The Yaquis with whom I lived also cultivated an intersubjectivity achieved not through shared race, nationality, class, educational background, or religious affiliation but rather through copresence and the cooperative performance of labor. Narayan's (1993) essay concerns positionality and the negotiation of a relationship between an anthropologist and her interlocutor, both of whom are, in fact, complex, many-faceted selves. In essence, I am simply extending Narayan's thesis, arguing that field*working* alongside Yaquis enabled me to identify on a level apart from race, class, ethnicity, and gender. In a place where truth is equated with labor in service of others, it is not so inconceivable that fieldworking establishes, through practical copresence, an altogether different subjectivity and generates another way of knowing grounded in relationality.

Yaqui Identity, Yaqui Community

I interpret Yaquis' demands, especially Yaqui women's demands, for my participation as a way of forging another plane of identification. Here, once again, women succeeded in negotiating the parameters of identity—but this time it was my own identity that was being shaped, even if only temporarily. As female and indigenous, Yaqui women are doubly marginalized. Still, the fact that Yaqui women exercise authority and garner respect within their homes and communities, the fact that women's ritual labor is recognized as contributing to Yaqui cultural continuity, the fact that the domestic and ceremonial spaces occupied and socialized by women are key sites in the constitution and communication of ethnicity—these and innumerable other examples attest to Yaqui women's agency in the production of both identity and community. It is important to remember that women's ritual labor and devotional works, practices that generate and exemplify the tangible essence of Yaquiness, ultimately depend on a system of reciprocity grounded in an ethic of responsibility.

While Yaquis obligate themselves to one another, they are also intimately obligated to and identify with the place they call home, *itom hiak bwia* (our Yaqui land). For Yaquis home is the desert where they first met the European others who would challenge Yaqui claims to their own land and threaten their very existence, the space of encounter in which, according to the Talking Tree story, Yaqui identity was forged on the eve of Spanish invasion. Home is the landscape dotted with enchanted openings to an esoteric and highly valued cultural knowledge, the land for which their ancestors struggled against armies and governments, first Spanish, then Mexican. Home is the river-fed valley from which Yaquis were exiled in the late 1800s and to which they returned in the early 1900s, the territory of their aboriginal ancestors now constructed as the homeland through narrative and the multifarious practices of emplacement. Place—specifically *this place* in southern Sonora—is integral to Yaqui identity in terms of both Yaqui autochthony and the confirmation and perpetual re-creation of themselves as a people. Yet if Yaqui ethnic identity has been constructed in relation to a specific experience of place and history, if it is continually negotiated in relation to the Yori other, if Yaqui cultural identity is constituted in the staging of elaborate public rituals and in the intimate quiet of household ceremonies, it may be lutu'uria that most succinctly encapsulates a sense of what Yaquiness means and how it is to be enacted.

As it connects and obligates individuals to one another, lutu'uria draws individuals and families into a vast network of reciprocal giving and mutual responsibility. It becomes foundational to the ritual system that binds Yaqui towns to the saints who, in turn, watch over them and bless them. Yet lutu'uria also creates self-identity and community. One of the most significant ways Yaquis maintain social and ritual bonds is through a gifting of labor that highlights and hinges on intersubjective relationships. The Yaqui concept of lutu'uria is a distinctive articulation of this vision of intersubjectivity, an acknowledgment that relationality is grounded in a willingness to serve. For Yaquis in southern Sonora, lutu'uria—truth—is the fulfillment of one's social and ritual obligations. Viewed as a behavior that is supremely Yaqui (si hiaki), lutu'uria is also a quality that one has; it is a readiness to shoulder responsibility, to labor with good heart, to cooperate. It is a demonstration of one's social maturity and one's humanity. Lutu'uria, labor freely given in service to others, is a performance of Yaquiness that produces community itself.

Notes

Chapter 1

1. "Nostalgia," Stewart writes, "is everywhere. But it is a cultural practice, not a given content; its forms, meanings, and effects shift with the context—it depends on where the speaker stands in the landscape of the present" (1988:227).

2. This brief overview of Yaqui history is intended merely to introduce the reader to significant issues and concerns arising from the Yaqui history of contact and conflict with non-Yaquis. Historical events (as they pertain to Yaqui discourses of ethnicity, place, and cultural belonging) will be referenced in greater detail in chapters 2 and 3. The information summarized here is drawn from scholars who have examined Yaqui history in depth, including Hewitt de Alcantara (1976), Hu-DeHart (1974, 1981, 1984), Lutes (1987), McGuire (1986), Moisés, Kelley, and Holden (1971), Padilla Ramos (1995), and Spicer (1980), and from the 1645 writings of Father Andrés Pérez de Ribas (1944). For a thorough treatment and analysis of Yaqui history readers should consult these sources.

3. Construction of the dam has decreased the Yaqui River to all but a trickle for most of the year.

4. My understanding of ethnicity and collective identity has been most heavily influenced by the concise and compelling five-part definition provided by Comaroff and Comaroff (1992) as well as by Hall (1980) and Knight (1990) and the essays in Wilmsen and McAllister (1996a).

5. Throughout this book I use the term "Yaqui" rather than "Yoeme," following the practice of the majority of my consultants.

6. See Molina and Shaul (1993) for a Yaqui–English resource.

7. Over the past few decades scholars have convincingly argued for the need to question the notion of an "essential" self or subject (Butler 1999; Kondo 1990; Mouffe 1992) and have challenged academics to acknowledge the complex ways in which "being" is accomplished through various processes of "becoming" (Abu-Lughod 1991). Kondo describes concepts of the self as "strategic assertions, which inevitably suppress differences, tensions, and contradictions within" (1990:10). McRobbie writes, "Identity requires acts of identification, and this, in turn, implies agency and process" (1992:723). The processes through which Yaqui cultural–ethnic identification occurs happen in both formal and informal circumstances; they are both conscious and unconscious. Identities

are negotiated in narrative and through ordinary discourse and in actions both ceremonial and mundane.

8. As Figueroa Valenzuela explains, "The Yaquis define themselves as such from birth. This, although a necessary condition, is not sufficient. In order to be Yaqui, it is also necessary to define oneself as Yaqui, but this is still not sufficient. To be Yaqui means, among other things, to behave as Yaquis do, that is, to believe, feel, and act as Yaqui, and above all, to be defined as Yaqui" (1994:349–350).

9. In order to protect the identities of those with whom I worked I have substituted pseudonyms for real names, and, when necessary, I have altered minor details (such as the location of an interaction or the description of a person's occupation) by which they might be readily identified.

10. Sonora's Mayos are an indigenous people culturally and linguistically related to the Yaquis and are not to be confused with the Maya of southern Mexico.

11. Most Yaquis refer to Spanish as "Castilla," referring to *castellano*, or Castilian Spanish.

12. Individuals often refer to the Yaqui language simply as *la lengua* or *el dialecto* (the dialect).

13. As Flores reminds us, "Remembering is a deeply embedded social practice that informs the present" (2002:xvi).

Chapter 2

1. Although we cannot be certain as to what motivated the Yaquis to allow the establishment of a Jesuit mission on their land, Hu-DeHart speculates that the Yaquis were concerned for their own security in the face of a rapidly growing presence of foreigners around them (1981:28). Also, Spicer (1980:17–19) notes that over the years various groups of Yaquis had paid visits to nearby Sinaloa to observe the work of the missionaries there. Spicer interprets the Yaqui invitation to the Jesuits as being rooted in both religious and practical concerns: he claims that while they were interested in new rites and teachings, they also desired "the practical advantages that they had seen in the Sinaloa and Fuerte River country of cattle and goats and other domestic animals and the new ways of planting and the new farm products like wheat and peaches" (1980:19).

2. As the most prominent and lengthy example of a myth uniquely identified with the Yaquis, the Talking Tree has attracted the attention of numerous scholars of Yaqui culture (Evers and Molina 1993; Giddings 1993; Painter 1986; Ruíz Ruíz and Aguilar 1994; Sands 1983; Savala 1980; Valenzuela Kaczkurkin 1977), beginning with Spicer (1954, 1980, 1984), who argues that the myth's principal significance lies in its separation of baptized mortal Yaquis from their unbaptized "enchanted" ancestors—people of diminutive stature called Surem

(1954:121). Spicer maintains that the Talking Tree story "provides sanction for the conception of the dual universe," sacralizing both Yaqui aboriginal land and the Jesuit-era pueblos (1980:172). In her analysis of different versions of the story, Sands (1983) links the myth's survival to an amazing "flexibility"—the Yaquis' capacity to conserve indigenous concepts while incorporating Christianity as a central part of their identity. And Evers and Molina (1993:35–39) argue that the narrative's concept of the world as dual (simultaneously Christian and enchanted) is key to the understanding and interpretation of Yaqui deer songs.

3. Even though Ramón did not give a title to his narrative, I refer to it as the Talking Tree story, the shorthand title assigned to it by Edward Spicer. It is best known in the academic literature by this title, and referring to the story as such connotes the intertextual quality of Ramón's performance.

4. I present Ramón's narrative in interview format, indicating Ramón Hernández with RH in the margin and the place where I interject to ask a question with KE. My original Spanish transcriptions of selected portions of this narrative can be found in the appendix.

5. At this point in the narrative Ramón performed a reported speech act. He drastically altered his tone and pace as if assuming the voice of one of the Surem.

6. In other versions of the story the "wooden pole" is described as a "talking stick" (*kuta nokame* in the Yaqui language), a tree trunk, or a tree with branches that appears to sing or hum (see Evers and Molina 1993; Giddings 1993; Sands 1983).

7. In the Yaqui language *yo* means "ancient" or "enchanted" and *mumu* means "bee." Literally, then, Yomumuli is the Enchanted Bee. Evers and Molina suggest that, as the talking stick gives off a humming or vibrating noise, "the young girl or her parent is named for another sound, perhaps also metaphorical of [the] sound she translates" (1993:37).

8. The Yaqui word *sea* has numerous associations, the most significant of which is *sea anía*—the beautiful "flower world" of Yaqui cosmology.

9. One dark, clear evening I expressed pleasure at seeing a falling star. My companion, a young Yaqui schoolteacher, warned me to muffle my enthusiasm, explaining that the "sea monsters" who are always peeking their heads out of the water might become aware that there are falling stars and would hide themselves beneath the cover of the sea. Falling stars protect human beings by killing the sea monsters.

10. In the past, traveling through the bush alone and even travel outside of the pueblo on foot were typically male practices.

11. This segment of Ramón's narrative may be an imported motif—it alludes to a story Spicer recorded during his research in Sonora in the 1940s "of a contest between a Yaqui bowman and the King of Spain. It was arranged that the Yaqui hero should shoot as far as he could in several directions and thus mark

the extent of the Yaqui territory. If he shot farther than the King, then the King would recognize the Yaqui possession of the land so marked out. The Yaqui bowman did shoot better than the King. A document was made out giving the bounds of the land; the King of Spain signed it, thus giving his sanctions to the Yaqui rights in a tribal territory" (1980:170).

12. Muriel Thayer Painter's Tucsonan Yaqui informants explicitly told her that the Surem exist in the *yo anía* (ancient or enchanted world) (1986:5). Through his work in both Arizona and Sonora Spicer also learned that the Surem are now the immortal inhabitants of the yo anía (1980:64–67, 172). The power and inspiration of the pascolas and deer dancers are associated with the Surem (Spicer 1980:67).

13. Velasquez's version was recorded in Kompwertam, Sonora.

14. This translation (from a Spanish translation of the original Yaqui) is my own; except for the ellipses, the text preserves the punctuation of the original written version.

15. I do not believe that Hu-DeHart, Spicer, and others are arguing that the Yaquis lacked a sense of group identity prior to the European presence. In fact, it is clear from the observations of newcomers during the colonial era that Yaqui group identity did exist before their sixteenth-century encounter with Spanish explorers and missionaries: the members of the rancherías along the Yaqui River could generate a force of over 8,000 warriors when necessary, and they clearly differentiated themselves from the Mayo people who lived in the river valley 80 kilometers to their south (Hu-DeHart 1981:11–14). But the Yaquis' relationship with their indigenous neighbors (in contrast to that which eventually emerged between themselves and the representatives of New Spain) was one that might more aptly be characterized, as the Comaroffs write, in terms of "symmetrical relations between structurally similar social groupings" (1992:54). In other words, the groups were distinct, but their relation to one another was that of relatively equal powers. Both the Yaquis and the Mayos belong to the Cáhitan language group, differing only in dialect; they had contiguous traditional territories, similar religious rites and material culture, a common mythology, and similar forms of marriage and kinship organization (Figueroa Valenzuela 1992). It is significant that the Yaquis' name for themselves, the Yoeme/Yoreme, is most strongly counterposed not to other local Indian groups (who are often called *otros Yoremes* [other people]) but to non-Yaqui "whites," labeled Yorim (strangers or foreigners). Hu-DeHart, Spicer, and others, espousing academic theories of Yaqui cultural change, posit that the *quality* of Yaqui collective identity was fundamentally altered as the presence of the other brought with it a new and radical power imbalance (as the Yaquis were incorporated first into an empire and later into a nation-state) and that *this* is ethnicity, distinctly different from other types of group identity.

16. Whatever its source, Ramón's ambivalence may index the continuing hegemony of certain forms of historical discourse in the present; no matter

how far we claim to have expanded our conceptual horizons, particular modes of historical accounting are still privileged (Hill 1988; see also Chernela 1988; Hulme and Whitehead 1992; Price 1990; Reeve 1988; Rosaldo 1980).

Chapter 3

1. There are large Yaqui communities in and around the Arizona cities of Tucson and Phoenix.

2. Because renting Yaqui land to non-Yaquis is not sanctioned by tribal authorities there is no official documentation of the number of these arrangements. However, multiple informants, Yaquis and non-Yaquis alike, offered similar estimates.

3. When I requested a translation of "Yori," Luz, like most of my Yaqui informants, said that a Yori is a *blanco* (white). See Hewitt de Alcantara (1976) for a discussion of transformations in Yaqui agriculture during the twentieth century.

4. This dichotomy can be found in Mexican political language of the late 1800s. After Mexican independence in 1821 the majority of Yaquis did not wish to acquiesce to the status of Mexican citizenship. Because they resisted the appropriation of their lands they were perceived to be a disorderly menace to the consolidation of a "modern" and "civilized" Mexico. Popular among many intellectuals at the time, academic discourses of social Darwinism and scientific racism were readily adopted by President Díaz and his cohort at the end of the nineteenth century in order to legitimize the subordination of rights and interests of both peasant and indigenous peoples (Knight 1990:78–79). Like the Apaches, who had for so long vexed the northern extension of the Spanish empire in New Spain, Mexico's Yaquis were seen as a barbarous, fierce people (see Alonso 1995; Hu-DeHart 1984:138). Surprisingly, such discourses can still be heard today as rural indigenous peoples are stereotyped and unfavorably compared to their more "civilized" mestizo–urban counterparts. For another interesting discussion of the misuse of the term *nomad* in the New World see Ramos's "Keywords for Prejudice" (1998:33–40).

5. Spicer (1980) published the first and most complete accounts of Yaqui cultural history and land mythology. Evers and Molina (1992b) write insightfully about how Yaqui actors orally and textually reinscribe the boundaries of their homeland and establish a connection between place and identity.

6. I have heard the Yaqui homeland referred to, in the Yaqui language, as itom hiak bwia (our Yaqui land). Consultants frequently translated the concept into Spanish as *las tierras Yaquis* (the Yaqui lands). When used in the context of discussions about Yaqui identity, these terms encapsulate Yaqui territory as an entity, distinguishing it from its surrounding state of Sonora. At the same time, "itom hiak bwia/las tierras Yaquis" designate the Yaquis' relationship with their homeland as aboriginal yet also forged through a history of hardship and perseverance.

In *Yaqui Deer Songs* Evers and Molina describe another (perhaps more formal) term for the homeland: "Yaqui is now the principal name the *Yoemem* apply to themselves. And they commonly now refer to the whole of their lands as *hia-kimpo*, literally translated 'in Yaquis,' or more truly as 'in the homeland'" (1993:43; see also Evers and Molina 1992a).

7. This interview, conducted and recorded in Spanish, was prompted by a series of stories about the Yaqui resistance that Inez had spontaneously shared with me on the day we first met. The stories, compelling in and of themselves and obviously well rehearsed, were made even more gripping by Inez's talent for dramatic narration. At that initial encounter I regretted that I did not have my tape recorder, so I requested a formal "interview" so that I could transcribe Inez's stories more accurately.

8. Huirivis, Rahum, and Belem are Yaqui pueblos to the northwest of Potam, occupying the territory closest to the Mexican city of Guaymas.

9. The deportations commenced in 1900 after the Battle of Mazocoba, reaching their height between 1906 and 1908 (Padilla Ramos 1995:66, 131). The majority of the Sonoran deportees to Central Mexico (Yaqui men, women, and children) were destined for servitude on the henequen plantations of Yucatán.

10. I am indebted to anonymous reviewers and friends who encouraged me to emphasize the discursive context in which these narratives are continually produced and reproduced.

11. The motivation behind the forced removal is clearly revealed in a telegram that was sent by Sonora's governor, Luis Torres, to President Díaz, requesting "authorization to send [Yaquis] . . . to Acapulco or Tonalá (in order to) deport them to some point from which they might never return" (quoted in Padilla Ramos 1995:104).

12. Henequen (*Agave fourcroydes*) thrives in the sunny, hot climate of Mexico's Yucatán peninsula. Sisal (*Agave sisalana*) is a different but related species that grows in other tropical areas. Both types are referred to as "sisal hemp" (Joseph 1988:13).

13. Padilla Ramos (1995:103) records one transport coordinator who claimed that his Yaqui charges were sold for 65 pesos per person, 10 of which he retained for his costs, the remainder going to the secretary of war.

14. The term *criollo* is ordinarily taken to mean a person of European ancestry born in Mexico (or any Latin American country). In this case, however, Luz employs the term in a more general way to identify non-Yaqui Mexicans as whites. Luz usually refers to Mexicans, the majority of whom are mestizo (of mixed European and indigenous ancestry) as *blancos* (whites).

15. Yaqui discourses of ethnic belonging often begin and end with blood: to be a Yaqui is equated (at least ideologically) with having Yaqui parents. Therefore, having children, especially with those who had forced them from their homeland, is portrayed as undesirable behavior.

16. The word "travel" itself is inappropriate in the Yaqui context, for, as Clifford points out, it "has an inextinguishable taint of location by class, gender, race, and a certain literariness" (1997:39). While discomfort with "travel" may be linked to social, class, or economic distance, we must also consider the possibility that such discomfort may be informed by the Yaquis' legacy of displacement.

17. INAH has a branch in the heart of Hermosillo's historic city center, housing offices, a museum, and a library.

18. See chapter 7 for a close examination of ritual kinship, reciprocity, and networks of dependence among Yaquis.

19. Geertz introduced the idea of the "model of" and "model for" in his classic essay "Religion as a Cultural System" (1973).

Chapter 4

1. In my attempt to interpret and to write about these stories and their places I look to sociologist Avery Gordon (1997). Gordon understands hauntings and enchantments not as quaint and folkloric but as socially significant—part of a thoroughly modern discourse. Gordon explains that her book *Ghostly Matters* is about "haunting, a paradigmatic way in which life is more complicated than those of us who study it have usually granted" (1997:7). In short, "it is essential to write about societies and people enthralled by magic, enchanted, possessed and entranced, disappeared, and haunted because, well, it is more common than you might have considered" (Gordon 1997:197). Gordon contends that such narratives should be taken seriously, because "to be haunted is to be tied to historical and social effects"; the "ghost is not simply a dead or missing person, but a social figure. . . . The way of the ghost is haunting, and haunting is a very particular way of knowing what has happened or is happening" (1997:190, 8).

2. Mazocoba, a battle fought between Yaquis and the Mexican army in the Yaqui Sierra de Bacatete in 1900, was catastrophic for the Yaquis. An estimated 400 Yaquis died, and 800 were taken prisoner; while General Tetabiate was not captured or killed in this clash, he was assassinated two years later (Hu-DeHart 1974:79; Spicer 1980:153). Most significantly, following the Battle of Mazocoba, the Mexican government initiated its program of deporting Yaqui citizens to Yucatán (Padilla Ramos 1995:66).

3. See Spicer (1980:144); Hu-DeHart (1984:88–89).

4. In his essay "Between Memory and History" Pierre Nora points to the power of *lieux de mémoire* (sites of memory), which include cemeteries and archives, statues and commemorations—deliberately constructed monuments to the past "where memory crystallizes and secretes itself" in a historical moment when "*milieux de mémoire*, real environments of memory," no longer exist (1989:7).

5. I do not know if the number of violent encounters has actually increased. Most people do not report attacks, and there is little confidence in local police,

who are frequently perceived as an arm of the "Yori government." In any case, I contend that such narratives of violent encounter are extremely important.

6. See the appendix for my original Spanish transcriptions of selected portions of Pedro Molina's narratives.

7. Evers and Molina's informants identify the Yaqui homeland as "Hiakim" (1992a). When questioned directly, my own informants referred to the Yaqui homeland as *itom bwía* (our land) or *itom hiak bwía* (our Yaqui land).

Chapter 5

1. Although Cecilia's mother and aunt share the plot of land on which their homes are built, they and their adult children run essentially separate extended family households. Each of the elderly sisters has her own kitchen, outhouse, and bathing facilities.

2. At the time of my fieldwork this translated to a value of between U.S. $7.70 and $10.00 for her day's labor. While whole cobs sold for one peso per kilogram, degrained cobs brought a better price: wet grains of corn sold for a minimum of eight pesos per kilogram; fully dried grains brought a minimum of nine pesos per kilo.

3. *Konti* means "surrounding" in the Yaqui language. The konti ceremony is an event in which the fiesteros (specially designated hosts of the fiesta) and their helpers honor the patron saint of the pueblo. The weekly konti involves a lengthy prayer session conducted in Latin. Fiesteros and their helpers take turns kneeling in front of the church's main altar, then process around the outside of the church, with several stops for the repetition of rosaries and the blessing of fiesteros. Cecilia played a significant role in Rahum's fiesta (the annual religious festival in honor of the patron saint) by assisting her sister, who had been selected as one of four *fiesteras* (female fiesta hosts) for the year spanning June 1997 to June 1998.

4. Ciudad Obregón, the second largest city in Sonora, is located just south of the Yaqui Zone. The latest Mexican national census figures available online are those for 2000 (XII Censo General de Población y Vivienda, Principales resultados por localidad, Sonora). According to INEGI, Obregón had 250,790 inhabitants in 2000 (INEGI 2000). Other unofficial sources estimate the population of Obregón to be closer to 450,000 (Enciclopedia Libre Universal 2007).

5. A house cross is a 1.5-meter-high wooden cross erected in the swept patio or yard in the center of the Yaqui compound. The cross is usually replaced or renewed every year during Lent, signaling a household's willing support of Lenten ceremonial societies and their activities. Most important household ceremonies occur in front of the house cross.

6. Both Yaqui chile and the traditional wakabaki are considered appropriate fare for important occasions.

7. *Lobos* (wolves) here refers to the *lobos marinos* (seals), which pass through this region on their yearly migration, making it Bahía de Lobos, or Seal Bay.

8. The Chapayekas are one of several Yaqui ceremonial societies. These masked dancers represent the soldiers of the Pharisees, evil ones in pursuit of Christ. During the Lenten season it is the Chapayekas who assume control of the pueblo. The duties of a Chapayeka are numerous and arduous. They include keeping constant vigilance over Potam's streets, observing absolute silence when the mask is donned, marching for hours under the hot sun during Semana Santa, sleeping for many nights on the hard cement floor of the church, sexual prohibitions, and obeying strictures against drinking.

9. The junior high is located a few kilometers to the west of Potam; the high school is in Vicam, 20 kilometers by road.

10. "Selling" means traveling to the city by bus and walking door to door in the city's middle-class *colonias* (neighborhoods).

11. Cecilia's work at her sister's home (a separate household) was a combination of paid and gifted labor. While the domestic chores and child care she undertook were part of the reciprocal exchanges that occur in every family, the 20-peso-per-day salary Cecilia earned for tending the store was perceived of as a wage by both sisters rather than as a redistribution of profits. Although many Yaqui couples and their children reside on a compound with parts of their extended families (sharing cooking and other facilities), the individual nuclear family units within the larger group remain relatively economically autonomous; income sharing is not a common practice in Yaqui extended families.

12. Here my characterization of Yaqui women's interventions as "tactical" is based on a consideration from the perspective of the national–regional economic system, where Yaqui women are identified as an economically vulnerable, politically disempowered ethnic minority. Michel de Certeau (1984) differentiates those responses that are tactical from those he considers strategic. According to Certeau, "a tactic is an art of the weak" (1984:37), whereas a strategy is formulated from a certain position of power. He writes, "Strategies are able to produce, tabulate, and impose [spaces] . . . whereas tactics can only use, manipulate, and divert these spaces" (Certeau 1984:30). Of course, the economic tactics of specific individuals can, *at the same time*, be thought of as "strategies," when considered on the local level, in terms of interpersonal and interfamilial relationships and power. A woman's decisions of how and when to labor may significantly impact (and may be affected by) her position in her community or family.

13. Established in 1965 under the Border Industrialization Program, maquiladoras are assembly plants located on the south side of the U.S.–Mexico border. Everything from electronics to chemicals, clothing to cassettes to automobile parts are assembled in maquiladoras. As the cost of labor and administration (as well as the "costs" entailed by environmental and labor laws and strong unions)

have been comparatively lower in Mexico than in the United States and in other "First World" nations, U.S. and other foreign companies invested heavily from the 1960s to the 1990s in the tax-free zone south of the border (Iglesias-Prieto 1997:xxiii–xxvi). Maquiladoras are "labor-intensive" factories "dedicated to the assembly of components, the processing of primary materials, or both, producing either intermediate or final products," which are then re-exported (Iglesias-Prieto 1997:xxiii). Iglesias-Prieto argues that the fragmentation of the production process itself combined with isolation from the parent company disempowers the worker and inhibits collective action (1997:17–18). Assembly work tends to follow the lowest labor costs: recent competition from China has precipitated the closure of hundreds of maquiladora plants in northern Mexico (see Rosenberg 2007). Since 2000 there has been a reported loss of tens of thousands of maquiladora jobs in places like Ciudad Juárez, Nogales, and other cities on Mexico's northern border (Moreno 2004), further unsettling an already vulnerable workforce.

14. In 2001 approximately 60 percent of Nogales's 300,000 people were employed in maquila industries (Ibarra 2003).

15. Lorenia is a typical maquiladora worker in another way as well. Along with the "feminization of poverty" (Pearce 1978), researchers have noted the feminization of some of the lowest-paying and most insecure sectors of Mexico's economy (Benería and Roldán 1987). Yet, as Jane Collins points out, age and ethnic background often combine in unpredictable ways in targeting a workforce: "Gender never operates simply, or in isolation, in these labor markets, but in connection with a host of other factors, including race, ethnicity, citizenship status and migrancy" (1995:182). Aihwa Ong's (1987) observations of factory workers in a Malaysian free trade zone resonate with the hiring practices of many multinational corporations in rapidly industrializing nations (including Mexico), where women workers are preferred to men because they are perceived to be more dexterous, less of a discipline problem, more amenable to repetitive work, willing to work for less money, and less likely to unionize (Iglesias-Prieto 1997; Ong 1987:151–155).

16. Although my evidence regarding education is anecdotal, it does seem that Yaqui teenagers and young adults are also availing themselves of educational opportunities to a greater extent. When I first conducted fieldwork in the summer of 1995 and then again in 1996–97, many of my most trusted consultants happened to be teachers. Of the eight teachers I knew best (men and women who were 25–45 years of age), only three had completely finished their teacher training through courses at either a traditional college or a normal school. I knew many other women and men of my generation and older who hadn't finished high school (la preparatoria)—individuals who had made it only through elementary school or who had been forced to leave school after junior high (la secundaria) in order to help out at home or in the fields. Only a tiny minority had been to college or normal school.

Ten years have passed since I began fieldwork in the 1990s. In stark contrast to Yaqui men and women of my own generation, all of the young people I know who were grade-schoolers in 1996–97 either have finished high school or are currently enrolled. Many others are now going to college, either four-year colleges, institutions that grant associate-level degrees, or normal schools. For instance, many younger members of Ana's own extended family are in college: Cecilia's oldest daughter is training to be a grade school teacher in an ordinary *normal*; Ana's niece is studying to be a high school biology teacher in a *normal superior*. Cecilia's son Ricardo was able to finish high school and has enrolled in a computer-programming program in Hermosillo. He lives with Marco and Ana on weekends, helping out at their house in exchange for their payment of his tuition. Competition to win a space in colleges and universities is perceived to be fierce, but whether in agroengineering or law, computer programming, accounting, or education, postsecondary education has become a reality for many.

Chapter 6

1. This sentiment highlights the historical continuity of Yaqui social organization. Spicer observed in 1937 that in the Yaqui community of Pascua, Arizona, it is "the household, which may be regarded, rather than the elementary family, as the fundamental social grouping" (1984:79). He found this to be equally true in Potam, Sonora (Spicer 1954, 1984).

2. This formulation is inspired by the seminal work of Judith Butler (1999 [1990]), who has unpacked the process of the performative constitution of gendered identities. Butler argues that "gender attributes . . . effectively constitute the identity they are said to express or reveal. The distinction between expression and performativeness is quite crucial, for if gender attributes and acts, the various ways in which a body shows or produces its cultural signification, are performative, then there is no preexisting identity by which an act or attribute might be measured" (1990:279). We must also bear in mind, as Lise Nelson (1999) argues in her critical reworking of Butler's theory, that this phenomenon is always spatially and geographically contingent.

3. Ranchera music is a traditional popular form played by small bands. Instrumentation typically includes guitars, an accordion, and at times a trumpet or other horns. Northern Mexican ranchera music is often played in a style referred to as *música norteña* (northern music), and some groups perform both traditional rancheras and corridos (Broyles-González 2002; Wikipedia n.d.). Groups hired for pueblo events (feast-day dances, fundraisers, quinceañeras, weddings, etc.) may be local or of regional fame.

4. Today, as in Spicer's time, household units are flexible in their composition (see Spicer 1984:79–80). I am aware of households with as many as five nuclear families, but the norm lies somewhere between one and three. While

some nuclear families do occupy their own compounds, residences tend toward bilocality, arising from the need for economic and social support. In a typical arrangement an elderly couple shares a compound with one or more sons or daughters, their spouses, and their children (see Spicer 1954:58).

5. A ramada is an open-air shelter that provides protection from rain and direct sunlight. Ramadas may adjoin one side of a house, or they may be free-standing. Roofing varies and may be constructed of thatch-covered carrizo panels, petates lashed together, or sheets of tin.

6. Writing about the centrality of homeplace and about her experiences growing up as an African American in a segregated community, literary and cultural critic bell hooks explains, "In our young minds houses belonged to women, were their special domain, not as property, but as places where all that truly mattered in life took place—the warmth and comfort of shelter, the feeding of our bodies, the nurturing of our souls. There we learned dignity, integrity of being; there we learned to have faith" (1990:41–42). There appear to be many similarities between bell hooks's childhood community and a Yaqui pueblo.

7. Historically rooted in pan-Mediterranean practices and beliefs, the Latin American honor–shame discourse clearly influences the negotiation of gender roles among Yaquis. Such "honor codes," argues historian Steve Stern, exist "both as cultural ideals and as a source of misleading stereotypes that recur in the lived culture as well as the scholarship about the culture" (1995:14). Stern explains that in colonial Mexico "a woman's duty to cultivate a well-developed sense of shame, a sensitivity to moral duty and reputation that screened her from social circumstances inviting opprobrium, called upon her to adopt social appearances that contrasted with those prescribed for honored men. These appearances included a submissive posture of obedience, support, and acceptance in household relations with husbands, fathers, and elders; a fierce regard for sexual propriety—virginity by daughters, fidelity by wives, abstinence by widows; and a respect for social place and decorum whose female version emphasized a sense of self-enclosure and discretion" (1995:14–15). Such ideals of honor and shame can and do become exaggerated stereotypes of a Latin American disposition, yet any scholar of this vast region must be aware of the historical persistence of these ideologies and the ways in which notions of honor and shame are either ignored, resisted, or invoked to justify the demand for certain modes of behavior (see Stern 1995).

Yaquis have experienced nearly 400 years of continuous contact with people of European descent. Yaquis have intermarried extensively with mestizos and other Indians, and they have adopted Catholicism, reshaping it in their own unique way. There has been a great deal of exchange between Europeans and Yaquis. This cultural give-and-take becomes readily apparent upon even the most cursory observation of the Yaqui sex–gender system (see Butler 1999), as Yaqui gender ideologies and practices resonate with those of Mexico's mainstream cultural milieu.

8. Roger Lancaster points out that the cultural process of naturalizing the abstract ideologies of honor and shame into ideal (and stereotypical) female dispositions is strongly associated with a specific role—that of "elevated motherhood" (1992:93). Academic discourses posit the existence of *marianismo*, a concept that is complementary but unequal to machismo (Lancaster 1992:310). Marianismo is a heuristic tool, a short-handed way for scholars of Latin American cultures to evoke a "complex of images of the ideal woman" (Lancaster 1992:93). As Lancaster explains, the "term draws on the Virgin Mary as the model for appropriate womanhood" (1992:93). This, as Ana María Alonso notes, is a "paradox," for, "like Mary, the ideal [northern Mexican] woman ... is both virgin and mother" (1995:85).

Throughout Mexico the attributes of virtuous motherhood are gathered up in the symbol of the Virgin Mary. But to an even greater degree the brown-skinned Virgin of Guadalupe, "the Indian Virgin Mary who appeared miraculously in early colonial times to symbolize the Virgin's specific protection of and devotion to Mexico's indigenous and mestizo peoples" (Stern 1995:342), is celebrated as a saint and national icon—"the Queen of Mexico" (Monsiváis 1997:37). While one can acknowledge that gender ideologies do not categorically limit or control behavior in any predictable manner, one must also realize that such ideologies do have some degree of impact upon every member of society, that they are meaningful and have concrete implications. Honor–shame discourses take various forms throughout Latin America and, along with the linked stereotypes of the "macho," the *abnegada* (self-sacrificing woman), and the "ideal mother," this ideological complex has had tangible effects upon Yaqui cultural practice as well.

9. Itom Ae has long been a meaningful figure to poteños. In the 1940s Spicer wrote that the name Itom Ae is often "applied by Yaquis to all the female images of the church which also go by the name of Mary, or the Virgin, and also to crosses used in ceremony. The applications of the term itom ae to all the images of Mary is regarded, however, by the maestros and other church officials as a loose usage. They feel that strictly it should be reserved for the single female figure which is placed at the top of the altar in most ceremonies, the small blue-robed image called Rosario or Conception" (Spicer 1954:115).

10. The social consumption of alcohol is a conspicuously male practice among the Yaquis and is generally regarded as an unacceptable behavior for women. There certainly are those women who drink, but during the time I lived in Potam I never saw an inebriated Yaqui woman. Alcoholic husbands are a major point of concern; women's talk often revolves around the subject of a husband's or father's recent binge, and some women go to curanderas in search of curative powders that they might covertly cook into a husband's meal in order to cure him of his proclivity for alcohol.

11. Although a woman is granted a certain immediate respect upon becoming a mother, age is also a significant factor; an elderly mother not only is venerated

within her own family but becomes a sought-after figure within the larger community. Regina's insistence that "the woman is *la que manda*" very specifically describes older, not younger, women. Indeed, while younger wives are sometimes central figures in their own families, those whose control becomes too overt or too obvious run head-on into the ideals of patriarchy. A young wife whose family leadership is displayed too publicly might be disparaged behind her back, her husband called a *mandilón*, a derogatory label stemming from the Spanish word *mandil* (apron), connoting a man who is too controlled by his wife, tied up in her apron strings.

12. Yaqui homeplaces embody what José Davíd Saldívar calls "the complex predicaments of gendered social space" (1997:85). Cultural and literary critic Jean Franco contends that while homeplace viewed as "sanctuary obviously makes it into a male-idealized otherness (the utopia) while locking women into . . . pacific domesticity," such spaces historically "gave women a certain territorial but restricted power base" (1999:13, 12).

13. La Mano Poderosa is frequently displayed on Yaqui home altars. It depicts Christ's wounded hand emerging from a cloud, with members of the holy family standing atop his outstretched fingers.

14. Many other events or portions of events are celebrated in the home, including wedding receptions; the procession, dance, and dinner for a quinceañera; and children's birthday piñatas.

15. In every Yaqui family the names of the dead are handwritten into a small, paperbound book called the *Aniimam* (meaning "souls" in the Yaqui language, an adaptation of the Spanish word *ánima* [soul]). Characteristically, the eldest woman in the family is the keeper of the *Aniimam*, and by maintaining and adding names to this book she becomes a repository of family memory.

16. Observed on November 1 and 2, the Days of the Dead encompass both All Saints' Day and All Souls' Day, or El Día de los Difuntos (also referred to as El Dia de los Muertos).

17. Juanita Garciagodoy observes that in rural, predominantly indigenous regions of Mexico the celebration of the Days of the Dead has an "earnest," folkloric character that is very different from the resistive, counterhegemonic, or "carnivalesque" parodies common to urban popular practice (1998:79–85). In Sonora it is an attitude of earnestness as well as the rootedness of Days of the Dead practices in Yaqui home space that serve to differentiate indigenous (Yaqui) from mestizo.

Chapter 7

1. At the time this was equivalent to a little over U.S. $13.00.

2. The pails are typically filled with chile (beef, potatoes, and olives in a thick chile pasillo salsa), atole (flour porridge flavored with sugar and cinnamon),

and wakabaki (garbanzo beans, beef, and vegetables in a clear broth soup), all homemade.

3. The exception to this is the baptism of consecutive children, which will be discussed shortly.

4. Women friends who have become coparents are expected to address one another as "comadre" rather than by their given names in order to acknowledge the relationship of respect. Alternatively, diminutives of these forms of address are used to signify endearment: comadres may be called "comadrita"; a child may address her madrina directly as "nina" or refer to her padrino as "nino."

5. The sketch of the fiesta that follows is provided to establish a baseline for a discussion of identity and the fiesta as well as a consideration of the role of reciprocity and relationality in organizing a fiesta. This is not meant to be an exhaustive account of fiesta activities, fiesta roles and responsibilities, or the order of fiesta events. The Yaqui fiesta's organization has been thoroughly described and analyzed by Spicer (1954:72–77, 1980:187–195). Although over half a century has passed since Spicer conducted his research, the fiesta's organization remains virtually unchanged, with only a few minor alterations. This continuity stands as a testament both to the importance of the fiesta itself and to the exactitude of the oral transmission of ritual expectations for this ceremony.

6. The Yaqui leadership structure is a thorough integration of political and religious aspects. The Yaqui *ya'uram* (leadership), or, as Spicer called them, the five "realms of authority," are "closely interlocked authorities, which may take the lead in certain important matters, but whose decisions are always subject to review by and adjustment with the other authorities" (1954:55, 96). Constituting the civil–ceremonial leadership of each of the Yaqui Ocho Pueblos, the five ya'uram are composed of (1) the church council, including the church governor, kiyostes, Matachines, and maestros; (2) the civil authorities, including pueblo governors; (3) the military authorities, including ceremonial captains and their underlings; (4) the Kohtumbre ("Customs Authority"), or ceremonial societies that assume control of the pueblos during Lent, including the Pilatos, the Chapayekas, and the Soldiers; and (5) the fiesteros, each contingent composed of a first captain (*kapita yo'owe*), a second captain (*kapita segundo*), a sheriff (*alawasin*), and a flag bearer (*alpés*), and their corresponding female companions and moros, or helpers (Spicer 1954:73, 1980:179–204; see also McGuire 1986:21–25).

7. The *–os* ending of the plural form *fiesteros* is inclusive of both male and female actors.

8. Spicer provides more examples, stating that even "the villagers who come to ceremonies and kneel in church, march in processions, and make the *muhti* [minor ritualistic acts of devotion performed by an individual before an altar; see also Spicer 1954:156] are also, in the Yaqui view, carrying out ceremonial labor. The people in the households also perform it when they set up altars

and receive church groups and ceremonial societies for death ceremonies and Lenten fiestas" (1954:177).

9. Detailed descriptions of these and other male vs. female ceremonial roles may be found in Spicer's "Church and Ceremonial Societies" (1954:78–93).

10. Scott (1985) utilizes Goffman's notion of front and back regions to discuss peasant resistance and to debunk the notion of false consciousness in situations of apparent compliance of the peasantry to the designs of the elite. In another study MacCannell (1973) employs the same concept to decode the search for authenticity in the tourist experience. Both scholars view frontstage and backstage regions as useful heuristic devices or ideals (MacCannell 1973) rather than as true dichotomies.

11. Admittedly, with my readings about the "frontstage" and "backstage" of performances and my overly rigid notions of "audience" and "performer," I was likely the only one surprised by this blending of spaces.

12. Here, Richard Flores's article "'Los Pastores' and the Gifting of Performance" (1994), a study of Los Pastores, a Nativity shepherd's play performed by Mexican Americans in the San Antonio region, is instructive. Flores examines the "structures of feeling" (Williams 1977) associated with the performance of Los Pastores in different venues. Following Marx, Flores distinguishes between the labor of performance as "free action associated with praxis" vs. labor that is the "alienated activity of human misery" (1994:277). In the backyards and patios of *mexicano* neighborhoods, among family and friends, the work of hosting the shepherds play and the performance of Los Pastores itself are labors of "gratitude" and acts of devotion (Flores 1994:279). Flores's analysis goes a long way toward illuminating the sensibilities that also underlie the Yaqui concept of ritual labor. Whether performed in household ceremonies, exchanged between close relatives, or contributed to the fiesta, the labor of tekípanoa becomes a "transformative gift" "founded on a process that accentuates the social relations that constitute it" (Flores 1994:280, 278). Such exchanges, based in reciprocity, strengthen and even generate the relations that create society.

Appendix
Narrative Transcriptions

Selected Portions of Ramón Hernandez's Narrative

Chapter 2

"The Mexicans? The Mexicans, well, they are just Mexicans." Los mexicanos? Los mexicanos, pues, ellos son mexicanos. Y a través del tiempo, pues, este, han traído muchas consecuencias nos, los mexicanos. A través del tiempo, en los tiempos pasados pues, la tribu Yaqui era una sola tribu Yaqui. Nada más. Una sola tribu. Sí. Antes de llegar los españoles. Pero sí, ya se había platicado, no? Por medio de su dioses, la tribu Yaqui. Y por medio de sus sueños, ellos platicaban, se entendían unos desastres se llegan por ellos. El sol era el padre de todos. Lo utilizaron como si fuera un papá, el sol. Y la luna, pues, este, también, la utilizaron como si fuera su mamá. La respetaban mucho. A la luna, mmm. Y a través del tiempo pues, parece que la tribu Yaqui antes de llegar los españoles, tenía una visión por medio de sabiduría. Ellos ya tenían sus propias costumbres, pero muy anticuadas, hmm? Y a través del tiempo después, no, una poetisa Yaqui dijo que con el tiempo iba ver otra generación, en otra forma. Y con el testamento de todo esto, no? Entendiendo bien, por medio de sus pensamientos, y por medio de hablar ellos, no, con los astros, y con toda clase de animales.

"In those times they passed the story along." En aquellos tiempos la escribían (pero por puras palabras, con puras palabras) de los Sures. Parece que hace cinco mil años o por aquí, no, pasó esa gente. . . .

En un tiempo, hasta acá, hasta Belem, en esa parte mandaban también, dominaron los estos, los Pimas. Los Pimas, no? Porque no pudo mudarse pa'al norte. Movieron para acá, no? Hacer siembras. . . . Y después del tiempo, pues, ya como empezó llegar los españoles aquí. Los mexicanos, los Yaquis. Ya se han platicado tantas veces, no? La de los Ocho Pueblos.

Esa fecha, no, desaparecieron de aquí los, los Pimas. Pero mucho más antes, estaban los Sures aquí. Es una teoría. He andado mucho yo, no? Haciendo pláticas. Investigando, no? En los Sures. . . . Y un tiempo, en la tierra encontré un metatito así. Metate así. Todavía está por allá. Una gente muy chaparrita así, los Sures. Hmm. Pero supone, no, que este que dicen, hmm, los antepasados, que sí existían esa gente. Y luego este, que muy, muy sabes también. Supieron que iban a andar los españoles aquí. Algunos montaron a la sierra y otros se huyeron bajo, bajo la tierra aquí. Hmm?

Está una poetisa Yaqui, no? Iban a ir por ella. Aquí en el cerro el Omteme, allí en esa parte, no, se apareció una madera, no? Una madera así, alta. . . . Hizo un sonido como telégrafo así, no? Así. Pero nadie entendió. Fueron por un sabio que vivía por allí. Hay otros sabios, no, y fueron por ellos también. . . . Ya creo que se enojó. Se enojó porque, "Cómo va a juntar esa gente aquí?" Y dicen esto "enojado," el Cerro Enojado, Omteme. Kawi Omteme. Y ya, hay que hacer la pregunta a todos animalitos, aves que iban por allí. Hacen la pregunta. . . .

"And so they went for the young woman." Y ya fueron por este, la muchacha, una poetisa Yaqui. Y pues ya llegaron allá. Y aceptó ella. Y dice, "Mañana, temprano voy para allá. Tengo que notificar a mi papá y todos. . . .

"Well, here I am. Now I am here." "Bueno, ya vine. Ya estoy aquí." Eran los saludos de ellos, no? "Haisa wewu, haisa wewu. Haisa wewu." Era el saludo porque todavía no conocían a Dios.

KE: No dijeron Dios em chaniabu?

RH: No. Todavía no sabían, hmm? Y entonces dijeron "Haisa wewu. Haisa wewu." Y ya la dio la explicación, lo que estaba pasando allí. "No l'entendemos nada. A ver si usted [entiende]." Era por el tarde, hmm, ahorita que empezar. A encender a un cigarro, del macuchus. Empezó a fumar. . . . "Bueno, señores," dijo, "ya m'enteré a todo. No hace nada, ese. Venir otras gentes. Vienen de allá del otro lado del mar. Gentes . . . como nosotros. Igualitos. Nada más que ellos son de allá y nosotros somos de aquí. Pero es la misma gente. Tienen el mismo espíritu, el mismo pensamiento de nosotros. El mismo corazón, los mismos ojos, la misma nariz. Todo. Ellos vienen para acá. De que adelante cuando llegan esas gentes, habrá otro cambio. Otro cambio, pues, de manera de vivir. Ellos llevan una cosa que se llama religión. Llevan, este, un palo así, el otro atravesado. . . .

"Esa gente ya vienen cercando para acá, están para acá . . . No más hay que prepararse. Con muchas flechas, arcos. Yo los digo con tiempo para que no les agarran de sorpresa. Cuiden su territorio aquí. Cuiden su territorio. Marquen los linderos. Marquen ustedes. Van a llegar."

"And that is what the Yaqui poetess said." Y así dijo la poetisa Yaqui. Hmm? Hmm. Entonces los Sures que andaban allí, en una noche se fueron. Envolvieron un pedazo de la, el Río Yaqui, así. Cada quien agarró su propio pedazo del río.

Selected Portions of Pedro Molina's Narrative

Chapter 4

"Here, many have heard it. Many." Aquí se han oído, muchos. Muchos se han oído. Nosotros también, oímos llanto en Rahum.

". . . when we heard weeping, very sharp." . . . cuando oímos un llanto, muy ladino. Nosotros lo oímos por acá. Y el otro, el güero, lo oyó pa'allá, pa' lado de la iglesia. Y al rato, otro. Ya, ya. Y, pues, "Vámonos!" . . . Fuimos. No sé que es

viento o que es, pero siempre se oye, se escucha ese llanto. . . . Sale un amigo allí, un soldado, dicen. Acá de la iglesia . . . en Rahum. Todas las noches camina . . . Llega esta por acá. Un soldado. Lo mataron, hace mucho. . . .

Y aquí, en esa parte, como a un kilómetro o dos kilómetros, hay un llanto también. Pero eso es llorar como que te lloraba. Pero ese que llora se llama Rosa. Le acusaron que era hechicera, todo, que se usaba antes. Y esa señora, era un miércoles. Allí le quemaba, con leña verde, porque era hechicera mala, dicen. Son creencias de la gente. Pobre, le mataron allí. Yo no lo vi.

"Where we used to go for firewood." Donde íbamos nosotros por la leña, hay una loma grande—larga—y allí [inaudible] . . . Tenía, tenía ruido, como baila el venado, pascola, tambor, cantos, canta así. En la noche que se oye. Yo hoara, dicen. Encanto. Y allí muchos, llegaron allí a, a, pa' bailar mejor. Encantarse.

"And over there, there's another." Y acá estaba otro. Y estaba otro en el Kében. Kébenia, le dicen. Kébenia. Allí está otro. Me platicaba una hermana de mi abuela. Angelina se llamaba esa viejita. . . . Ella murió de los 115 años. Ella platicaba cuando este . . . era un charco de agua. Allí oían tocar a veces . . . en veces, veía ese, y no ponen ese, que bailan el venado? . . . Ella cuidaba allí, cuidaba chivas. Ella me platicaba ese. Que encantaron [cerca del charquito]. Un señor se encantó allí. Era tampaleo. . . . Hay otro también que dicen Harón Kawi. . . . Cerro encantado. Pues, aquí había muchos. Encantos. Y en la sierra también, las pilas, que le dicen. Encantos.

Spanish–English Glossary

In many cases the definitions I provide in this glossary are specific to the Yaqui context.

abnegada a selfless, self-sacrificing woman

adobada preserved; meat preserved with chiles

agua water

aguantar to endure, to bear

ahijado godchild

alabanza hymn, praise

amarrado tied

amarrar to tie, to bind

ándale, ándele an imperative meaning "get going," "there you go," "okay, then"; also used as an expression indicating affirmation or agreement

angelito little angel; Yaqui child who plays the role of protector of Christ during Holy Week

antes before, in the past

asaltante assailant

así like that

así, no más just like that; like that, nothing more

atole porridge made from flour; Yaquis usually flavor atole with cinnamon

atole de bledo grass-seed porridge

barrio neighborhood

blanco white

bolo coins given as a gift at a christening. For Yaquis *bolo* has a very specific meaning: it is the ritual gift given to godparents, parents of the groom, and new fiesteros, consisting of three large tin pails brimming with food, a basket of tortillas, and hand-embroidered napkins

borracho drunk

brujo witch

bueno good; when used as an interjection, *bueno* translates as "okay," "well," or "all right"

bulto form, shape

buñuelo fritter, a deep-fried flour pastry drizzled with honey

caballeros horsemen; refers to the cavalry, the ceremonial guardians of Jesus during Lenten and Holy Week processions

cabo de año one-year anniversary of a death, a fiesta to mark the end of the mourning period; also known as *luto de año*, *aniversario*, or simply fiesta

caldo clear broth soup

caliente hot

calle principal main street

campesino peasant

campo country, countryside

cancha ball court or field, basketball court

cantora female "singer"; Yaqui female ritual specialist

carne meat, beef

carne con chile beef in a chile sauce

carnitas chopped pieces of barbecued pork

carrizo cane, reed, a bamboolike plant that occurs naturally along streams and riverbeds in southern Sonora

casa house

casado married

casar to marry

castilla Spanish (Castilian)

castillo castle

cerrito little hill

cerro hill

Cerro Enojado Angry Hill, Angry Mountain; Spanish name for Kawi Omteme

chalupa literally, "canoe"; tostadas topped with beans, lettuce, cheese, and chile powder in Yaqui territory

chicharrones pork cracklings, deep-fried pork skin and fat

cigarro cigar; how Yaquis commonly refer to cigarettes

cohetes small fireworks that explode from the top of a castillo

colonia neighborhood

comadre co-mother

comal metal plate or disc on which tortillas are cooked

compadrazgo elaborate system of coparenthood stemming from godparenting relationships

compadre co-father or co-parent, the relationship between godparent and parent

compadres de pila baptismal co-parents

compañero companion

Comunidades Yaquis Yaqui Communities

corona homemade paper flower wreaths used to adorn graves

criollo creole, person of European ancestry born in a Latin American country

cruzado crossed, referring to persons of mixed racial heritage

cuarentena quarantine, usually the 40-day postpartum quarantine

Cuaresma Lent

cuartel barracks, encampment

curandero(a) male or female healer

decir to say, to tell

día day

dialecto dialect, language

dicho saying

Dios God

director(a) male or female principal of a school

doble jornada double day or double workday; refers to the combined burden of wage labor and housework most often borne by women

don, doña Mr., Mrs. (also Ms., Miss); terms of respectful address for men and women

dulce sweet

dulcería candy shop

duritos chips

ejido public land granted to landless peasants, worked cooperatively

empanada bread pastry with fruit, meat, or vegetable filling

encanto enchantment

esposa wife, spouse

esposo husband, spouse

etnia ethnic group

falluquero street vendor

fiesta religious celebration, usually on a saint's feast day; party

fiestero(a) male or female host of the annual fiesta for a pueblo's patron saint

frijoles beans

frijoles puercos beans made with *chorizo* (pork sausage) and cheese

frontera border, frontier

gordita open-faced taco, made by garnishing a small, thick tortilla with beans, potatoes, beef, and cheese

gracias thank you, thanks

guardia headquarters; adobe building and attached outdoor shelter in each of the major pueblos that serves as court, meeting place, and administrative seat of the Yaqui tribal government and military society

güero light-complected

hacendado landowner, owner of a hacienda

harina flour

helados popsicles, frozen treats

henequén sisal hemp

hombre man

horchata ground rice drink

lengua tongue, language

llano plain, flat expanse of ground

lobo wolf
lobo marino seal
lotería lottery, a game somewhat like bingo
machaca shredded dried beef
machismo masculinity, virility, sexism, male chauvinism
machista sexist, chauvinist
madre mother
madrina godmother
maestro teacher, expert, authority; a cohort of Yaqui lay ministers originally
     established to assist Jesuit missionaries, Yaqui maestros continue to lead prayer
     rituals in nearly every significant Yaqui ceremony
maíz maize, corn
maldito troublemaker
mamá mom, mommy, mama
manda promise, vow to God or a saint
mandar to send, to give orders, to lead, to be in charge
mandil apron
mandilón man who is dominated by a woman
maquiladora cross-border assembly plant, also known as a *maquila*
mar sea
marianismo images of ideal womanhood based upon the Virgin Mary
marimacha tomboy, female who displays masculine qualities
menudo clear broth tripe soup
mesita little table; the small, delicate table on which food is offered to Yaqui
     ancestors on the Day of the Dead
mestizo person of mixed race, particularly of Indian and European parentage
metate flat stone for grinding maize
mole sauce made from a mixture of chiles and sometimes chocolate and peanuts
monte wilderness, bush
moros helpers of fiesta sponsors
muchacha young woman
muchacho young man
muerto dead, a dead person
mujer woman
muy very
muy Yaqui very Yaqui
ni modo no matter
niña little girl
niño little boy
nómada nomad
norteamericano North American, designation often given to persons from
     the United States

norteño northerner, person from northern Mexico

novenario ninth-day wake

novia fiancée, girlfriend, bride

novio fiancé, boyfriend, groom

Ocho Pueblos (Sagrados) Eight (Sacred) Pueblos of the Yaqui people

olla pot

otro other

otro lado other side of the international border

padre father

padrino godfather

padrinos godparents

pan bread

pan dulce sugar-dusted roll, sweet bread

panela round loaf of fresh cheese produced locally on Yaqui dairy ranches

panga canoe or small open boat

panteón cemetery

papá dad, daddy, papa

papel picado sheets of decorative cut paper in a variety of colors

partera midwife

patrón boss or patron

petate reed mat

pico de gallo what Yaquis call fruit salad

Pilato Pontius Pilate; ceremonial role performed by Yaqui men portraying persecutors of Jesus during Lent and Holy Week

pinole drink made from cornmeal

piñata papier-mâché container full of candy; Yaquis call birthday parties *piñatas* as well, especially a first birthday

pobre poor

pobrecito poor thing

Porfiriato period of reign of Mexican president–dictator Porfirio Díaz (1876–1910)

Potam Viejo Old Potam

poteño inhabitant of Potam pueblo

pueblo town

pues well, then; often used as an interjection, adding emphasis to whatever has just been stated

puñito fistful

pureza purity

quelites wild greens

quinceañera 15-year-old girl; this word is also used to designate the mass and party celebrating a girl's fifteenth birthday, her coming of age

ramada shelter

ranchera traditional popular music played by small bands
ranchería hamlet, small settlement
ranchito little ranch
rancho ranch
ratero thief
rebozo shawl
reducción reduction; common Jesuit practice of gathering (reducing) inhabitants of smaller, dispersed Indian communities into larger, more densely populated pueblos
regalar to give as a gift
reserva reserve; plot of land set aside for habitation by an indigenous group, somewhat akin to a reservation
Reserva Yaqui Yaqui Reserve
respeto respect
rezo prayer, prayer session
Río Yaqui Yaqui River
Santísima Trinidad Holy Trinity
santo saint, holy
Semana Santa the Christian Holy Week, the week preceding Easter
sociedad society, cooperative; name by which Yaqui farming cooperatives are known
socio associate; member of Yaqui farming or fishing cooperative
sombra shadow
sombrero hat; cowboy hat is the preferred style among Yaqui men, as with other northern Mexicans
sureño southerner, person from southern Mexico
tacos dorados golden tacos, deep-fried tacos
telenovela soap opera
temastianes catechists
tierno tender
tierra land
tímido timid
tortillería tortilla factory, small workshop for production and sale of tortillas
tribu tribe
vergüenza embarrassment, shame
viajar to travel
virtudes virtues
zafra harvest
Zona Indígena Indigenous Zone
Zona Yaqui Yaqui Zone; another name for Zona Indígena

Yaqui–English Glossary

achai father
ae, maala mother
alpés (alpesim) a female flag bearer
anía world
aniimam souls
baa'am water
baka carrizo; bamboolike cane or reed native to Yaqui region
batwe river
bledo wild grasses, the seeds of which are used to make atole
bwaana to cry, to weep
bwía land, earth
Chapayeka Lenten masked dancer representing a soldier of the Pharisees in
  pursuit of Jesus; *chapa* (folded or crooked), *yeka* (nose)
chiokoe utte'esia thank you (short form)
choki star
Dios em chaniabu may God help you
Dios em chaniabu kechem al-lea may God bless you with happiness
Dios emchiokoe ket tu'i may God also repay you with goodness; response to
  a greeting
Dios emchiokoe utte'esia thank you
Dios enchi jiokoe may God forgive you
haisa wewu *haisa* (how), *wewu* is not translatable
hiak Yaqui
huya anía wilderness world
in achai my father
inim bwan bwía this weeping land
inim bwan bwía-po here in this weeping land
Itom Ae Our Mother
itom bwía our land
itom hiak bwía our Yaqui land
kawi hill, mountain
Kawi Omteme Angry Mountain
kiyohtei female altar attendant or ceremonial flag bearer; at times the pronun-
  ciation is Hispanicized to *kiyoste*, and *kiyohteim* is the plural form

Kohtumbre "customs" religious society or brotherhood

konti surrounding; ceremonial procession to various Stations of the Cross around the perimeter of the churchyard

kus cross

kuta stick, pole, tree trunk

kuta nokame talking stick

lutu'uria truth; the fulfillment of traditional social obligations

macuchus Yaqui tobacco, native tobacco; also known as *hiak vivam*

mapoam strings of tiny beads worn as bracelets

mochomo ant

mumu bee

munim beans

omte angry

pascola old man of the fiesta, a ritual clown dancer who entertains crowds at fiestas, weddings, and other ceremonial events

sea, sewa flower

sea anía flower world

Sea Hamut Flower Woman, also known as Yomumuli; the wise woman who prophesied the coming of the whites to the Surem

sea hiki flowers embroidered on clothing, "fantasy flowers"

sea taka flower body; inborn gift of special powers of perception

si hiaki very Yaqui (referring to behavior)

Surem little people; the precontact ancestors of the Yaquis

tapanko the tapesti after it has been set with food offerings for the dead

tapesti a small, high table used during Day of the Dead rituals

tekípanoa work, labor; applies especially to ritual labor

tenanche(im) female who bears an image of the Virgin in Yaqui ceremonies

teneboim cocoon rattles

torim large, tree-dwelling rodents

wakabaki Yaqui clear broth made with vegetables, garbanzo beans, and beef

ya'uram one of five major bodies of Yaqui leaders or authorities

yo ancient, enchanted

yo anía ancient or enchanted world

yo hoara enchanted home, enchanted place

Yoeme, Yoreme Yaqui person, human being; plural form: Yoemem, Yoremem

Yori foreigner, "white person," non-Yaqui (refers specifically to a non-Yaqui Mexican); plural form: Yorim, Yoris (Hispanicized)

Bibliography

Abu-Lughod, Lila (1986). Veiled Sentiments: Honor and Poetry in a Bedouin Society. Berkeley: University of California Press.

——— (1991). Writing against Culture. *In* Recapturing Anthropology: Working in the Present. Richard Fox, ed. Pp. 137–162. Santa Fe: School of American Research Press.

Alonso, Ana María (1995). Thread of Blood: Colonialism, Revolution, and Gender on Mexico's Northern Frontier. Tucson: University of Arizona Press.

Bakhtin, M. M. (1986). Speech Genres and Other Late Essays. Michael Holquist and Caryl Emerson, eds. Vern W. McGee, trans. Austin: University of Texas Press.

Barth, Fredrik (1969). Introduction. *In* Ethnic Groups and Boundaries: The Social Organization of Culture Difference. Fredrik Barth, ed. Pp. 9–38. Boston: Little, Brown and Company.

Barthes, Roland (1972). [1957] Mythologies. New York: Hill and Wang.

——— (1977). Image—Music—Text. London: Fontana.

Basso, Keith (1996). Wisdom Sits in Places: Landscape and Language among the Western Apache. Albuquerque: University of New Mexico Press.

Bauman, Richard (1977). Verbal Art as Performance. Prospect Heights, IL: Waveland Press.

Bauman, Richard, and Charles Briggs (1990). Poetics and Performance as Critical Perspectives on Language and Social Life. Annual Review of Anthropology 19:59–88.

Benería, Lourdes, and Martha Roldán (1987). The Crossroads of Class and Gender: Industrial Homework, Subcontracting, and Household Dynamics in Mexico City. Chicago: University of Chicago Press.

Benjamin, Walter (1977). [1928] The Origin of German Tragic Drama. J. Osborne, trans. London: New Left Books.

Broyles-González, Yolanda (2002). Ranchera Music(s) and the Legendary Lydia Mendoza: Performing Social Location and Relations. *In* Chicana Traditions: Continuity and Change. Norma Cantú and Olga Nájera-Ramirez, eds. Pp. 183–206. Urbana: University of Illinois Press.

Bruner, Jerome (1991). The Narrative Construction of Reality. Critical Inquiry 18:1–21.

Butler, Judith (1990). Performative Acts and Gender Constitution: An Essay in Phenomenology and Feminist Theory. *In* Performing Feminisms: Feminist Critical Theory and Theatre. Sue-Ellen Case, ed. Pp. 270–282. Baltimore: Johns Hopkins University Press.

——— (1999). [1990] Gender Trouble: Feminism and the Subversion of Identity. New York: Routledge.

Casey, Edward (1996). How to Get from Space to Place in a Fairly Short Stretch of Time. *In* Senses of Place. Steven Feld and Keith Basso, eds. Pp. 13–52. Santa Fe: School of American Research.

Certeau, Michel de (1984). The Practice of Everyday Life. Steven Rendall, trans. Berkeley: University of California Press.

Chavez, Leo (1998). [1992] Shadowed Lives: Undocumented Immigrants in American Society. 2nd edition. Belmont, CA: Wadsworth/Thomson Publishers.

Chernela, Janet (1988). Righting History in the Northwest Amazon: Myth, Structure, and History in an Arapaco Narrative. *In* Rethinking History and Myth: Indigenous South American Perspectives on the Past. Jonathan D. Hill, ed. Pp. 35–49. Urbana: University of Illinois Press.

Cixous, Hélène, and Catherine Clément (1986). The Newly Born Woman. Betsy Wing, trans. Minneapolis: University of Minnesota Press.

Clifford, James (1983). On Ethnographic Authority. Representations 1(2): 118–145.

——— (1986). Introduction: Partial Truths. *In* Writing Culture: The Poetics and Politics of Ethnography. James Clifford and George E. Marcus, eds. Pp. 1–24. Berkeley: University of California Press.

——— (1997). Routes: Travel and Translation in the Late Twentieth Century. Cambridge, MA: Harvard University Press.

Collins, Jane (1995). Transnational Labor Process and Gender Relations: Women in Fruit and Vegetable Production in Chile, Brazil, and Mexico. Journal of Latin American Anthropology 1(1):178–199.

Comaroff, John, and Jean Comaroff (1992). Ethnography and the Historical Imagination. Boulder: Westview Press.

Curcio-Nagy, Linda (2000). Faith and Morals in Colonial Mexico. *In* The Oxford History of Mexico. Michael C. Meyer and William H. Beezley, eds. Pp. 151–182. New York: Oxford University Press.

Davis, Natalie Zemon, and Randolph Starn (1989). Introduction. Theme issue, "Memory and Counter-Memory," Representations 26:1–6.

Douglas, Mary (1990). Foreword: No Free Gifts. *In* The Gift: The Form and Reason for Exchange in Archaic Societies, by Marcel Mauss. W. D. Halls, trans. Pp. vii–xviii. London: Routledge.

Eicher, Joanne B., ed. (1995). Dress and Ethnicity: Change across Space and Time. Oxford: Berg.

Eicher, Joanne, and Barbara Sumberg (1995). World Fashion, Ethnic, and National Dress. *In* Dress and Ethnicity: Change across Space and Time. Joanne Eicher, ed. Pp. 295–306. Oxford: Berg.

Ellen, R. F., ed. (1984). Ethnographic Research: A Guide to General Conduct. London: Academic Press, Harcourt Brace and Company, Publishers.

Enciclopedia Libre Universal (2007). Ciudad Obregón (Sonora). *In* Enciclopedia Libre Universal en Español. Electronic document, http://enciclopedia.us.es/index.php/Ciudad_Obreg% C3%B3n_(Sonora), accessed July 21, 2006.

Evers, Larry, and Felipe S. Molina (1992a). Hiakim: The Yaqui Homeland. Journal of the Southwest 34(1):1–2.

——— (1992b). The Holy Dividing Line: Inscription and Resistance in Yaqui Culture. Journal of the Southwest 34(1):3–46.

——— (1993). [1987] Yaqui Deer Songs/Maso Bwikam: A Native American Poetry. Tucson: Sun Tracks and the University of Arizona Press.

Feld, Steven, and Keith Basso, eds. (1996). Senses of Place. Santa Fe: School of American Research.

Fernández-Kelly, María Patricia (1983). For we are sold, I and my people: Women and Industry in Mexico's Frontier. Albany: State University of New York Press.

Figueroa Valenzuela, Alejandro (1992). Organización de la identidad étnica y persistencia cultural entre los Yaquis y los Mayos. Estudios Sociológicos 10(28):127–148.

——— (1994). Por la tierra y por los santos: Identidad y persistencia cultural entre Yaquis y Mayos. Mexico City: Consejo Nacional para la Cultura y las Artes.

Fiske, John (1990). Introduction to Communication Studies. 2nd edition. London: Routledge.

Flores, Richard R. (1994). "Los Pastores" and the Gifting of Performance. American Ethnologist 21(2):270–285.

——— (1995). Los Pastores: History and Performance in the Mexican Shepherd's Play of South Texas. Washington, D.C.: Smithsonian Institution Press.

——— (2002). Remembering the Alamo: Memory, Modernity, and the Master Symbol. Austin: University of Texas Press.

——— (forthcoming). Los Pastores and the Gendered Politics of Location. *In* Mexican American Religions: Spirituality, Activism and Culture. Gaston Espinosa and Mario T. Garcia, eds. Pp. 206–220. Durham, NC: Duke University Press.

Foucault, Michel (1980). Power/Knowledge: Selected Interviews and Other Writings 1972–1977. Colin Gordon, ed. Colin Gordon, Leo Marshall, John Mepham, and Kate Soper, trans. New York: Pantheon Books.

Fowler-Salamini, Heather, and Mary Kay Vaughan, eds. (1994). Women of the Mexican Countryside, 1850–1990. Tucson: University of Arizona Press.

Fox, Richard G., ed. (1991). Recapturing Anthropology: Working in the Present. Santa Fe: School of American Research Press.

Franco, Jean (1989). Plotting Women: Gender and Representation in Mexico. New York: Columbia University Press.

——— (1999). Critical Passions: Selected Essays. Mary Louise Pratt and Kathleen Newman, eds. Durham, NC: Duke University Press.

Friedland, Roger, and Deirdre Boden, eds. (1994). NowHere: Space, Time and Modernity. Berkeley: University of California Press.

Garciagodoy, Juanita (1998). Digging the Days of the Dead: A Reading of Mexico's Días de Muertos. Niwot: University Press of Colorado.

Geertz, Clifford (1973). Interpretation of Cultures. New York: Basic Books.

Giddings, Ruth Warner (1993). [1959] Yaqui Myths and Legends. Harry Behn, ed. Tucson: University of Arizona Press.

Goffman, Erving (1959). The Presentation of Self in Everyday Life. Garden City, NY: Doubleday.

Gordillo, Gastón (2004). Landscapes of Devils: Tensions of Place and Memory in the Argentinean Chaco. Durham, NC: Duke University Press.

Gordon, Avery (1997). Ghostly Matters: Haunting and the Sociological Imagination. Minneapolis: University of Minnesota Press.

Grossberg, Lawrence, ed. (1996). On Postmodernism and Articulation: An Interview with Stuart Hall. In Stuart Hall: Critical Dialogues in Cultural Studies. David Morley and Kuan-Hsing Chen, eds. Pp. 131–150. London: Routledge.

Gupta, Akhil, and James Ferguson (1992). Beyond "Culture": Space, Identity, and the Politics of Difference. Cultural Anthropology 7(1):6–23.

Gutmann, Matthew C. (1996). The Meanings of Macho: Being a Man in Mexico City. Berkeley: University of California Press.

Hall, Stuart (1980). Race, Articulation and Societies Structured in Dominance. In Sociological Theories: Race and Colonialism. Pp. 305–345. Paris: UNESCO.

——— (1996). New Ethnicities. In Stuart Hall: Critical Dialogues in Cultural Studies. David Morley and Kuan-Hsing Chen, eds. Pp. 441–449. London: Routledge.

Harris, William Richard (1908). By Path and Trail. Salt Lake City: Intermountain Catholic Press Company.

Harvey, David (1990). The Condition of Postmodernity: An Enquiry into the Origins of Cultural Change. Cambridge, MA: Blackwell Publishers.

Herzfeld, Michael (1985). The Poetics of Manhood: Contest and Identity in a Cretan Mountain Village. Princeton, NJ: Princeton University Press.

Hewitt de Alcantara, Cynthia (1976). Modernizing Mexican Agriculture: Socioeconomic Implications of Technological Change 1940–1970. Geneva: UN Research Institute for Social Development.

Hill, Jonathan D. (1988). Rethinking History and Myth: Indigenous South American Perspectives on the Past. Urbana: University of Illinois Press.

hooks, bell (1990). Yearning: Race, Gender, and Cultural Politics. Boston: South End Press.

Hu-DeHart, Evelyn (1974). Development and Rural Rebellion: Pacification of the Yaquis in the Late Porfiriato. Hispanic American Historical Review 54:72–93.

———— (1981). Missionaries, Miners and Indians: Spanish Contact with the Yaqui Nation 1533–1820. Tucson: University of Arizona Press.

———— (1984). Yaqui Resistance and Survival: The Struggle for Land and Autonomy, 1821–1910. Madison: University of Wisconsin Press.

Hulme, Peter, and Neil L. Whitehead (1992). Wild Majesty: Encounters with Caribs from Columbus to the Present Day. Oxford: Clarendon Press.

Ibarra, Ignacio (2003). Maquila Turnaround Foreseen. Arizona Daily Star, December 26. Electronic document, http://search.ebscohost.com/login.aspx?direct=true&db=nfh&AN=2W61911319328&site=ehost-live, accessed January 29, 2008.

Iglesias-Prieto, Norma (1997). Beautiful Flowers of the Maquiladora. Austin: University of Texas Press.

INEGI (2000). XII Censo General de población y vivienda 2000. Principales resultados por localidad, Sonora. Electronic document, www.inegi.gob.mx, accessed July 21, 2006.

Jameson, Fredric (1972). The Prison-House of Language: A Critical Account of Structuralism and Russian Formalism. Princeton, NJ: Princeton University Press.

———— (1981). The Political Unconscious: Narrative as a Socially Symbolic Act. Ithaca, NY: Cornell University Press.

———— (1991). Postmodernism, or, The Cultural Logic of Late Capitalism. Durham, NC: Duke University Press.

Joseph, Gilbert (1988). Revolution from Without: Yucatán, Mexico, and the United States 1880–1924. Durham, NC: Duke University Press.

Kelley, Jane Holden (1978). Yaqui Women: Contemporary Life Histories. Lincoln: University of Nebraska Press.

Knight, Alan (1990). Racism, Revolution, and Indigenismo: Mexico, 1910–1940. In The Idea of Race in Latin America, 1870–1940. Richard Graham, ed. Pp. 71–113. Austin: University of Texas Press.

Kondo, Dorinne (1990). Crafting Selves: Power, Gender, and Discourses of Identity in a Japanese Workplace. Chicago: University of Chicago Press.

Lancaster, Roger (1992). Life Is Hard: Machismo, Danger, and the Intimacy of Power in Nicaragua. Berkeley: University of California Press.

Lauretis, Teresa de (1987). Technologies of Gender: Essays on Theory, Film, and Fiction. Bloomington: Indiana University Press.

Lefebvre, Henri (1991). [1974] The Production of Space. Donald Nicholson-Smith, trans. Malden, MA: Blackwell Publishing.

Limón, José (1994). Dancing with the Devil: Society and Cultural Poetics in Mexican-American South Texas. Madison: University of Wisconsin Press.

Linnekin, Jocelyn, and Lin Poyer, eds. (1990). Cultural Identity and Ethnicity in the Pacific. Honolulu: University of Hawaii Press.

Lomnitz-Adler, Claudio (1992). Exits from the Labyrinth: Culture and Ideology in the Mexican National Space. Berkeley: University of California Press.

Low, Setha, and Denise Lawrence-Zuñiga, eds. (2003). The Anthropology of Space and Place: Locating Culture. Malden, MA: Blackwell Publishing.

Luckert, Karl W. (1975). The Navajo Hunter Tradition. Tucson: University of Arizona Press.

Lutes, Steven (1987). Yaqui Indian Enclavement: The Effects of an Experimental Indian Policy in Northwestern Mexico. *In* Ejidos and Regions of Refuge in Northwestern Mexico. Anthropological Papers of the University of Arizona, 46. N. Ross Crumrine and Phil C. Weigand, eds. Pp. 11–20. Tucson: University of Arizona Press.

MacCannell, Dean (1973). Staged Authenticity: Arrangements in Social Space in Tourist Settings. American Journal of Sociology 79(3):589–603.

Marx, Karl (1978). Theses on Feuerbach. *In* The Marx–Engels Reader. 2nd edition. Robert C. Tucker, ed. Pp. 143–145. New York: W. W. Norton and Company.

Massey, Doreen (1994). Space, Place, and Gender. Cambridge: Polity Press.

Mauss, Marcel (1990). [1950] The Gift: The Form and Reason for Exchange in Archaic Societies. W. D. Halls, trans. London: Routledge.

McGuire, Thomas (1986). Politics and Ethnicity on the Río Yaqui: Potam Revisited. Tucson: University of Arizona Press.

McRobbie, Angela (1992). Post-Marxism and Cultural Studies: A Post-Script. *In* Cultural Studies. Lawrence Grossberg, Cary Nelson, and Paula A. Treichler, eds. Pp. 719–730. New York: Routledge.

Moisés, Rosalio, with Jane Holden Kelley and William Curry Holden (1971). A Yaqui Life: The Personal Chronicle of a Yaqui Indian. Lincoln: University of Nebraska Press.

Molina, Felipe S., and David Leedom Shaul (1993). A Concise Yoeme and English Dictionary. Tucson: Tucson Unified School District Bilingual Education and Hispanic Studies Department.

Molina, Felipe, David Shaul, and Herminia Valenzuela (1999). Yoeme–English, English–Yoeme Standard Dictionary. New York: Hippocrene Books.

Monsiváis, Carlos (1997). Mexican Postcards. John Kraniauskas, trans. London: Verso.

Moore, Henrietta (1986). Space, Text, and Gender: An Anthropological Study of the Marakwet of Kenya. New York: Cambridge University Press.

——— (1988). Feminism and Anthropology. Minneapolis: University of Minnesota Press.

Moreno, Jenalia (2004). Mexican Manufacturers Adapt to Recover U.S. Work Lost to Cheaper Chinese Labor. Houston Chronicle, September 12. Electronic document, http://web.ebscohost.com/ehost/detail?vid=3&hid=103&sid=29d a3880-e0f3-4680-b7f3-8ef173cecbba%40sessionmgr104, accessed January 28, 2008.

Morrison, Kenneth M. (1992). Sharing the Flower: A Non-supernaturalistic Theory of Grace. Religion 22:207–219.

Mouffe, Chantal (1992). Feminism, Citizenship and Radical Democratic Politics. In Feminists Theorize the Political. Judith Butler and Joan Scott, eds. Pp. 369–384. New York: Routledge.

Nabokov, Peter (2002). A Forest of Time: American Indian Ways of History. New York: Cambridge University Press.

Narayan, Kirin (1993). How Native Is a "Native" Anthropologist? American Anthropologist 95(3): 671–686.

Nelson, Lise (1999). Bodies (and Spaces) Do Matter: the Limits of Performativity. Gender, Place and Culture 6(4):331–353.

Nora, Pierre (1989). Between Memory and History: Les Lieux de Mémoire. Representations 26:7–25.

Ong, Aihwa (1987). Spirits of Resistance and Capitalist Discipline: Factory Women in Malaysia. Albany: State University of New York Press.

Ortner, Sherry (1973). On Key Symbols. American Anthropologist 75(5):1338–1346.

Padilla Ramos, Raquel (1995). Yucatán: Fin del sueño yaqui. Hermosillo, Sonora: Instituto Sonorense de Cultura.

Painter, Muriel Thayer (1986). With Good Heart: Yaqui Beliefs and Ceremonies in Pascua Village. Tucson: University of Arizona Press.

Pearce, Diana (1978) The Feminization of Poverty: Women, Work and Welfare. Urban and Social Change Review 11(1–2):28–36.

Pellow, Deborah (2003). The Architecture of Female Seclusion in West Africa. In The Anthropology of Space and Place: Locating Culture. Setha M. Low and Denise Lawrence-Zuñiga, eds. Pp. 160–183. Malden, MA: Blackwell Publishing.

Pérez de Ribas, Andrés (1944). [1645] Historia de los triunfos de Nuestra Señora de Fe entre gentes las más bárbaras y fieras del nuevo orbe. Vol. 2. Mexico City: Editorial Layac.

Price, Richard (1990). Alabi's World. Baltimore, MD: Johns Hopkins University Press.

Radding, Cynthia (1989). Peasant Resistance on the Yaqui Delta: An Historical Inquiry into the Meaning of Ethnicity. Journal of the Southwest 31(3): 330–361.

Ramos, Alcida Rita (1998). Indigenism: Ethnic Politics in Brazil. Madison: University of Wisconsin Press.

Reeve, Mary-Elizabeth (1988). Cauchu-Uras: Lowland Quichua Histories of the Amazon Rubber Boom. *In* Rethinking History and Myth: Indigenous South American Perspectives on the Past. Jonathan D. Hill, ed. Pp. 19–34. Urbana: University of Illinois Press.

Rodman, Margaret C. (2003). Empowering Place: Multilocality and Multivocality. *In* The Anthropology of Space and Place: Locating Culture. Setha M. Low and Denise Lawrence-Zuñiga, eds. Pp. 204–223. Malden, MA: Blackwell Publishing.

Rosaldo, Michelle Z. (1974). Woman, Culture and Society: A Theoretical Overview. *In* Woman, Culture and Society. Michelle Zimbalist Rosaldo and Louise Lamphere, eds. Pp. 17–42. Stanford, CA: Stanford University Press.

Rosaldo, Renato (1980). Ilongot Headhunting, 1883–1974: A Study in Society and History. Stanford, CA: Stanford University Press.

————— (1989). Culture and Truth: The Remaking of Social Analysis. Boston: Beacon Press.

Rosenberg, Matt (2007). Export Assembly Plants for the United States. Electronic document, http://geography.about.com/od/urbaneconomicgeography/a/maquiladoras.htm, accessed January 28, 2008.

Ruíz Ruíz, María Trinidad, and Gerardo David Aguilar Z. (1994). Tres procesos de lucha por la sobrevivencia de la tribu yaqui: Testimonios. Hermosillo, Sonora: Universidad de Sonora.

Saldívar, José Davíd (1997). Border Matters: Remapping American Cultural Studies. Berkeley: University of California Press.

Sands, Kathleen M. (1983). The Singing Tree: Dynamics of a Yaqui Myth. American Quarterly 35(4): 355–375.

Savala, Refugio (1980). The Autobiography of a Yaqui Poet. Kathleen Sands, ed. Tucson: University of Arizona Press.

Schechner, Richard (1997). Waehma: Space, Time, Identity, and Theater at New Pascua, Arizona. *In* Performing the Renewal of Community: Indigenous Easter Rituals in North Mexico and Southwest United States. Rosamund Spicer and Ross Crumrine, eds. Pp. 151–183. New York: University Press of America.

Scott, James (1976). The Moral Economy of the Peasant: Rebellion and Subsistence in Southeast Asia. New Haven, CT: Yale University Press.

————— (1985). Weapons of the Weak: Everyday Forms of Peasant Resistance. New Haven, CT: Yale University Press.

Sharp, John (1996). Ethnogenesis and Ethnic Mobilization: A Comparative Perspective on a South African Dilemma. *In* The Politics of Difference: Ethnic Premises in a World of Power. Edwin Wilmsen and Patrick McAllister, eds. Pp. 85–103. Chicago: University of Chicago Press.

Shaw, Rosalind (2002). Memories of the Slave Trade: Ritual and the Historical Imagination in Sierra Leone. Chicago: University of Chicago Press.

Shorter, David (2002). Santa linium divisoria/Holy Dividing Lines: Yoeme Place-Making and Religious Identity. Ph.D. dissertation, University of California, Santa Cruz.

———— (2003). Binary Thinking and the Study of Yoeme Indian *lutu'uria*/Truth. Anthropological Forum 13(2):195–203.

Soja, Edward (1989). Postmodern Geographies: The Reassertion of Space in Critical Social Theory. London: Verso Press.

———— (1996). Thirdspace: Journeys to Los Angeles and Other Real-and-Imagined Places. Malden, MA: Blackwell Publishers.

Solidaridad (1995). Solidaridad en Sonora: Evaluación, memoria 1989–1994. Hermosillo: Estado de Sonora.

Spicer, Edward (1954). Potam: A Yaqui Village in Sonora. American Anthropological Association 56(4), pt. 2, memoire no. 77.

———— (1969). Northwest Mexico: Introduction. *In* Ethnology. Evon Z. Vogt, ed. Pp. 777–791. Vol. 8: Handbook of Middle American Indians. Robert Wauchope, gen. ed. Austin: University of Texas Press.

———— (1971). Persistent Cultural Systems: A Comparative Study of Identity Systems That Can Adapt to Contrasting Environments. Science 174:795–800.

———— (1980). The Yaquis: A Cultural History. Tucson: University of Arizona Press.

———— (1984). [1940] Pascua: A Yaqui Village in Arizona. Tucson: University of Arizona Press.

———— (1988). People of Pascua. Kathleen M. Sands and Rosamond B. Spicer, eds. Tucson: University of Arizona Press.

Stern, Steve J. (1995). The Secret History of Gender: Women, Men, and Power in Late Colonial Mexico. Chapel Hill: University of North Carolina Press.

Stewart, Kathleen (1988). Nostalgia—A Polemic. Cultural Anthropology 3(3):227–241.

———— (1996). A Space on the Side of the Road: Cultural Poetics in an "Other" America. Princeton, NJ: Princeton University Press.

Taussig, Michael (1993). Mimesis and Alterity: A Particular History of the Senses. New York: Routledge.

Turner, John Kenneth (1969). Barbarous Mexico. Austin: University of Texas Press.

Turner, Victor (1969). The Ritual Process: Structure and Anti-Structure. Ithaca, NY: Cornell University Press.

Valenzuela Kaczkurkin, Mini (1977). Yoeme: Lore of the Arizona Yaqui People. Tucson: University of Arizona Press.

Vélez-Ibañez, Carlos (1996). Border Visions: Mexican Cultures of the Southwest United States. Tucson: University of Arizona Press.

Vincent, Joan (1974). The Structuring of Ethnicity. Human Organization 33(4):375–379.

Vološinov, V. N. (2000). [1973] Marxism and the Philosophy of Language. Ladislav Matejka and I. R. Titunik, trans. Cambridge, MA: Harvard University Press.

Wade, Peter (1997). Race and Ethnicity in Latin America. London: Pluto Press.

Weismantel, Mary (2001). Cholas and Pishtacos: Stories of Race and Sex in the Andes. Chicago: University of Chicago Press.

White, Geoffrey (1991). Identity through History: Living Stories in a Solomon Islands Society. Cambridge: Cambridge University Press.

Wikipedia n.d. Norteño (music). Electronic document, http://en.wikipedia.org/wiki/Norte% C3%B1o_%28music%29, accessed January 29, 2008.

Williams, Raymond (1977). Marxism and Literature. Oxford: Oxford University Press.

Wilmsen, Edwin N. (1996). Introduction: Premises of Power in Ethnic Politics. In The Politics of Difference: Ethnic Premises in a World of Power. Edwin N. Wilmsen and Patrick McAllister, eds. Pp. 1–24. Chicago: University of Chicago Press.

Wilmsen, Edwin N., and Patrick McAllister, eds. (1996a). The Politics of Difference: Ethnic Premises in a World of Power. Chicago: University of Chicago Press.

——— (1996b). Preface. In The Politics of Difference: Ethnic Premises in a World of Power. Edwin N. Wilmsen and Patrick McAllister, eds. Pp. vii–ix. Chicago: University of Chicago Press.

Index

Days of the Dead, 156n16; in colonial
Mexico, 111; and food, 107–9;
Yaqui, 107–11; and Yaqui
ethnicity, 111
deportation: stories about, 49–50;
of Yaquis, 44–45, 47–48. *See also*
displacement
devotional labor: and altars, 105–6;
and identity, 84–85, 134. *See also*
tekípanoa
Día de los Angelitos (Day of the Little
Angels), 106
Día de los Difuntos. *See* Days of the
Dead
Díaz, Porfirio, 6, 43–44, 147n4
displacement: stories about, 43–44,
46–47; of Yaquis, 41–43
domestic ceremonies: as ethnic
assertion, 106; and ethnicity,
132–33; Yaqui, 106
domestic space: and ethnicity, 98–99;
female gendered, 100, 103–4; in
Potam, 98–99; protection of, 104;
and ritual, 99; and women, 130–32;
women's sacralization of, 99,
104–6; women's socialization of,
98–99
Douglas, Mary, 119

economic life: and Yaqui ethnicity, 83
education, 152n16
Eight Pueblos. *See* Ocho Pueblos
embodiment: of ethnicity, 75–76
empeñar (pawning), 114
emplacement, 60; of violence, 64
employment: and Yaqui women, 40
enchanted places. *See* yo hoara
endurance: and ritual life, 80–81; and
Yaqui identity, 80–81
ethnic belonging, 148n15
ethnic identity: and devotion, 135;
origins of, 24–25, 36 (*see also*

ethnogenesis); as relation, 36;
Yaqui, 5, 14, 144n8; Yaqui women's,
74–75. *See also* ethnicity; identity
ethnicity, 35; defined, 11; and gender,
10–11, 96; studies of Yaqui, 13–14;
theories about, 143n4; Yaqui,
146n15. *See also* ethnic identity;
identity
ethnogenesis, 32; defined, 25; theories
about, 35; Yaqui, 35, 37–38. *See also*
ethnic identity, origins of
Evers, Larry, 32; and homeland,
148n6; and *sea anía*, 78; and
Talking Tree story, 145n2, 145n7;
and *yo anía*, 67–68

feminization of poverty, 152n15
Ferguson, James, 54
fieldwork, 16–18
fiesta (religious celebration), as cultural
display, 122–23; 113, 119–25, 157n5;
and ethnicity, 132–33; and ethnic
meaning, 122–23; food in, 121–22;
gendered division of labor in, 121;
men's work in, 122; reciprocity in,
123–25; women's work in, 122; as
utopian moment, 123
fiestero(a) (fiesta host), 120–21;
defined, 3; responsibilities of,
123–25, 138; selection of, 123;
women's duties as, 120
Flores, Richard R., 113, 137, 144n13,
158n12
Franco, Jean, 156n12
frontstage and backstage, 131–32

Garciagodoy, Juanita, 156n17
gender: and domestic labor, 100;
performativity, 153n2; Yaqui
women's, 73–75, 80
generosity: as cultural value, 114–15
ghost, 62–63

Yaquis (*cont.*)
  of, 25–26 (*see also* reducción). *See
  also* Yoeme
ya'uram (Yaqui leadership complex),
  120–21, 157n6
yo anía (enchanted world), 67–68
Yoeme: defined, 11–12; linguistic root,
  12. *See also* Yaquis
yo hoara (enchanted home), 57; and
  cultural knowledge, 55; defined, 68;
  stories about, 55, 67, 68–69

Yomumuli, 145n7
Yori (non-Yaqui Mexican), 2;
  defined, 12
Yucatán, 45, 47; Yaquis in, 48–49;
  Yaqui women in, 48

Zona Indígena (Indigenous Zone), 7,
  8, 10; employment in, 40 (*see also*
  Yaquis, and employment); farming
  in (*see* agriculture, Yaqui); map of,
  9 (fig. 2). *See also* Yaqui, Reserve

About the Author

Kirstin Erickson is an associate professor of anthropology at the University of Arkansas in Fayetteville. She has conducted ethnographic research with the Yaquis in northern Mexico since 1996 and has published three articles about Yaqui historical narrative and identity: "'They will come from the other side of the sea': Prophecy, Ethnogenesis, and Agency in Yaqui Narrative," *Journal of American Folklore* (2003); "Moving Stories: Displacement and Return in the Narrative Production of Yaqui Identity," *Anthropology and Humanism* (2003); and "Paisajes encantados: La memoria, el sentido de lugar e identidad en la narrativa yaqui," *Cuadernos de Literatura* (2007).

Dr. Erickson received her Ph.D. from the University of Wisconsin–Madison in 2000. In 2005 she collaborated with Minnesota artist Dawn Zero Erickson on Material Devotions, a textile–silkscreen production exhibited at the Rochester Art Center Museum in southern Minnesota. The exhibit featured seven original textile pieces by Dawn Erickson accompanied by text from Kirstin Erickson's writings on Yaqui healing and material culture.

Her current research is an ethnographic and historical examination of how a Hispanic, Native American, and Anglo intercultural borderland is inscribed on the northern New Mexico landscape through pilgrimage, tourism, and commemorative practices.